M000287124

Homosexuality

2|2010   011 LAD 6/09
2at VPL   1 FRV

Homosexuality
Its Nature and Causes

D. J. West

AldineTransaction
A Division of Transaction Publishers
New Brunswick (U.S.A.) and London (U.K.)

First paperback printing 2008
Copyright © 1967 by Donald J. West.

All rights reserved under International and Pan-American Copyright Conventions. No part of this book may be reproduced or transmitted in any form or by any means, electronic or mechanical, including photocopy, recording, or any information storage and retrieval system, without prior permission in writing from the publisher. All inquiries should be addressed to AldineTransaction, A Division of Transaction Publishers, Rutgers—The State University, 35 Berrue Circle, Piscataway, New Jersey 08854-8042. www.transactionpub.com

This book is printed on acid-free paper that meets the American National Standard for Permanence of Paper for Printed Library Materials.

Library of Congress Catalog Number: 2008001554
ISBN: 978-0-202-36236-6
Printed in the United States of America

Library of Congress Cataloging-in-Publication Data

West, D. J. (Donald James), 1924-
　Homosexuality : its nature and causes / D.J. West.
　　p. cm.
　Originally published: Chicago : Aldine Pub. Co., [1968, c1967].
　Includes bibliographical references and index.
　ISBN 978-0-202-36236-6 (alk. paper)
　　1. Homosexuality. I. Title.

HQ76.W4 2008
306.76'6--dc22　　　　　　　　　　　　　　　　　　　2008001554

PREFACE

The subject of homosexuality, and especially male homosexuality, has received a great deal of publicity in recent years, both in England and America. The furor began with the first of Kinsey's famous reports on sexual behaviour, which brought out the fact that a far higher proportion of the population than was commonly supposed deviated from accepted standards of normality and morality. Taking courage from the apparent safety of large numbers, the sexually unorthodox and their sympathisers began to challenge the criteria of normality, and to question whether sexual habits that were so widespread and so deeply entrenched could justifiably be written off as totally immoral.

Similar arguments took place in England, and were given impetus by some disquieting trials of prominent homosexuals, whose fate began to look more like that of the scapegoat than the criminal. The government-sponsored inquiry, which produced the Wolfenden Report, and the recommendation that the law against adult consentual homosexuality should be repealed, ensured an indefinite continuation of the public debate. Now, with the passing of the Sexual Offences Act, 1967, public controversy may subside in England, but it will never again be possible to ignore and avoid the topic to quite the same extent.

Meantime, in the United States, a similar controversy has been going on, but with characteristically different overtones. If one dare make any generalisation about so diverse and dynamic a nation, it seems to the European that Americans feel unduly threatened by relatively harmless deviations, whether in morals, politics, or dress. Hence, except in Illinois, a Wolfenden-type reform seems unlikely. Instead, the homosexual minority has taken advantage of the popular movement against social discrimination to try to assert some basic civil liberties: They want to be allowed to congregate in bars of their choice, to hold meetings, to run clubs, to publish magazines, to serve in the armed forces and enjoy the privileges of veterans, and to share the common immunity from undue police surveillance. All this by-passes the issue of freedom of sexual expression in private. But perhaps that is of comparatively little importance, since what happens in private only rarely comes to the notice of the courts.

All this politico-legal controversy has tended to overshadow the more fundamental questions concerning the nature and causes of homosexuality. In this field, no striking discoveries have resulted from the increased public interest. Nevertheless, a body of factual data has accumulated, and a number of theories are available. It has been my chief purpose to summarise as clearly as possible what is known, to draw what practical conclusions may be possible, and to point out where we are still groping and ignorant.

In presenting this work to an American audience, there is little risk of being misunderstood. Our cultures are broadly similar, and so are the psychological problems from which we suffer as individuals. Even so, it is arguable (by Englishmen, of course) that male homosexuality is more frequent in the United States because American women are socially more dominant, exacting, and frightening. It has also been alleged that American homosexuals are addicted to fellatio more than to buggery because of unsatisfied needs for oral gratification (in the Freudian sense). I mention these speculations in a preface, rather than in the text, for the reason that I can find no certain information on the facts of the matter or on their interpretation. The possibility of significant differences in the causes or manifestations of homosexuality between cultures that are very similar raises the question how far one can generalise about homosexuality in cultures far removed from our own. On this aspect, as on many others of equal importance, information is simply not available, and there is still a fresh field for the enterprising researcher. This book is of necessity no more than a somewhat parochial account of some of the sexual tribulations of a particular culture at a particular point in time as seen in the light of a strictly limited supply of factual information and research. Should it be possible to revise this book yet again after still another decade, one hopes the changes will be much greater.

CONTENTS

Introduction
    1. DEFINITIONS   PAGE 9
    2. A THEORETICAL APPROACH   15

I: Homosexuality in Various Communities
    1. PRIMITIVE PEOPLES   17
    2. HISTORICAL TIMES   21
    3. ANIMAL BEHAVIOUR   29

II: The Incidence of Homosexuality Today   33

III: Homosexual Types
    1. PHYSICAL FEATURES   44
    2. IDENTIFYING PSYCHOLOGICAL CHARACTERISTICS   48
    3. REACTIONS TO BEING A HOMOSEXUAL   53
    4. MASCULINE—FEMININE: ACTIVE—PASSIVE   59
    5. TRANS-SEXUALISM AND 'CHANGE OF SEX'   62
    6. LESBIAN TYPES   65

IV: Some Legal Problems
    1. THE LETTER OF THE LAW   72
    2. ENFORCING THE LAW   84
    3. CIVIL DISABILITIES   91
    4. ETHICAL AND RELIGIOUS ISSUES   96

V: Some Social Problems
    1. INTOLERANCE AND ITS EFFECTS   102
    2. HOMOSEXUAL SOCIETY   107
    3. CHILD MOLESTATION   114
    4. SEDUCTION OF YOUTHS   120
    5. IMPRISONMENT AND ITS EFFECTS   124
    6. MALE PROSTITUTION   132
    7. VENEREAL DISEASES   138

7

Contents

VI: Two Typical Cases   PAGE 141

VII: Glands and Heredity
  1. THE PHYSICAL BASIS OF SEX   151
  2. SEX PERFORMANCE, DESIRE AND PREFERENCE   153
  3. THE HORMONAL CONTRIBUTION TO LUST AND
     DEVIANCE   155
  4. A BIOLOGICAL ANOMALY?   160
  5. AN INHERITED FACTOR   166

VIII: The Psycho-Analytic Approach: An Introduction   172

IX: Some Psychological Factors
  1. SEARCHING FOR EXPLANATIONS   187
  2. PARENTAL BEHAVIOUR   188
  3. DEVELOPMENT OF SEX ROLES   196
  4. MORE PSYCHOLOGICAL INTERPRETATIONS   201
  5. EXPLANATIONS OF LESBIANISM   207
  6. BISEXUALITY   214

X: The Odd, The Mad and The Violent
  1. COVERT, LATENT AND REPRESSED HOMOSEXUALS   216
  2. HOMOSEXUALITY AND PARANOID SCHIZOPHRENIA   219
  3. SEXUAL VIOLENCE   223

XI: Treatment for The Individual
  1. PROSPECTS OF CURE   230
  2. DECIDING THE AIMS OF TREATMENT   237
  3. TECHNIQUES OF TREATMENT   247
  4. BEHAVIOUR THERAPY   256

XII: Conclusions
  1. CAUSES   261
  2. PREVENTION BY TOLERANCE?   266
    REFERENCES   274
    INDEX   302

INTRODUCTION

1. Definitions

Not so long ago, sexual topics were avoided in polite conversation and young persons were carefully shielded from too early awareness of what was considered the more unpleasant side of life. Ideas have changed, and works on hitherto taboo subjects, such as marital adjustment and birth control, now circulate freely. But although lip service is paid to the ideal of an open attitude to sex, prudery and obscurantism linger on, especially in relation to homosexuality. On this topic attitudes of ignorance still abound, varying from an almost superstitious dread, through abhorrence and contempt, to an amused and prurient fascination. Since 1954, when the British Government set up a Departmental (Wolfenden) Committee to look into English Law on homosexuality and prostitution, the legal issue has been repeatedly aired in the Press, on Television and in both Houses of Parliament. The judgements expressed have often been warped by the heat of controversy, and by the superficiality of the information discussed, but at least the public debates have broken the long conspiracy of silence and brought some serious social and psychological questions out of the atmosphere of the schoolroom smut and into the arena of rational scrutiny. More and more people want to know the facts of the matter, and this book sets out to give the general reader a sober account of the information available, as well as to consider the implications calmly in the light of common sense and modern knowledge.

Unfortunately, though strongly held opinions abound, hard facts about homosexuality and its possible causes are difficult to obtain. Scientific research of necessity progresses slowly, and it will take many years to make up for past

9

neglect. Even now, serious medical and sociological investigations in this subject are scandalously few considering the importance of the questions in human terms. Although the cupboard has been opened, and the skeleton glimpsed, many people dislike the revelation and resist looking any closer. This resistance becomes acutely apparent when a social investigator wants to get down to business and proposes some definite line of research. Gordon Westwood [378], who carried out one of the very few sociological inquiries into homosexual behaviour in England, commented on the repugnance which his investigation aroused, the refusal of Trusts and Foundations to entertain the project as suitable for a grant, and the unwillingness of social organizations to allow their interview rooms to be used for the purpose, once they realized that homosexuals would need to enter the premises. Until a large section of the public is prepared to face the facts squarely and rationally, and to support adequate research, our knowledge will remain rudimentary. This book must inevitably raise many more questions than can be answered at present.

Homosexuality simply means the experience of being erotically attracted to a member of the same sex, and men or women who habitually experience strong feelings of this kind are called homosexuals. Those who act upon such feelings by participating in mutual sexual fondling or other forms of sexual stimulation with a partner of the same sex are known as 'overt'[1] or practising homosexuals. Those whose erotic feelings for the opposite sex are absent altogether, or slight in comparison to their homosexual feelings, are called exclusive or obligatory homosexuals. This is the type doctors usually have in mind when they refer without further qualification to 'homosexuals', or when they speak of 'true' homosexuals or 'inverts', or when they consider the condition more or less permanent and unchangeable. Indeed, it is this exclusive, obligatory

---

[1] Sometimes the term 'overt' is used to describe a person who fully recognizes and admits to himself or others that he is homosexually inclined, though he may not necessarily put his inclinations into practice.

type of homosexual who presents the chief problem for contemporary society, and who is the main concern of this book. The thought of intimate contacts with their own sex disgusts many normal persons, but many of these exclusive homosexuals, especially male homosexuals, are even more appalled by the prospect of relations with the opposite sex. Even if women provoke in him no positive revulsion, the exclusively homosexual man finds that feminine attractions leave him quite uninterested and unaroused sexually or emotionally. For this reason he would probably be impotent if he tried to force himself to have sexual relations with a woman. Many female homosexuals on the other hand, are able to give a man the satisfaction of intercourse, though they themselves obtain little or no sexual excitement. This physiological difference between the sexes goes some way to account for the observation that female homosexuals tend to be less frequently 'exclusive' in their sexual conduct.

In contrast to the exclusive variety, those who take to homosexual activities only on odd occasions, usually when deprived of contact with the opposite sex (for instance during imprisonment), are called 'facultative' homosexuals. Such persons have the ability to use the homosexual outlet as a convenient substitute, like others might use masturbation, without it interfering with their normal heterosexual capacity or feeling. The term bisexual is used to describe persons who can find full erotic satisfaction with persons of either sex. These three classes of bisexual, facultative homosexual, and exclusive or obligatory homosexual, conveniently describe common patterns, but one must not be too categorical. In reality one encounters every conceivable gradation of feeling, attitude and behaviour, from absolutely exclusive heterosexuals at one end of the scale, to complete inverts at the other extreme [302].

In its widest sense, the term sexual perversion, or sexual deviation, covers all conditions in which erotic interest centres upon anything other than simple copulation. It embraces masturbation, sadism, cross-dressing (transvestism), peeping Tom activities (voyeurism), genital exposure (exhibitionism), fetishism and so on. The range of activity defined as 'perverse' varies from one culture to another. Masturbation and kissing are generally excluded from the list of perversions by Western authorities. These apart, homosexuality is by far the commonest form of sexual perversion all over the world. But homosexuals hate to be called perverts, because of the pejorative tone the term has acquired, and because the word suggests unjustly that they have chosen their unpopular way of life in deliberate defiance of heterosexual society.

It is now realized that homosexuality is an extremely common condition and that the only reason why psychiatrists and law courts are not completely swamped with cases is that the great majority of those affected neither seek psychological advice nor fall into the hands of the police. Apart from the specialized writings of psycho-analysts, medical literature devotes but scant consideration to homosexuality, and even this is not always well informed or free from bias. The subject has never received the serious attention of scientific researchers that its importance warrants. Yet homosexuals are so numerous that nearly everyone, whether he realizes it or not, has one or more among his acquaintances. But it is not just on account of the number of such persons that the matter is of general concern. Occasional homosexual feelings may be experienced by anyone, and those responsible for training children, administering the law, or advising on public morals cannot fulfil their duty to the community if they keep themselves in ignorance of certain facts. Homosexuality is a part of life that intelligent people should know about and understand. Unhealthy ignorance causes an almost unbelievable amount of misery and frustration.

This book deals mainly with male homosexuality, because in men the condition causes more obvious social problems and has been studied more intensely by psychiatrists. Homosexuality in women is sometimes called lesbianism, the name deriving from Lesbos, an island in the Aegean, where the Greek poetess Sappho lived in the fifth century B.C. She gathered about her a circle of female admirers and wrote passionate verses in praise of lovely maidens. Lesbians have usually been less vocal and unobtrusive than male homosexuals, so less has been written about them, and they have not been legislated against nor so fully investigated. Indeed, the existence of lesbianism as a commonplace condition continues to be largely ignored or denied in polite society. Some commentators have suggested that lesbians owe their immunity from arrest and imprisonment to the masculine pride of legislative authorities, who tend to resist a public admission that many women prefer to bestow their sexual favours elsewhere.

Although homosexuality has sometimes been looked upon as a dangerously seductive vice, the sexual pleasures involved are in no way unusual. As with ordinary attraction between men and women (heterosexuality), homosexual feelings are a mixture of varying proportions of animal passion and sentimental fondness. Since normal copulation between persons of the same sex is impossible, homosexuals depend for reaching climax (orgasm) on methods of mutual stimulation that normal couples would regard as mere incidental indulgences leading up to intercourse. Kissing, fondling, close bodily contact, and mutual masturbation are common forms of love-making with which both male and female homosexuals begin their sexual careers, and many never progress beyond this. Between men, however, there are the additional possibilities of inserting the penis into the partner's mouth (fellatio) or anus (buggery or sodomy). Use of the latter technique generally indicates some degree of practice or sophistication, since without the necessary relaxation and dilation the insertion can be quite painful, as many patients who have undergone rectoscopic examinations will be aware.

The one who inserts the penis during the act of sodomy is called the 'active' partner, the one who receives it is the 'passive' partner. Although these roles are commonly interchanged, those who habitually prefer the passive role are popularly credited with being particularly deeply rooted in their perversion. Some male homosexuals preserve a semblance of masculinity by limiting themselves to active sodomy, and may even deny their perversion by pretending that their partner is nothing more to them than a poor substitute for a woman. Between women, a common form of mutual simulation is by rhythmic mutual apposition of the genitals (tribadism), a technique less suited to male anatomy. The use or an artificial penis or 'dildol', gripped in the vagina of one woman and inserted in simulation of intercourse, strikes the imagination of the prurient male, but is probably a comparatively unusual lesbian technique. Most of these methods of stimulation, such as mouth-genital contacts and sodomy, are not limited to homosexuals. It has been shown that the anal area is physiologically an active erotic zone to much the same degree in both sexes [223], and in some countries sodomy between husband and wife has long been known as the poor man's contraceptive, or as a remedy for the lax or torn vagina produced by multiple childbirths. The real distinguishing feature of homosexuals is not that in love-making they prefer particular methods of stimulation, but that they prefer a partner of their own sex.

Although the matter will be dealt with more fully later, it is worth emphasizing at the outset that, however much some male homosexuals like to pretend to be women, in fact, in the essentials of physique, genital equipment and physiological sex responses they are no different from other men, and lesbians are the same as other women. This point gives rise to the one small advantage that might be claimed for homosexual love play, namely that the participants, being of the same sex, have an immediate appreciation of each other's stimulatory needs. In heterosexual intercourse, the different timing of the woman's mounting sexual tension, the role of indirect stimulation of the clitoris by traction on the labial hood, and the woman's need for release of vascular engorgement and muscle-tension by a definite orgasm, are all points which may cause dissatisfaction among the inexperienced.

A Theoretical Approach

The ideal heterosexual relationship fulfils both the need for love and the need for sexual release; but as everyone knows some heterosexual men are women-haters at heart, using their wives or mistresses as mere machines for sexual purposes, but otherwise neglecting them or maltreating them. Likewise, some wives lavish more interest and affection on Platonic friends of their own sex than upon their husbands. Such attitudes amount to homosexual perversion on the moral plane; but in compliance with common usage this book limits the use of the term 'homosexuality' to physical, erotic reactions.

2. A Theoretical Approach

In view of the guilty secrecy with which our society has long surrounded sexual deviation, and the uncompromising denunciations by moralists of what is traditionally known as 'unnatural vice' or 'degeneracy', it is no surprise that the average person looks on homosexuality with rooted aversion, and that his ideas about it are crude. Male homosexuals have been variously regarded as degenerate personalities, moral pariahs who obstinately persist in tasting forbidden fruits, effete, 'pansy' types incapable of natural manliness, dangerous seducers of the young, victims of circumstance, sufferers from psychological disorder, cases of glandular disease, or even the forerunners of a new biological type—the third sex. None of these views completely fits the known facts. After perusing the account which follows the reader will form his own conclusion, but it may be useful to know from the outset the author's own outlook. It seems to him that children are not born with the sex instinct specifically directed to one sex or the other. Exclusive preference for the opposite sex is an acquired trait, and involves the repression of a certain amount of homosexual feeling which is natural to the human being. Some adults fail to become completely inhibited in this respect, and though they have normal, happy relations with the opposite sex, they can still enjoy occasional homosexual activities as well. One may perhaps disapprove of their

15

behaviour, but they are not necessarily psychologically ill. On the other hand, the completely homosexual man, one who is repelled rather than attracted by feminine charms, really suffers from an abnormal inhibition, the origin of which can often be traced to psychological causes early in life. In such a case, the flight from heterosexual relations is a neurotic symptom, produced in much the same way as other irrational fears and inhibitions. Freud put the same basic idea more elegantly when he wrote: 'Freedom to range equally over male and female objects—as it is found in childhood, in primitive states of society, and early periods of history, is the original basis from which, as a result of restriction in one direction or another, both the normal and the inverted types develop.'[1]

[1] Freud, S. *Three Essays on the Theory of Sexuality* (translated J. Strachey). London, 1949, p. 23, footnote.

CHAPTER I

HOMOSEXUALITY
IN VARIOUS COMMUNITIES

1. Primitive Peoples

To most people of modern Anglo-American culture homosexual indulgence appears self-evidently abnormal or immoral, but many older communities have taken different attitudes. Some societies have been more rigidly condemnatory than ourselves, others have treated it with indifference or denied its occurrence, others have looked upon it as expected and appropriate behaviour for young unmarried people, and some have accorded special social or religious status to the occasional sex deviant. In a survey of anthropological literature the investigators Ford and Beach found that in 49 out of 76 (that is 64 per cent) of the primitive societies about which information was available some form of homosexual activity was considered normal and acceptable. In some societies male homosexuality was universal [103]. They quoted several examples of this. For instance the Siwans, a small North African tribe, who lived by raising crops and domestic animals, expected all men and boys to engage in homosexual sodomy, and thought a man peculiar if he did not have both male and female affairs. Among the Kerski of New Guinea the young men were introduced to anal intercourse at puberty by older men, and thereafter spent the rest of their bachelorhood doing the same to other initiates. They had to pass through these two stages of first passive and later active homosexual sodomy before they could achieve full social status and have relations with women [25]. The Kiwai had similar customs; they believed sodomy helpful in making young men strong [225]. The Aranda of Australia carried the custom a stage further. Their youths commonly went through a stage of homosexual 'marriage' in which they lived as a 'wife' with an older bachelor for several years until the elder partner would break away and take a female wife.

In a small Melanesian island community referred to by William Davenport [74] as East Bay, the boys up to age six or seven characteristically played in a rough and tumble way, grabbing and pinching at each others genitals, but from about the fifth year they were taught to avoid touching girls, and always to keep a respectable distance from the opposite sex. After puberty, young bachelors were given high social status, but were required to live apart in a men's house and avoid heterosexual contacts. Masturbation was regarded as a safe and proper outlet for the unmarried of both sexes. For men, homosexual relationships were also permitted and were regarded as perfectly normal. Between two young men, physical relations were usually alternately active and passive, but when the partners were a youth and an older man the latter was expected to take the active role and repay the favour with presents. Curiously enough, though anal copulation was considered enjoyable no one appeared to understand how mouth-genital contacts could give any sexual pleasure. After marriage, the men could still indulge in homosexual activity provided they also satisfied their wives. However, the idea that any man might be exclusively homosexual, lacking all interest in women, had apparently never occurred to these people until they were asked about it by the investigators. Questioned privately, adult males most commonly reported both homosexual and heterosexual interests, but more often with a preference for the latter.

Some cultures, like the Andamanese, the Ute of Colorado, or the Tahitians were very permissive in regard to heterosexual love affairs between young unmarried people, but regarded homosexual activity as extremely aberrant [283]. In contrast, the Cubeo Indians of the North-west Amazon were unusually strict in preventing pre-marital heterosexuality but permitted semi-public displays of adolescent homosexuality, during which girls might stroke each others nipples to produce erections and boys could indulge in mutual masturbation [140]. The Manus of New Guinea were equally rigid in moral discipline with regard to heterosexual relations, which they surrounded with a host of taboos and inhibitions, but they viewed homosexual acts with laughing unconcern [257].

Some communities had a recognized class of men, variously called *berdaches, alyhas,* or *shamans,* who were intermediate in social status between men and women. They dressed like women, performed women's tasks, and even got married to men. Sexually they took the passive role in sodomy. Special ceremonies had to be gone through before a man was recognized as a proper *berdache.* In some tribes the *berdaches* carried their pretence to femininity so far that they imitated female functions, scratching themselves to simulate menstrual blood or stuffing their clothes with rags to simulate pregnancy.

George Devereux made a study of the homosexual system among the Mohave Indians, a warrior race who inhabited the south-west of North America. Youths who did not fit in with the usual pursuits of the male members of the tribe went through an elaborate ceremony which changed their sex status. Henceforth they were *alyhas,* who lived and dressed as women and were permitted to set up house with a 'husband'. The *alyha* usually made an industrious wife, and had a quite respectable position in the community. The *alyha's* husband, however, had to suffer a certain amount of teasing, especially when his 'wife' insisted that he observe obsolete taboos in honour of an entirely imaginary pregnancy. In this community there was also a recognized class of exclusively homosexual women [79]. Marise Querlin [300] quotes a description by Dominique Troare, a Sudanese schoolmaster, of institutionalized marriages between women of the Bobo-Nienegués. These usually took place between older childless widows and young girls, the older woman contributing a substantial bride-price in order to improve her status from that of a despised sterile woman to that of titular husband. Male lovers were allowed to visit surreptitiously in order to produce children for the marriage. In general, however, the occurrence of extensive lesbianism, institutionalized or otherwise, has rarely been noted by anthropologists.

The Big Nambas, a cannibal race of the New Hebrides, were also noted for their institutionalized homosexuality [160] as were the Zuni Indians of North America [24]. Ruth Benedict was particularly impressed by the fact that the *berdaches* had a definite position in the social structure and were able to lead useful lives. Often they excelled and took the lead in women's occupations, but some of their husbands were weaklings who preferred a self-supporting *berdache* to an economically dependent wife. Ruth Benedict inclined to conclude that the sense of guilt and inadequacy and the social failure of many homosexuals today is a secondary consequence of the strain of social disapproval and not the result of the condition itself. Like the Zuni, the Siberian Chukchee also had a class of men-women who enjoyed great prestige. They were called *shamans*, and were credited with supernatural powers. They lived as 'wives', taking the passive role in sodomy. Their 'husbands' were allowed to have female mistresses as well, and sometimes the *shamans* too had mistresses and fathered children of their own [283]. In Chukchee society, the high price of brides and the existence of a large floating population of unmarried labourers, was held responsible for the popularity of transvestite shamanism as a way of escape. Anthropologists have pointed out that, where a society expects men to live up to a difficult ideal, one usually finds some institutionalized method of escape for those who cannot make the grade.

In some tribes, though homosexual practices took place between adult males, sodomy was avoided. Others would not tolerate homosexual practices in any shape or form. Malinowski says of the Trobrian Islanders that, although they permitted affectionate intimacy and embraces between male friends, perverse acts were effectively kept down by contempt, ridicule, and scoffing. Exposed culprits would kill themselves. The Trobrianders' language included phrases descriptive of sodomy, but individuals always insisted that such acts were a thing of the past. Homosexual practices were common among the natives confined in gaols, mission stations and plantation barracks, but Malinowski attributed this to the forcible segregation of men used to regular sex activities [248]. Other tribes, even stricter than the Trobrianders, used to put to death any men found committing sodomy.

It seems that in different communities every shade of attitude has prevailed, from severe condemnation, through various shades of indifference, to institutional recognition. Where homosexual conduct was said not to exist at all this probably indicated that strong pressures had been brought to bear against its open manifestation. On the other hand, no primitive society, not even the most permissive, has accepted the open practice of exclusive homosexuality as a permanent way of life by large numbers of adults.

2. Historical Times

Homosexuality is as old as humanity and occurs as much in advanced civilizations as it does in primitive cultures. In the 'Terminal Essay' to his translation of *The Arabian Nights*, Sir Richard Burton [47] instances with monotonous pertinacity one example after another of homosexual practices past and present. He claims that such practices have always been endemic over a vast area of the globe, including the countries bordering the Mediterranean and a great part of the East, especially India, China, Japan, and the Pacific islands. His rambling discourse covers such diverse matters as male brothels both ancient and modern, scandals in French society under the Second Empire, lewd treatment of prisoners in Egypt during the Napoleonic wars, male prostitutes on the caravan trails of the Middle East, the uninhibited behaviour of South Sea Islanders, romantic male love in classical Greece, and the debauches of the Caesars. After wading through all this it is hard to resist the conclusion that homosexual behaviour constitutes

21

a fundamental human tendency that may crop up at any time. Sometimes it is found linked with the religious beliefs and ceremonials. Burton states that 'in Rome as in Egypt the temples of Isis were centres of sodomy', and similar practices took place among 'grand priestly castes from Mesopotamia to Mexico and Peru'. (Vol. x, p. 227.)

References to the matter in the Old Testament writings indicate that among the ancient tribes of Israel homosexuality was both practised and condemned. The fact that homosexuality had ritualistic significance for alien religions lent special force to this condemnation. Genesis xix contains the story of a group of debauched men of Sodom who stormed the house where Lot was, demanding: 'Where are the men which came in to thee this night? Bring them out to us that we may know them.' Lot offers his virgin daughters instead. The same story with slight modifications also appears in Judges xix. In this case a female concubine was proff. 1 in place of the man they sought. The history of David and Jonathan (1 Samuel xx, 2 Samuel i) whose love was 'passing the love of women', and the story of the love of Ruth and Naomi (Ruth i) have been cited as examples of homosexual romance [105].

In classical Greece homosexuality achieved social recognition as an acceptable and expected form of love between normal males. most appropriate between youths and somewhat older men who could set a good example [88]. When Plato wrote so sublimely of the emotions and aspirations of love he was describing what we should call perversion. Male homosexual sentiment permeated the whole fabric of Greek society. Homosexuality meant more to the Greeks than a safety valve for excess of lust; it was in their eyes the highest and noblest of passions. They idealized the love of man for man as much as present-day Western civilization idealizes romantic love between men and women [231].

The subservient role played by Greek women probably helped foster this curious attitude. Greek civilization was essentially a man's world. Their literature dealt almost

22

entirely with male pursuits and the masculine point of view. Courage and nobility of mind, indeed all the most admired virtues, seemed essentially manly attributes. The women lacked education and lived in seclusion in their own rooms. There was no domestic life as we know it, so that men of culture looked always to their own sex for stimulating companionship [353]. On matters of sex the Greeks had an uninhibited outlook. They held sensual enjoyment an important part of life and were not afraid to express their sentiments. The human body, and especially the body of the athletic young male, was admired as an object of great beauty, a fitting subject for eulogistic poems and exquisite sculpture. The influence of this ideal on the art of the period is well known.

It seemed natural to the Greeks that men should be passionately attracted by beautiful youths, and it was usual for an older man to take under his wing some favourite youth and to act as his special friend and mentor. The Doric states observed this custom especially strictly. A man failed in his duty if he did not become the guardian of one younger than himself whom he could instruct in the manly virtues, and a youth felt disgraced if he failed to win such a friendship [34].

Homosexual sentiment abounds in ancient Greek legends, and was prominent in the heyday of Greek civilization as well as during is decay. Writers pictured homosexual love as a lofty passion that raised men above themselves. In his *Symposium* Plato wrote:

And if there were only some way of contriving that a state or army should be made up of lovers and their loves, they would be the very best governors of their own city, abstaining from all dishonour, and emulating one another in honour, and when fighting at each other's side, although a mere handful, they would overcome the world. For what lover would not choose rather to be seen by all mankind than by his beloved, either when abandoning his post or throwing away his arms? He would be ready to die a thousand deaths rather than endure this. Or who would desert his beloved or fail him in the hour of danger?

23

The veriest coward would become an inspired hero, equal to the bravest, at such a time; Love would inspire him.

(Jowett translation.)

The Spartan and Theban armies were organized on just this theory, regularly making sacrifices to Eros before battle. The celebrated Theban Band, long supposed invincible, consisted of pairs of lovers fighting side by side. When finally they were annihilated at the battle of Chaeronea, even their conqueror wept at the sight of the three hundred lying dead together.

The Greeks did not encourage indiscriminate infatuations. Socrates' fascination for youths brought him no credit. Moreover, the cult of effeminacy in young men and the buying or selling of sexual favours evoked the strongest disapproval. The penal code of ancient Athens included various provisions against homosexual abuses, some of which dated from Solon's enactments in the sixth century B.C. Though relations between adult citizens were permitted, Solon forbade a slave to have association with a free-born youth on pain of a public whipping. Though others might do as they thought fit, later legislation provided for the removal of all civil rights from any Athenian citizen who prostituted his body for money. The legal code also took special care to protect children from seduction. For an outrage against a minor a man could be sentenced to death or to a heavy fine. A father (or guardian) who prostituted his son for gain was liable to severe punishment, as was the man who took advantage of the boy, although the boy himself, provided he was under age, suffered no legal penalty [82].

Romanticized homosexual love, with its association of excellence and manliness, contrasts sadly with the homosexuality practised as a luxurious vice by Oriental potentates who patronized effeminate court favourites and boy prostitutes. Even among the Greeks, their drama goes in for occasional coarse lampooning of boy infatuations on a level with modern music-hall jokes. With the Roman in-

24

flux, idealism seemed to disappear. In Roman literature homosexuality became a subject of amusement or contempt, and in practice it was linked with orgiastic debauchery and prostitution [206]. The satires of Juvenal and the writings of Petronius attribute every possible sexual vice to the Roman rulers. In the Satyricon, Petronius portrays a society bent upon pleasure without restraint. The tale opens with the attempted seduction of a young man by a much older one, but the young man learns nothing from his unpleasant adventure and at once tries forcibly to seduce a still younger person. Suetonius's *Lives of the Caesars* is a sorry tale of debauchery. Nero's disgusting and cruel orgies, in which men and women suffered equally, reached the depths of squalor. He had Sporus, his favourite, castrated, after which he went through all the ceremonies of marriage and made the unfortunate youth his 'wife'. Apparently many emperors were tarred with the same brush, even Julius Caesar whom one senator, the older Curio, called 'every woman's man and every man's woman'. True or not, the taunt reflects the morals of an age in which such behaviour was commonplace.

Study of the sexual habits of Greece and Rome serves to confirm what has already been deduced from anthropological studies, namely that homosexual instincts soon make themselves apparent whenever they are given a free rein. The consequences can be good or bad according to how the community handles the situation. In Greece homosexual love was made to serve the highest ideals of the time. For the later Romans, homosexual lust merely added variety to their debaucheries. Not since the decline of classical Greece has male homosexuality been raised to the status of a desirable ideal, though pale reflections of ancient Sparta have from time to time appeared in various militaristic systems. At the time of the Crusades, the cult of masculine valour, the hero-worship, the great emphasis on manly fortitude and valour, the tradition of the pure woman to be admired from afar, doubtless helped to foster homosexual tendencies. The homosexual behaviour attributed to such bands as the Templars must be understood in the light of this background. A somewhat similar situation prevailed in recent times in Nazi Germany when the Hitler Youth banded together for the sake of a mystic, manly ideal that over-rode all family ties [274].

Leaving the ancient world and coming nearer home, the history of our own civilization shows that the cultivation of a severely repressive attitude has consistently failed to eradicate the homosexual problem. In each century one finds the question of homosexuality arising. Even in periods when detection meant death the practice was known to be widespread. The popular notion that this is a social problem of the present day, due to a recent relaxation of moral standards, can be disproved by the briefest excursion into history [359].

Elizabethan literature has homosexual allusions. Shakespeare himself wrote sonnets apparently addressed to a youth. According to Montgomery Hyde, that other great dramatist Christopher Marlowe only escaped execution for homosexual offences through being murdered in the nick of time in a public house brawl. In 1631, for acts of sodomy, the Earl of Castlehaven and two of his servants were dispatched on the scaffold and the gallows respectively [173]. In the eighteenth century convictions and executions still continued, but the male brothels and homosexual clubs thrived in London [176]. A renowned meeting place, the White Swan, headquarters of the Vere Street Coterie, was exposed in 1810, and seven men were sent to the pillory in the Haymarket. A huge mob gathered and behaved with unusual brutality. Street vendors hawked missiles, which the angry crowd hurled at the prisoners, causing severe injuries.

A curious little eighteenth-century book entitled *Plain Reasons for the Growth of Sodomy in England* (Anon., *c.* 1730) [9] shows that even in those days homosexuality was considered a social problem. The author attributes the prevalence of the vice to the molly-coddling of boys and the cultivation of effeminate habits by young men. He deplores

26

the custom of sending young boys to kindergartens run by women. He thinks the young men's habits of foppish attire, continental manners, indolence, and tea-drinking breed milksops. The influence of the Italian opera he considers particularly pernicious, for it is well known (he alleges) that sodomy is thought a trivial matter in Italy, so that no sooner does a stranger set foot in Rome than the procurers rush to ask if he wants a woman or a young man.

The nineteenth century was full of scandals, from the suicide of the Foreign Minister Castlereagh because of the fear (probably delusory) of being denounced, to the imprisonment of the playwright Oscar Wilde after three sensational trials [189]. Wilde was convicted largely on the evidence of self-confessed male prostitutes and blackmailers who turned Queen's Evidence and thus went free. When Wilde was sentenced, it is said, prostitutes in the street outside the Old Bailey lifted their skirts to dance in glee, and sermons on the subject were delivered throughout the country. The learned judge expressed his utmost indignation at the evidence of corruption of the most hideous kind and regretted that the maximum penalty he was allowed to give was totally inadequate. But even in 1895 there were some more sober counsels. The famous editor W. T. Stead wrote: 'Should everyone found guilty of Oscar Wide's crime be imprisoned, there would be a very surprising emigration from Eton, Harrow, Rugby, and Winchester to the gaols of Pentonville and Holloway.'

Historical studies of famous persons can give a false impression that the incidence of homosexuality was particularly high in former times. One has to keep in mind how very common such behaviour is today, and that one would expect any group of persons whose intimate lives have been recorded to contain a quota of homosexuals. The Kings of England, for example, whose renown is based on accident of birth rather than specially good or specially bad characteristics, include several whose homosexual tendencies were well known. William Rufus's behaviour was so scandalous that he was refused a sanctified burial by the Church. Edward II kept the notorious Picrs Gaveston and other favourites. James I's favourite, Robert Carr, is said to have escaped punishment for murder because he threatened to make public his relations with the King, and William III is said to have been in love with Albemarle. Those interested in historical by-ways may perhaps identify other homosexual monarchs, but the exercise merely shows that kings share the common passions of humanity.

In an effort to establish a better public image, homosexual propagandists often cite names of great historical personages whose deviant sexual tendencies have become publicly known. Such reasoning is as muddled as that of the anti-vice campaigner who cites criminals as evidence that homosexuals are evil. The discovery that many famous or infamous men have shared this common characteristic is worth about as much as a discovery that a proportion of them had fair hair.

The fact that writers have always been prone to expose their private emotions to public scrutiny may have given rise to a similarly false impression of an unduly high incidence among the literary fraternity. Verlaine boasted that he was one of:

> The chosen ones, the servants of the good Church,
> Of which Plato would be Pope and Socrates the nuncio.

André Gide made no secret of his male loves [132]. In one of his works, *Corydon*, he creates a fictitious doctor who expounds at great length a scientific justification for homosexual practices. Marcel Proust, author of the analytic masterpiece, *A la recherche du temps perdu*, infused life into his love passages by drawing upon his own passionate experiences as a homosexual lover. He had a liaison with one Albert Le Cuziat, keeper of a male brothel, to which he even contributed some of his family furniture [254].

If the indecent haste with which the homosexual interests of the late Somerset Maugham were exposed in the press the moment he died is any guide, the homosexual propagandists of the future will have a lot more of this kind of ammunition.

3. *Animal Behaviour*

The fact that many species of animals have been seen to behave homosexually has been put forward as support for the view that homosexual responsiveness forms part of the natural, biological heritage of both the human and animal kingdoms. Dr. F. A Beach, an expert on animal sexuality, puts it this way: 'In our society sexual contact between members of the same sex is considered extremely undesirable. Various social goals and ethical laws are violated by the homosexual individual, but to describe his behaviour as "unnatural" is to depart from strict accuracy' [17].

Interpretations of animal reactions are sometimes less straightforward than at first appears. The behaviour of some of the lower species differs so much from human conduct that concepts like homosexuality scarcely apply [77]. For instance, the snail having both masculine and feminine genitals, can copulate as a male at one time and as a female at a later date. In some species of lizard the male anatomy allows them to penetrate each other easily and copulation occurs as often between two males as between a male and female. The male toad cannot identify the sex of his mate until he has clasped her (or him) in the sexual position. If the partner chirps and jumps away this means he has got hold of another male and must try again.

In animals closest to man in evolution, the mammals and primates, whose copulatory mechanisms so closely resemble our own, matings between members of the same sex occur quite frequently and spontaneously in the natural state. When stated as a formal research finding, this may cause some surprise, which only goes to show how little we think about what we do not want to know about. The sight of dogs mounting each other and making copulatory movements is a familiar street spectacle, and countrymen know how often cows and cockerels do the same. Indeed, when cows begin to mount each other this furnishes a useful sign that they are at the right phase for breeding. In obtaining semen for artificial insemination, a young bull is often used as a 'teaser' to induce mounting and ejaculation in the breeding bull. If this is done regularly the bull soon comes to react more readily to his own sex than to a female.

In natural surroundings, mammalian homosexual behaviour generally takes place when animals are strongly aroused, and usually occurs in addition to heterosexual behaviour rather than in place of it. It has been noticed most often among young males. Usually one of the larger, more powerful and aggressive males mounts a smaller, younger, and more submissive partner. In many species, the threatening or aggressive behaviour which maintains safety, status and territory appears indistinguishable from male courtship behaviour. Both forms of conduct involve the same gestures, rituals and modes of attack [365]. Behaviour which in a man would signify a strong homoerotic urge of the 'active' type might be just a by-product of the aggressive, assertive tendencies of the male mammal. This cannot be the whole story, however, since many animals will mount another of the same sex only if no female can be found [102]. Among some primates, however, which are the animals nearest to man on the evolutionary scale, mature males have been seen to establish unmistakable homosexual alliances even when females were readily available [395]. It seems to be a general rule that the more intelligent species, those that come closest to mankind in versatility and learning power, such as the dolphin [238], display the greatest variety of auto-erotic and homoerotic behaviour.

Conditions which encourage homosexual conduct in animals have been studied with a view to discovering factors which might have importance in the human situation. Few animals in the natural state develop an exclusive preference for the same sex in the way that humans sometimes do; but one can induce such a preference in adult male rats by prolonged segregation from females. Jenkins showed that the longer the male rats were kept apart the more homosexual behaviour they manifested. While some of them reverted to heterosexuality quite quickly when given the opportunity, others evinced little interest and continued for an indefinite period to prefer their own kind [195]. In another experiment with rats, Rasmussen [308] demonstrated that males given an electric shock whenever they attempted to copulate with females were discouraged from further attempts at heterosexuality and became 'homosexuals'.

Experiences which occur early in an animal's life have a greater and more lasting effect. Once an inborn instinctive drive finds release in a particular mode of behaviour, this tends to persist. The following reaction of birds, studied by Konrad Lorenz [237], provides a good example. Newly hatched goslings have a tendency to attach themselves to the nearest moving object. Normally the object is their mother, and they follow on behind her wherever she goes. If, during the critical period of imprinting, as it has been called, the goslings are separated from the mother bird they can be made to follow humans instead. In some species, the imprinting experience determines sexual as well as social responses. When they come to the mating season the affected birds will perform pathetic rituals and copulatory attempts towards the human objects to which they had become attached as babies.

Even higher animals, whose social and sexual reactions are less stereotyped and more dependent upon learning, pass through critical periods of development during which appropriate responses may be established once and for all or else not at all. Thus, dogs kept in kennels away from humans during their first few months of life can never become satisfactory pets later on [107]. Very striking demonstrations of the importance of early environmental experience in determining adult social and sexual behaviour have been produced in Harlow's experiments with monkeys. Separation of baby animals from their mothers, and from other monkeys, during the first six months of life (equivalent to two to three years of a child's life) produced

31

irreversible disturbance of behaviour. When they were put into a normal group of monkeys the experimental animals remained isolated, irritable, and subject to attacks of frenzy and self-mutilation. As they grew older, they failed either to make or to respond properly to normal sexual approaches, for the most part limiting themselves to solitary masturbation. Some of the females did become pregnant, in spite of their disturbance, but these proved incapable of caring for their offspring in a proper manner [158, 159].

It seems that in monkeys early contacts with other animals, especially contact with other young monkeys with whom they can engage in sex play, is an essential element in the learning of normal adult heterosexual responses. Such observations lend colour to the psycho-analytic contention that emotional experiences of infancy may have a lasting effect upon the sexuality of a human animal. They may also cause one to reflect upon the possibly deleterious consequences of our cultural prohibitions against the sexual interests and sexual play of young children.

CHAPTER II

THE INCIDENCE
OF HOMOSEXUALITY TODAY

Often it is easier to study the ways of primitive tribes and historic civilizations than to examine contemporary culture, for only by dint of great mental effort can a man stand back and view dispassionately his own cherished beliefs and customs. In attempting to estimate the frequency of homosexuality in the community today one must guard against the tendency to minimize what is unpleasant or inconvenient. Estimates by normal folk, based on their personal observations, are always too low. They do not care to suspect their own acquaintances, and the deviants themselves are at pains to disguise their peculiarity from family and friends. A well-known psychiatric authority, in the preface to the second edition of his book on sexual perversions, remarked that he had been astonished by the number of acquaintances and colleagues who had consulted him since the appearance of the first edition, although they had shown no outward sign of abnormality [4].

Police statistics prove that male homosexuality is common, but give no real indication of the true extent, since the majority of illegal acts of this kind take place secretly behind closed doors. The number of prosecutions depends more upon official policy than anything else. *The Times* for 13 May 1954, drew attention to the rapid increase in prosecutions for homosexuality in recent decades; from an average of 13 per year per million males over ten during the years 1900 to 1909, to a figure of 107 in 1952. *The Criminal Statistics* for England and Wales [179] reveal a substantial total of 5,435 indictable homosexual crimes[1]

[1] Counting Home Office offences 16, 17, and 18, i.e. buggery, attempts, etc. and indecency between males.

'known to police' in 1963, compared with an average of 748 over the five years 1930 to 1934. The figure went down to 4,389 in 1965, largely through smaller numbers in the category of indecency. This merely suggests that lately the police have not been taking so much interest in the less serious varieties of homosexual offence.

Men who are themselves homosexual are relatively well placed for judging the proportion of their fellows similarly inclined, except that, in their understandable desire not to be thought too freakish, some of them like to exaggerate. The promiscuous ones sometimes say that almost any young man can be got to indulge given the right circumstances; but they cannot know this for sure, since they only make the attempt with men they think unlikely to rebuff them. In any case, an isolated response to persuasion does not indicate a natural preference for homosexuality. More reliable are the observations of homosexuals who have lived among groups in training establishments, in the army, or in small communities where everyone's life history is known. These regularly report certain knowledge of other sexual deviants in their group. The anonymous homosexual author of a conscientious little book *The Invert* [8], after some sober consideration of this kind, ends up with an estimate that up to five per cent of men are predominantly homosexual. The assertion that one in twenty of all adult males are predominantly homosexual seems at first almost incredible. It means that the few thousands dealt with annually by the police represent no more than a tiny and probably untypical minority of unfortunates.

For practical purposes the psychiatrist and the sociologist need not know the exact proportion of practising homosexuals in the community so long as they understand the virtually limitless extent of the problem. But the more scientifically minded have long wanted to have an exact figure. The earliest estimates made by such investigators as Havelock Ellis were little more than shrewd guesses based on common-sense considerations plus the testimony of confessing homosexuals. Ellis himself believed that two to five

34

per cent of Englishmen were predominantly homosexual [92].

The Germans attacked the matter more systematically. Dr. Magnus Hirschfeld [172, 173] circulated a questionnaire to 3,000 German male technology students and 5,721 metal workers. According to the replies 2·3 per cent of them were exclusive homosexuals and 3·4 per cent were partial homosexuals. Since only a half of those who were sent forms returned an answer, the result cannot be reliable. Hirschfeld sought to obtain confirmation by questioning homosexual men who, by virtue of their experiences, would know the extent of the homosexual activity among their own business and social groups. By this means he arrived again at approximately the same figures.

Most of the estimates of incidence have been made in America. In 1929 G. V. Hamilton published a survey of the lives of 100 married men and 100 married women. Seventeen of the 100 men reported having had some homosexual experience after the age of 18 [157]. In 1947 an American psychologist, F. W. Finger [98], reported the results of a questionnaire study submitted to a class of adult students in advanced psychology. He prepared the students for the questionnaire by a course of preliminary instruction and assured them of the secrecy of their replies. By this means he secured answers from 111 members of the total class of 138. Of those who replied 27 per cent admitted at least one adult homosexual episode leading to orgasm.

In 1948 all previous work on these lines was put in the shade by the publication of a monumental survey on the sexual behaviour of American men prepared by the zoologist Dr. A. C. Kinsey and his collaborators [207]. These investigators collected a sample of over 4,000 American men, representing as far as possible a cross section of the white community. They gave all the men confidential interviews in which they questioned them exhaustively about their sexual habits. They estimated that in the United States about 4 per cent of white males were exclusively homosexual all their lives, and that over a third admitted at least some adult homosexual experience. Their criterion of homosexual practices was contact with another man leading to orgasm. They introduced a seven-point rating scale of homosexuality, giving a maximum of six points to those who had orgasms only with other men, a minimum of 0 points to men who had orgasms only with women, and a mid score of three to men who had orgasms equally with either sex. They found that there were more men with the intermediate scores than with the maximum of 6, so that partial homosexuals were even commoner than complete inverts. They found, for example, that nearly a quarter of all men indulged in some homosexual activity, and that 10 per cent were more or less exclusively homosexual in their outlets, for a period of at least three years consecutively.

In considering these findings one must keep in mind that Kinsey concerned himself with bodily indulgence rather than the investigation of subjective feelings. The evidence of societies in which homosexual practices are universal, and the frequency of homosexual incidents in prison camps and other places where men are confined together without women, shows that most normal men are potentially capable of enjoying homosexual experiences. Kinsey has shown that a very high proportion of normal men do in fact indulge occasionally even when women are available. But the man who only occasionally, and perhaps only in special circumstances indulges in homosexual excitements, and then returns happily to his wife, is less of a social or psychiatric problem than the man who is incapable of ever enjoying a woman. Kinsey's percentages are swollen by the large number of uninhibited and highly-sexed men who will satisfy themselves with either a male or female partner. The real psychological problem, however, is the hard core of complete homosexuals, represented by Kinsey's 4 per cent, who eschew women all their lives.

One important outcome of the Kinsey exploration was the conclusion that homosexuality is not an all-or-none condition, and that it is not always permanent and unalterable. Many men who were predominantly homosexual in their teens and early twenties married later and settled down to normal sex relations. On the other hand as high a proportion as 10 per cent of the younger married men admitted having concurrent homosexual experience, and there were also some who changed from exclusively heterosexual habits to exclusively homosexual ones. Another interesting point was the evidence from older men. Their testimony gave no indication of any substantial change in the incidence of homosexuality from one generation to the next.

Kinsey's work met with a storm of criticism, much of it abusive and ill-informed. The viewpoint of the majority of critics was succinctly expressed by the naïve comment of the doctor who wrote, in the *Practitioner*, vol. 172, 1954, p. 357: 'These unseemly explorations during growth are better unrecorded; one would certainly get just as high percentages from the obliquities of other appetites, of gluttonies and pilferings. It would have been a cleaner world if Kinsey had stuck to his rats.'

In fact no one has been able seriously to dispute Kinsey's findings with regard to the prevalence of homosexuality. He and his collaborators were alive to the need for caution. They remark in their report:

We ourselves were totally unprepared to find such incidence data when this research was originally undertaken. Over a period of years we were repeatedly assailed with doubts as to whether we were getting a fair cross section of the total population or whether a selection of cases was biassing the results. It has been our experience, however, that each new group into which we have gone has provided substantially the same data. Whether the histories were taken in large cities, in small towns, or in rural areas, whether they came from one college or from another, a church school or a state university or some private institution, whether they came from one part of the country or from another, the incidence data on the homosexual have been more or less the same [207].

Kinsey and his colleagues checked their figures in a

variety of ways. They were acutely aware of the dangers of lies, exaggerations, and suppressions, and took great pains to guard against them. The interviewers were experienced and specially trained, and of course familiar with the slang terms and mode of life associated with different sexual patterns. A deliberate cheat would have soon put himself under suspicion by inconsistent responses to the many interrelated questions fired at him in the course of the interview. 'Retakes' of case histories, in which the same persons were questioned again after a lapse of years, and also comparison of the results of different interviewers, confirmed the substantial accuracy of the data collected, particularly with regard to the incidence of homosexual activity. The investigators tackled the possibility of unfair selection by approaching whole groups, such as college classes and fraternities, or all the occupants of particular lodging houses. Bias due to the omission of persons unwilling to co-operate was eliminated when everyone in a group was prevailed upon to give the required information. The figures for these complete groups, as well as those for almost complete groups, were much the same as the figures for the total sample.

They applied other checks. They compared the incidence of homosexuality in different places, in different religious and social groups, and at different age levels, all of which showed that their over-all percentages were reasonably representative and consistent. When possible they checked their findings against some independent criterion. The statements of married couples were compared one with the other, and the testimony of men and women on the incidence of activities involving both sexes was compared. Recollection on such points as the age when pubertal changes took place were compared with the results of direct observation. The checks all served to confirm the essential soundness of their estimates. In fact their investigation was about as painstaking and as scientific as such a project could be. The figures in the report may not be 100 per cent accurate, but at least they give a better picture of the true state of affairs than any previous research. Some slight inaccuracy either way would be of little practical significance. A knowledge of the exact percentage of homosexuals in various grades of society is of academic interest, but a realization that they abound everywhere is a conclusion of interest to all.

The popular press in England gave the Kinsey investigation a shoddy reception. Some newspapers hypocritically condemned the publication as pornographic or morally subversive and at the same time printed sensational excerpts under lavish headlines. In Doncaster magistrates went so far as to order confiscation of copies of Kinsey's second book, but later decided against declaring it obscene.

For a reasonable appraisal of Kinsey's work one must consult psychological literature [126, 218]. One recurrent criticism is that Kinsey limited himself to a study of actual behaviour, refraining from any deep examination of emotional attitudes or attempts at psychological discussion [30]. This was deliberate, for Kinsey wanted to keep his research strictly objective and leave the theorizing to others. But psychiatrists in particular have been irked by the absence of any meaningful interpretations of the behaviour reported by Kinsey. A too rigid adherence to the 'objective' behaviouristic approach can be misleading, for in matters of human sexuality what a person feels is often more important than what he does. Quantitative observation tells only a part of the story. Judged solely on the criterion of the number of orgasms per week, a man may appear to have a full and satisfactory sexual life when, in reality, he is being driven to over-indulgence on account of inner fears and compulsions. In the case of homosexual behaviour, Kinsey did not distinguish clearly between casual homosexual adventures, such as might be thought a part of normal development, and the compulsive seeking out of fresh contacts by the confirmed sexual deviant. Kinsey might have found out a lot more if he had taken into account the underlying motives behind sex behaviour, but his discoveries are none the less important for lacking completeness. His donkey work has given a firm factual basis for further research, and one only hopes psychologists and psychiatrists will make the most of it.

Publication in 1953 of the second Kinsey report [208], this time on the sexual behaviour of American women, brought to light a wealth of information on the extent of female homosexual practices. Of course previous investigators had dealt with the same question, but never before had anyone conducted such a large-scale inquiry. In 1929 Katharine Davis had published a survey of the sex habits of 2,200 American women, 1,200 of them college graduates [75]. She found that more than a sixth of the women had had overt homosexual experiences. The frequency was higher in the case of college graduates and single women. There were as many again who had had intense emotional relationships with other women, but without actual bodily indulgence. In a later American study, published in 1940, in which a group of 153 women were questioned, less than four per cent admitted actual sexual practices with other women, but as many as 21 per cent reported having had more intense mental or physical attachments to women than to men friends [223].

The Kinsey research went into greater detail and showed that active lesbianism, although widespread, is less common than overt male homosexuality. The fact that convention allows kissing and other manifestations of affection between women might give a false impression. In his sample of American men Kinsey found that by the time they reached the age of 45 at least 37 per cent had had some homosexual contact leading to orgasm in the course of their adult life, although of course in many cases it was a rare or isolated experience. In contrast, the corresponding figure for his sample of nearly 6,000 white women was only 13 per cent. He also found that many of the women who reported homosexual experiences had had them during only a short period of their lives. Relatively few women remained predominantly homosexual for many years and nearly all of those who did were unmarried women. In his sample about 4 per cent of the single women remained more or less exlusively homosexual in their outlets throughout the period from 20 to 35 years of age. The corresponding figure for single men was about three times as great. The permanent, complete homosexual was thus decidedly less common among women.

A substantial proportion of male homosexuals have sexual experiences with many different people, but Kinsey found that lesbians more often restrict themselves to one or two partners. It seems to be a general rule among both homosexuals and heterosexuals that men are more promiscuous than women. One reason for this may be that men are more easily tempted into unfaithfulness because they are more easily aroused sexually by psychological stimuli, such as the sight of a good-looking person or the recollection of past pleasures. It is quite normal for young men to be aroused to the point of erection several times a day without having any actual physical contact. Women, on the average, are less readily excited by casual suggestions or associations in the absence of bodily stimulation. The partner's physical appearance is not of such paramount importance to women, and they can go without sex for longer periods than men because they are not being so frequently aroused.

Kinsey's views as to the relative infrequency of promiscuity among lesbians conform to the impressions of most observers and are confirmed by Hans Giese's five-year study of 2,000 homosexual men and 100 homosexual women. According to him, female homosexual relationships are usually lasting and firm, whereas the males are usually inconstant and unstable [133]. Few confirmatory studies of homosexual incidence have appeared. In between the publication of Kinsey's two books, R. T. Ross [319] reported results from an anonymous questionnaire sent to American male college students asking them for particulars of their experiences of masturbation, homosexuality and sexual intercourse. The proportions of positive admissions were substantially similar to those obtained by Kinsey and earlier by Finger [98]. Ross concluded that it appeared quite

41

possible to reproduce Kinsey's data using other techniques.

England has earned abroad a reputation for a particularly high incidence of 'vice Anglaise', which is popularly assumed to have some connection with the habit of sexual segregation at boarding schools. However, the Wolfenden Report [177] stated frankly that no inquiries comparable to the Kinsey studies had been made in England, and that most of the medical witnesses who gave evidence said they could not tell what figures woud be likely to be obtained in England. The only systematic inquiry the Wolfenden Report could quote was an investigation by Davidson and Spencer of a hundred unselected Oxford Undergraduates. According to the research report published later [345], 35 per cent admitted having participated in some sort of homosexual interest. Of these 35 students, 27 said their homosexual interests were fading, although 13 of them admitted physical sex acts, for the most part mutual masturbation with other adolescents. The remaining 8 confessed to a persistent and troublesome homosexual inclination, and seemed quite likely to become permanent, obligatory deviants.

Whatever the exact incidence of obligatory homosexuality, when it appears that something like a million English men must be involved the enormity of the social problem can no longer be denied. The hope of controlling a plague of this dimension by individual psycho-analysis, or by imprisonment, is plainly futile, unless the entire 'normal' population takes to acting as therapists or jailers to the defiants. Homosexuals who come to official notice in medical practice or in prison constitute such a small minority that it would be unsafe to regard them as representative. Michael Schofield made an amusing calculation (based upon a 5 per cent incidence and a rate of one sex act per deviant per week) showing that the chances of any one homosexual act becoming 'known to the police' were less than one in ten thousand, and that the chances of any one homosexual being convicted in a given year were less than one in five hundred.

The ubiquity of homosexual practices, among animals

and humans alike, and the fact that such practices have continued unabated in spite of moral and legal condemnation, supports the view that such behaviour arises out of a natural biological propensity. Put another way, homosexuals are so numerous they cannot all be serious misfits or outstandingly peculiar.

CHAPTER III

HOMOSEXUAL TYPES

1. *Physical Features*

What sort of people are homosexuals? The word con-
jures up a particular type—the effete, precious-mannered
young man with mincing gait and feminine tone of voice.
In practice the majority of homosexuals possess no such
obvious signs. The affectedly effeminate group is a minority
which attracts undue public attention and gives rise to a
stereotyped idea of the male homosexual that is about as unfair as the stereotype of the beak-nosed, money-grabbing
Jew. Those who imagine that they can invariably pick out
'one of them' at a glance are certainly mistaken. Homosexuals are to be found anywhere and everywhere, in all
types of occupation and in every social class, but as most
of them possess no obvious distinguishing features, either
of appearance or manner, the unsophisticated remain in
ignorance of their existence.

Male homosexuality has long been associated in the
public mind with Bohemian artistic and theatrical circles.
Before ever Oscar Wilde suffered his legal exposure, his
band of 'precious' young men provoked unfavourable
comment. The Gilbert and Sullivan comic opera *Patience*,
first performed in 1891, contained the famous song about
the 'particularly pure young man'. Other groups also have
a reputation for homosexuality, for instance sailors and
boxers, who are the reverse of effete or theatrical, which
only goes to confirm that there is no special character
common to all homosexuals. Moralists have proclaimed
that homosexuals are degenerate types, and prison officials,
such as Sir Norwood East, have pointed out the high
incidence of homosexuality among criminals and person
of weak mentality [78]. In contrast, as homosexual

literature never tires of pointing out, the greatest writers and musicians include a goodly proportion of known homosexuals. The realistic viewpoint accepts homosexuality as a universal potentiality that may develop in response to a wide variety of factors. Neurotic fears of sex, disappointment in love, an all-male background, guilt about women, all these things may contribute and tip the scales towards a homosexual development. Thus the mere fact that a man is homosexually inclined tells us nothing about his character. He may have developed that way as a result of too many scruples about women, or he may have cultivated homosexuality because it affords easy sexual gratification without trouble or responsibility. The possession of homosexual inclinations no more defines a man's character than the possession of a nervous twitch.

Acceptance of the fact that homosexuality affects a substantial proportion of the population means the abandonment of some common notions about homosexual 'types'. The popular idea that all male homosexuals have effeminate body build, girlish outlook and mannerisms, or a weak character, is a complete misconception. Among the homosexual multitude all types of physique and character may be found. Misconceptions about physique readily arise on account of a minority of male homosexuals who affect peculiar mannerisms amounting to a crude caricature of femininity, including simpering attitude, swaying gait, over-smooth movements, and lisping voice. The motives behind this odd behaviour, which may be so habitual as to become automatic and unconscious, vary from a real desire to play a woman's role to a need to advertise for a mate. When such mannerisms become extreme, the man-in-the-street recognizes them and gets the impression that all male homosexuals must be half women.

Psychiatrists holding the view that the cause of homosexuality must lie in some inborn biological quirk have looked so hard for traces of femininity that sometimes they have found them. A wide variety of physical traits have been allegedly associated with homosexuality, including

45

small stature, excess fat, wide hips, smooth skin, a feminine distribution of pubic hair, narrow shoulders, a boyish face, luxuriant hair, an inability to whistle and a 'too good-looking' appearance. That some of these traits are contradictory is sufficient ground for caution. In all probability feminine traits occur as often among normal men as among homosexuals, but homosexuals who happen to be effeminate are readily spotted and remembered.

Systematic studies of samples of known homosexuals have failed to demonstrate any consistent deviations from the average measurements of comparable groups of normal men [390]. Weil, examining a group of 380 mature male German homosexuals, concluded that they had a significantly greater height, longer legs, and wider hips than a normal group. However, another investigator, Wortis, criticized his findings and claimed that the results were vitiated by the fact that the normal and homosexual groups came from different districts with different average heights [391]. Comparing Weil's homosexual measurements with published data from other groups of German males showed no significant difference in height or hip and shoulder width.

In another series of measurements, published by Henry and Galbraith, the ratio of shoulder width to pelvis width was further from the feminine average in a group of homosexuals than in a corresponding group of normal men [167]. All such investigations have to be viewed with scepticism because of the great difficulty of securing an unselected group of male homosexuals.

In one American study of 342 psychotic male patients, 37 of whom were known to be repeatedly and persistently indulging in homosexual practices, no significant peculiarities in height, weight, torso length, or hip-shoulder measurements could be discovered among the homosexual group. An apparent difference in pubic hair distribution impressed the investigators, a proportion of the homosexuals having genital hair tending towards the female type with a horizontal upper margin. But the figures were too small to be statistically significant. One can but agree with Barahal's conclusion: 'Experience has shown that body measurements are so variable, even in the so-called normal group, that . . . it is impossible to reach any conclusion from such measurements. The same applies to other traits and characteristics frequently attributed to homosexuals, such as those pertaining to hair distribution, mannerisms, pitch of voice, and so forth' [15].

More subtle modern methods of evaluating physique have proved equally unrewarding. W. H. Sheldon, who devised a method of typing body-build by measurements made on standardized photographs of the nude figure, found that the muscular, athletic or mesomorphic physical type was correlated with a vigorous, outgoing temperament such as might be regarded as ideally 'masculine'. One might have expected this category to be poorly represented among male homosexuals, but when Sheldon applied his technique to samples of young male criminals, he found that the homosexuals among them had no distinctive contours. He still thought that they might be picked out by less easily measurable features like soft skin, feminine hands and tone of voice, but that was really just his personal opinion [335].

A J. Coppen [63] used two particularly sensitive indices of sexual physique developed by Tanner and Reynolds. One involved measuring the relation of shoulder (biacromial) width to hip (bi-iliac) width; the other was based on the ratio of bone thickness to the thickness of the layer of subcutaneous fat in the calf of the leg as viewed on an X-ray film. The measures were applied to a group of homosexual male patients attending psychiatrists, a group of male neurotics under treatment, and a control group of male members of a large business who were attending for Mass radiography. The fat-bone measures revealed no significant differences, but the shoulder-hip measures deviated significantly towards the feminine in the homosexual group, and also in the neurotic group. Coppen concluded that the peculiarity was not directly related to sexual abnormality, but was one associated with all kinds of

47

psychiatric disturbance. What one doesn't know, of course, is whether the same peculiarity would be detectable in a group of homosexuals who were not psychiatric patients.

2. *Identifying Psychological Characteristics*

Generalizations about homosexual temperament are no safer than generalizations about homosexual physique. Clinical psychologists have tried to develop tests to distinguish homosexuals from normals. Some of these are really tests of neurotic tendency, working on the supposition that anxious or inhibited responses to words or pictures with sexual connotations indicate conflicts about sex and probable homosexuality. As will be explained later, however, the supposed connection between homosexual and neurotic tendencies is much disputed. Other tests depend on the assumption that male homosexuals will react more like women than like normal men. To give a very simple example, in the 'Draw-a-Person' test, the majority of men and women choose to draw first a figure of their own sex. If a man draws a woman first this has been held to suggest homosexual tendencies. Grygier, in a most competent survey of the tests so far developed, concludes that none is satisfactory [149]. However, using a test of his own on male homosexual neurotic patients, he found that they differed from other male neurotics in traits of passivity, narcissism (i.e. self-preoccupation), and need for warmth, comfort and support, in all of which respects they tended to give responses typical of women [150]. When his analysis of material collected by Michael Schofield is published, it may be possible to be more definite about the meaning of these differences, but meantime they should be treated with some reserve. Many male homosexuals, especially perhaps those who are not neurotics, preserve masculine interests and attitudes apart from their erotic preferences. Furthermore, what is accepted as typically masculine or feminine in tastes and attitudes varies with age, social class, and educational background. When the American investigators Terman and Miles first introduced a psychological test for

48

masculine and feminine mental traits they applied it to male homosexuals with odd results [360]. Their test was a 456-item questionnaire, including word associations, statement of moral attitudes, interests, opinions, character preferences, and so on. The average man and woman gave radically different scores on the test. It is now generally admitted that this is due at least as much to individual training factors as to innate differences between the sexes. Be this as it may, it is interesting that male musicians and artists gave score averages that were almost female, whereas women athletes, doctors, and scientists gave scores that were almost male.

The test was given to 77 men described as passive homosexuals and to 46 said to be active homosexuals. The first group produced scores more typical of females than males, whereas the second group scored more 'masculine' than the average soldier. The authors were inclined to conclude that there were two qualitatively different types of male homosexuality. In my view a more likely cause for the differences was the way the two groups were selected. For the passives they first contacted a subject in gaol, and he brought his friends, who in turn brought their friends. Most of them were prostitutes. The second group was recruited from the U.S. Disciplinary Barracks at Alcatraz. It is not surprising that the aggressive criminal group were more masculine than the average, or that the prostitutes, whose chief advertisement is an imitation of femininity, should give female scores. The results merely show that there is as wide a range of temperaments among homosexuals as in the population at large.

Slater devised a male-female vocabulary test which he believed to be more discriminating than the lengthier Terman and Miles test. It depended upon the principle that certain words were more familiar to men than to women and vice versa. The average score of 37 male homosexuals who were given the test deviated in the expected direction, that is towards femininity, but there were wide variations of score and the homosexuals were clearly a mixed group [338].

Clarke [59] who gave this test to another group of male homosexuals who were attending a psychiatric hospital, found no evidence that they had excessive feminine interests, although they knew slightly less of the more masculine words than a control group of heterosexuals. The detection of interests or attitudes more typical of members of the opposite sex is the principle underlying a number of questionnaires. According to some authorities, such as Krippner [217], the Panton or Mf scales of the M.M.P.I. will pick out homosexuals successfully in three cases out of four. Other workers, such as Aaronson and Grumpelt [1], point out that male homosexuals who have pronounced masculine attitudes may slip through undetected by these questionnaires.

Masculine intellectual interests or attitudes in a woman, or feminine artistic interests in a man, may sometimes accompany homosexuality, but even so they do not necessarily indicate a generally neurotic personality. The belief that the majority of homosexuals are either excessively anxious, conflict-ridden persons; or else primitive, impulsive types with poorly developed social conscience, probably arises from the concentration of attention upon psychiatric patients and prisoners, two untypical groups who happen to be readily available for examination. Dean and Richardson [76] analysed the responses of male college graduates on the M.M.P.I., a standard American personality questionnaire which picks out with a fair degree of efficiency persons suffering from or liable to breakdown from neurotic illness. Apart from the femininity of interest revealed by their responses on the Mf scale, the forty overt homosexuals tested gave response patterns not substantially different from those of their heterosexual colleagues. The investigators found no general tendency to severe personality disturbance among the homosexuals. Other psychologists have come to opposite conclusions. Raymond Cattell [55], using the 16 PF questionnaire, found that convicted homosexuals produced a pattern of responses significantly different from the normal, and resembling that characteristic of anxiety neurotics. But in this instance, as in so many such researches, the method of selecting the homosexual sample may have determined the result.

Another fallacy about homosexuals is the belief that they necessarily share the same personality peculiarities or the same reasons for their aversion to the opposite sex. As will appear from the discussions in the second part of this book, the homosexual condition is probably the common end result of a variety of different causes. The submissive man may find homosexuality a refuge from domination by intimidating women, whereas the aggressively independent type may wish to avoid the cloying sentimentality of feminine attachments. Evelyn Hooker [181, 183], in investigations based upon volunteers from American homosexual organizations, found a wide diversity of personality patterns rather than any characteristic trait, and the most striking finding that emerged was how many homosexuals appeared to be well-adjusted personalities. The responses of two-thirds of the men given projection tests were, according to all three judges who scored them, indicative of average or superior adjustment. Certainly, in the great majority of instances, it would have been quite impossible to deduce that the subject was homosexual from the personality traits revealed.

The fact that some cases of homosexuality can be successfully diagnosed by psychological tests does not necessarily mean that the deviants have identifiable personality characteristics. Some of the tests work by recording involuntary or unobtrusive reactions to sexual situations, which give away the true nature of the subject's dominant erotic interests. For example, in some research at Chicago [170] it was demonstrated that measurement of changes in the size of the pupils while looking at pictures reliably distinguished between (known) homosexual and heterosexual males. The former naturally reacted more to pictures of men, the latter to pictures of women. Emotional reactions of interest or fear can be detected in a variety of physiological measures, such as changes in the electrical resistance of the skin due to sweat reactions (psycho-galvanic reflex) or changes in volume of the finger tip due to capilliary blood pressure fluctuations (pleythysmographic response). These form the basic ingredients of lie-detector tests, which serve to diagnose deviancy from emotional reactions occurring in response to trick questions or ambiguous pictures suggestive of homosexual situations. (See page 95.) Greater and possibly more discriminating emotional reactions can be obtained if the subject is willing to submit to test while watching overtly erotic or anxiety-provoking sexual films. This method has been used in some research in California [215].

In the Rorschach Test, in which the subjects are asked what they can see in a series of ambiguous shapes, it has been suggested that certain responses are characteristic of male homosexuals, although not necessarily indicative of personality disturbance otherwise [380]. Among the signs considered significant are frank, undisguised references to genital shapes (presumably indicative of sexual preoccupations and anxieties) and references by males to feminine topics. In an American Army Unit, it was found that descriptions of a sex organ rarely accounted for more than 40 per cent of the total resemblances identified by normal men, but in the records of soldiers suspected of homosexuality the proportion of such responses often exceeded 40 per cent [33]. Evelyn Hooker, although generally sceptical of the Rorschach signs, did find that a feminine emphasis (i.e. seeing female clothes, producing feminine associations) was statistically more frequent among homosexuals. Such evidence might suggest a diagnosis of homosexuality, but would not be conclusive [182].

In another test, using small models, subjects have been given a background set and a number of male and female figures to arrange in any manner they choose. It has been claimed that heterosexuals tend to place males and females together more often than do homosexuals. Kuethe [219], using prisoners as subjects, found that heterosexual inmates, when reconstructing model displays from memory, tended to produce arrangements in which males and females were closer together than in fact had been the case, whereas the homosexual inmates erred by placing pairs of male figures too close together. Another method of detection uses pictures flashed briefly on a screen by a tachistoscope [139]. Persons who are trying to repress their homosexual interests are said to give themselves away by their slowness and inaccuracy in the perception of homosexually suggestive pictures.

3. *Reactions to being a Homosexual*

Although no personality type characteristic of homosexuals in general has been identified, certain well-recognized attitudes and reactions to the condition do occur quite frequently. Most important of these, and most noticeable among the kinds of people seen by psychiatrists, is the pronounced sense of guilt about their sexual feelings from which many deviants suffer. Psycho-analysts usually attribute this to a carry-over from early neurotic conflict. They suggest that the guilt feelings precede the deviation, and are responsible for the individual turning away from normal sexual outlets in the first place. Other authorities contend that society's abhorrence of deviants, and the difficult, secretive lives that deviants must lead, adequately explain their sense of guilt [361].

Doubtless there is some truth in both views, but, whatever the reason, some homosexuals absorb and exaggerate this condemnation, and go through life in an agony of self-torture over their immoral desires. They strive after continence, but sooner or later yield to temptation, paying for it in untold pangs of remorse and self-disgust. The sense of guilt may grow so acute that the individual feels he can fit in nowhere and do nothing right because the burden of shame and inferiority paralyses all initiative and destroys all pleasure in human contacts. An actual example of this kind is described in Chapter 6. The biography of another such case, under the pseudonym Martin Beardson, was published by Jean Evans [94]. In this American example, an

53

intelligent and sensitive young man, enraged at his own homosexuality, wanders off from family and college in a vain search for freedom from the compulsions of the flesh. He lapses into poverty and vagrancy and falls inevitably into the hands of the police.

That homosexuals sometimes exaggerate the seriousness with which others view their deviation was suggested by Kitsuse's research [209] among American undergraduates. Given the same kind of clues, the likelihood of being suspected or identified as homosexual was greater for men than women. Conviction that a colleague was homosexual usually built up gradually, and sometimes resulted in ostracism, but quite often it made no great difference to ordinary social relationships. No instances of physical violence or denunciation to the police were reported, but as the author pointed out the group consisted of young middle-class intellectuals who might be unusually tolerant.

According to one professional woman, herself a homosexual, lesbians, who have no reason to fear actual prosecution as criminals, are still conscious of society's condemnation. They suffer as much as male homosexuals from feelings of loneliness and being misunderstood, and from a fear of their own degrading impulses. Some of them seek relief in alcohol [245]. On the other hand, in more permissive cultures, men have indulged in homosexuality freely and without guilt, and even now, in some delinquent groups, young men can indulge without worry or guilt so long as they can rationalize the activity as purely for gain. (See page 136.)

Depressive and suicidal reactions are also common among homosexuals. Karl Lambert [222], in a study of 200 neurotic soldiers, found a history of attempted suicide or severe depression to occur much more often among those with homosexual tendencies. O'Connor [231], reporting on a small series of suicides and attempted suicides, found a homosexual problem present in a half of the cases. Suicides have long been known to occur more frequently among the unmarried; and threatened public exposure of sexual devia-

54

tion sometimes precipitates suicide. (See page 87.) This
liability to depression and suicide may indicate an underlying instability of temperament, but on the other hand the
social difficulties encountered by homosexuals are also quite
sufficient to account for it.

Many homosexuals succeed in time in conquering up to
a point their initial sense of shame. Sometimes consultation
with a doctor who will accept them as they are gives them
a new feeling of assurance. Mixing with other homosexuals
who take their condition as a matter of course eases their
conscience and also removes their feeling of isolation. They
gain the security of a group membership, and discover a
milieu in which they can express themselves freely without
fear of persecution. This sense of belonging to a group,
even though a persecuted minority, gives considerable
relief to the guilt-ridden homosexual. A short time ago in
England homosexuals could imagine themselves the worst
freaks or sinners on earth simply because they had no
knowledge of the many thousands of others similarly
affected. With increasing experience of life and accumulated contacts with other homosexuals, guilt feelings recede,
but signs of underlying insecurity often remain. Many
suffer throughout their lives from an abnormal sensitive-
ness, a quickness to feel slighted, a suspicion that they are
not properly accepted by their colleagues. Some develop a
protective brazen front, an 'I'm as good as the next one'
attitude. Such over-compensation for inner insecurity has a
lot to do with the aggressively brazen behaviour of those
groups already mentioned who affect outrageous manners.
Evelyn Hooker [180] has suggested that some of the traits
and attitudes said to be typical of the warped personality of
some homosexuals are in fact characteristics regularly
found among all rejected minority groups: they are really
'traits of victimization', that is defensive responses to a
hostile world. For example, the obsessive concern of homosexuals with their problem recalls the obsessive concern of
Jews and negroes with race and colour. Special attitudes,
such as 'protective clowning' and 'hatred of himself and his

own group' as well as 'attitudes of dependence and passivity' are all commonly found both in homosexual and in other minority groups.

Identification with homosexual minority groups, who oppose conventional moral assumptions, probably hardens the deviant's tendency towards counter-rejection of the values of the society that spurns him. In order to test this, Kendrick and Clarke [203] applied an attitude measure (The Semantic Differential Technique of C. E. Osgood) to a group of homosexual men referred to a psychiatric hospital, and a control group of ostensibly heterosexual volunteers. In this test, the subjects evaluate a variety of concepts by choosing among a series of descriptive adjectives the one they consider most appropriate. The investigators expected, and found, that the homosexuals made more derogatory choices than the heterosexuals in evaluating certain aspects of family and social life. Such contempts as 'British justice', 'Myself as I am', 'Sex' and 'Punishment' evoked less favourable attitudes among the homosexuals. Although the homosexuals' attitudes were distinctive, they were not pathologically extreme or indicative of a persecution complex or paranoid state. (See page 219.)

Reference to the homosexual's position in the wider society calls attention to the different kinds of problems, and hence the different range of reactions, likely to be encountered during the successive phases of a deviant's lifetime. The histories of some homosexuals suggests the enactment of a pre-ordained tragedy. Trouble to come may be heralded by temperamental difficulties in boyhood, by shyness, timidity or distaste for the things considered suitable for a growing male. At adolescence, when so many youngsters pass through an experimental phase of temporary homosexuality, the individual deviant becomes less conspicuous. A little later, as other youths drift away with their steady girl friends, and people begin to make hints about him, the young homosexual may be forced to admit to himself for the first time that he is an isolate and a pervert. He must either reconcile himself to living like an old-maid in his parental home, or move out and seek a life among others of his kind. At this point, many migrate to the big cities where they visit the 'gay' spots, join up with established homosexual groups, pick up the current slang, and generally organize their lives within the sub-culture of deviants. Eventually, except for formal relationships during working hours, and occasional visits to the old folks, some homosexuals virtually confine themselves to their own cliques and give up the society of normal people altogether. A few get themselves into occupations where suspected sexual deviation won't count too much against them. Designing, acting and personal service occupations (e.g. waiters, stewards, hairdressers) are thought to attract male homosexuals; and on account of this some normal young men decline to take up these careers.

The deviant who has 'come out' into homosexual society, and fully accepts his inverted feelings, has then to go through the experiences of falling in love and having affairs of greater or lesser intensity or exclusiveness. Many strive to duplicate the heterosexual model of monogamous marriage, but both nature and social circumstances work against this solution. Male homosexuals are men first and deviants second. In a male partnership, where both have jobs and social independence, conflicts of interest and leadership must arise. The heterosexual custom of engagements, or preparatory companionship over a long period, has never caught on among homosexuals, who enter upon their affairs much more lightly. The absence of child-rearing responsibilities and of any legally or socially binding marriage contract makes for the dissolution of homosexual affairs in the face of difficulties. Men cannot live together permanently as a couple or go about together constantly without exciting damaging comment. All the same, as Horowitz [186] demonstrated by means of questionnaires addressed to volunteers from homosexual organizations, satisfying and lasting unions occur more often than is generally realized by authorities who see only the more unstable, problem types. However, apart from unfavourable outside circumstances, something in the nature of many of these relationships seems to lead to frequent breaks. The masculine urge for sexual freedom, and the masculine responsiveness to casual sexual approaches, frequently leads to jealousy and quarrels. Curiously enough, some of the most stable male homosexual unions are those in which the partners pursue their sexual interests independently. One such case is described in Chapter 6. Lesbians, who have a lesser urge towards promiscuity, seem to preserve their affairs longer and more faithfully.

Male affairs rarely last a lifetime, and in the course of the numerous re-shuffles older men tend to get more and more left out. Some, of course, have never been seriously interested in pseudo-marriage, preferring a life of brief encounters. Many ageing homosexuals, having organized their lives and interests around sexual adventures, to an extent almost unimaginable to staid married people, find eventually that they are left without family, roots or purpose. Some of them can be seen wearily trailing their old haunts, trying to bribe themselves back into the company of young men, or loitering pathetically around public lavatories. Others retire to a grimly isolated existence. The dread of growing old is a noticeable feature of male homosexuals, some of whom try desperately to preserve some semblance of youth by wearing the fashions of the younger generation, looking after their figures, and cultivating a bright young style of conversation. The normal man, restricted as he may be by family routine, has little cause to envy the so-called 'gay' life.

It should be clear by now that homosexuals vary so much that the search for a pattern common to all is doomed to failure. Writers on the subject, even medical writers who should know better, carelessly throw out generalizations without an atom of validity. One reads that homosexuals are depraved, or exhibitionists, or (and this usually from the homosexuals themselves) that they are more 'alive' and 'sympathetic' than the humdrum mass of humanity. In reality some homosexuals suffer from neurotic fears and anxieties, and some are self-assured and hard as nails; some are vain and ostentatious and some are shy and quiet; some are cowardly and some are heroes; some are effeminate and some are brutes. Since all these types are represented, psychologists can all too easily pick out examples to suit their own pet theories. Those who choose to believe the condition is a sign of moral degeneracy, on a par with drug addiction, alcoholism, and criminal tendencies, can find plenty of examples among the prison and criminal population of men who readily satisfy any and every sexual whim without the slightest pang of conscience. On the other hand, those who believe that the over-attachment of the young boy to his mother causes homosexuality can equally well pick out examples, especially among only children, of shy, pampered men who have never broken away from an adoring mother. Those who believe that homosexuality springs from narcissism—that is to say, love of self to a pathological degree coupled with inability to form a give-and-take relationship with other people—can readily point out vain, attention-seeking individuals who are prepared to put on a show of simpering mannerisms for the benefit of any male willing to dally with them. The question of causation will be dealt with later. Suffice for the moment to say that there is probably some truth in all these divergent views. Seemingly anyone can develop homosexuality given the right conditions, but the causes will differ from one case to the next. A mentally defective criminal and a musical genius may both be homosexual, but their characters and the influences that have moulded them will be radically different.

4. Masculine—Feminine: Active—Passive

The notion that all male homosexuals have effeminate characters and all lesbians have masculine traits is not without a certain justification, for a minority among homosexuals do show a marked temperamental bias towards features more characteristic of the opposite sex. This observation has been used to argue for the existence of a special group, the true inverts, who supposedly possess a constitutional disposition to contrary sexual habits [145]. But the argument loses its force in the face of modern anthropological research which shows that many of the temperamental characteristics popularly defined as 'masculine' or 'feminine' are the result of cultural training and are not biological sexual distinctions. Margaret Mead [258], in particular, has called attention to wide differences in the traditions of masculinity and femininity. Among the Tchambuli, for example, there is a sharp division between male and female roles, but in contrast to our own culture it is the Tchambuli women who do the productive work, dominate in social organization, and take the initiative in sexual relations. The men have a more decorative function. Supported by female labour, they spend their time on art and in the production of ceremonial dances. The ideal Tchambuli woman is efficient, business like, loyal, and comradely; but for the Tchambuli man it is normal to indulge in affected manners, catty gossip, and jealous squabbles.

Among the Mungudumors, another primitive people studies by Margaret Mead, both men and women were far more aggressive than is normal for the most masculine in our culture. Their society had no place for tolerance and affectionate relationship, and their men were in a perpetual state of jealous hostility, fighting and insulting each other in a ceaseless battle to possess the best women. The male ideal was a life in splendid isolation within a stockade housing many wives to look after him and only a few puny male relations who would not challenge his supremacy. The wives were only a degree less hostile, quarrelling among themselves and refusing to help each other's children. Both men and women liked brief, passionate sexual contacts in which foreplay consisted of biting, scratching, ripping clothes, and tearing ornaments.

From observations of this kind Mead contends that dominance or submissiveness in social behaviour are not sex-linked characteristics, and that therefore any society that defined masculinity and femininity in such terms will inevitably have a large number of temperamental misfits. Some theorists label all such misfits 'latent homosexuals', but this is wrong. Temperamental non-conformity does not necessarily imply deviant sexual impulses, although the difficulties that these misfits encounter in their attempts to establish normal relations may cause some of them to seek refuge in homosexuality [259].

Some psychiatrists believe, and there is evidence to support their view, that male homosexuals fall into two contrasting categories known respectively as *active* and *passive*. The active type is forceful and masculine in his love-making, while the passive is gentle, yielding, coy, and liking to be chased. If sodomy occurs, it is the active partner who penetrates the passive. The active type tends to display his masculinity, to cultivate athletic pursuits, and to reject all feminine traits. The passive type is more likely to adopt pseudo-feminine mannerisms. The use in homosexual circles of such slang expressions as 'bull' and 'butch' or 'cow' and 'queen' shows that some at least must conform to type.

According to some theorists different causes operate to produce these two types. The passive type, often regarded as the 'true' invert, is thought more likely to possess feminine physique or to have some glandular disturbance, whereas the active type is merely looking for a substitute for a woman. But the evidence on these points is flimsy. The homosexual man with predominantly passive sex habits does not necessarily affect feminine manners or possess feminine physique. Wortis quotes two cases of passive male homosexuals with markedly effeminate mannerisms who had undoubtedly masculine physique [391], and I have come across several men (the history of one is given later) habitually passive in their sexual relations who were effeminate neither in body nor in manner. A great many homosexuals, possibly the majority, prefer mutually reciprocated sex activity where neither partner dominates. Many adopt the active or passive roles as occasion demands. Some begin by taking only the active role in sodomy, thinking that by so doing they avoid being really 'queer', and end up by taking the passive role in order to please more youthful partners. Others gravitate from a passive to an active role as they grow older. Furthermore, sexual practices may be culturally determined more than a matter of individual choice. Edouard Roditi [316] mentioned that whereas in the United States mouth-genital contacts are favoured by many male homosexuals in preference to sodomy, in some Moslem countries even the lowest type of male prostitute will refuse to agree to this practice on the grounds that only animals would do such a thing. Nevertheless, a minority among homosexuals do allow dissatisfaction with their gender to determine their style of love-making, since in this, as in their dress, manners, gait, speech, interests and occupation they try their best to act like persons of the opposite sex. Such firm cross-sex identification is really a different condition from ordinary homosexuality [45]. The two do not necessarily go together or have the same cause.

5. *Trans-sexualism and 'Change of Sex'*

Most homosexuals do not really identify themselves with the opposite sex. Men who mimic girls' manners or put on female dress to excite their homosexual friends do not usually wish to lose their boyish figures or change their genitals. Indeed were such a transformation to occur they would immediately cease to attract other male homosexuals. In other words their effeminacy remains rather less than skin deep, an indication of the kind of sexual attentions they are asking for rather than of any genuine desire to become women. As for the 'butch' lesbians who mimic men, the same considerations apply. Most of them dislike males. They aim not to become men, but to supplant men, especially in relation to female admirers.

Nevertheless, a minority of homosexuals do like to think of themselves as belonging to the opposite sex. In men this may show as a passion for housewifery, cosmetics and dressing up. If they have sexual relations with other men they insist on adopting the passive role, this being the only one appropriate to their 'femininity'. In many cases, how-ever, their interest in playing a female social role ex-ceeds their interest in homosexual activity. Sometimes the insatiable desire for the role of the opposite sex goes beyond mere cross-dressing, and the individual insists that he is actually changing sex, or that he has been assigned to the wrong sex at birth. They often pester doctors to arrange operations to remove their unwanted sexual characteristics, and they clamour for a change of sex on their birth certi-ficates [277] and for recognition of their status by em-ployers, tax authorities and so forth. This pre-occupation with change of sex is known technically as trans-sexualism. In point of fact, physical examination in such cases almost invariably reveals a biologically normal and sexually mature person whose claim to belong to the other sex has no physical basis [26]. In a review of the published information on seventy-five cases of trans-sexuals and transvestites, Hous-den [187] found reports of anomalous physical characteris-tics in only five instances, and one or two of these were rather doubtful. He concluded that the root cause was nearly always psychological, and that doctors who en-couraged belief in the possibility of a physical change of sex were doing a dis-service to these patients.

Trans-sexualism is a comparatively rare condition. It nearly always begins to manifest before puberty. It is quite distinct from ordinary homosexuality, and although it may be accompanied by homoerotic feeling this does not neces-sarily follow. Married men with families may have the same delusion and insist on a sex change in spite of the fact that they function heterosexually. Women trans-sexuals, how-ever, appear to be nearly always lesbians [306].

Cross-sex identification or trans-sexualism is something more than the simple urge many men have to wear women's clothes. This perversion, known as transvestitism, may sometimes represent a half-way stage on the road to trans-sexualism, but many transvestite males are perfectly mascu-line in their attitudes and heterosexual in orientation. They just have a fetishistic fascination for female garments.

Homosexual Types

These curious psychological states may bring men into trouble with the law on charges of masquerading as women, or for homosexual importuning even though homosexuality it not their primary concern. In one case known to me, a trans-sexual youth was arrested as a female prostitute and conducted in the first instance to a women's prison. He had been taking hormones to make his breasts swell. With appropriate clothes and cosmetics he had deceived men into thinking he was a girl, and in some cases, with the aid of dim light and some strapping to disguise his genitals, he had got his clients to commit buggery under the impression that they were having heterosexual intercourse. All this in aid of proving his true female identity and his right to an operation for change of sex!

Although psychotherapy often proves ineffective in cases of trans-sexualism, a surgical attack can at best convert a normal body into a rather freakish imitation of the opposite sex. Some details of the procedures used for changing a man into a pseudo woman have been described by Savitsch [323]. The process takes a long time and involves considerable pain and risk. The final outcome may possibly allow the man to simulate intercourse, but the process is likely to prove painful and unsatisfying, owing to the lack of muscle tonus and nerve supply in the artificially constructed vagina. As the surgeon Charles Wolf [387] put it: 'Only those who propose to become old maids can submit to the operation without fear of the consequences'. Moreover, the vagina is at best a fake, since there are no internal organs, and no possibility of producing babies. The masculine skeleton, including the big feet and hands, the large larynx and deep voice, and many other unalterable signs of maleness which remain, bear witness to the incompleteness of the transformation.

In view of all these disadvantages, one may wonder why surgeons ever attempt these operations. One reason is that the patients force their hand by serious threats of suicide, or by self-mutilations which necessitate surgical repairs, or by first having castrations performed by private surgeons in countries where anything can be got for money and then presenting themselves for repair of the damage. Following extensive newspaper publicity in connection with the case of 'Christine' Jorgensen, Professor Hamburger, the Danish endocrinologist, received hundreds of pathetic letters from people all over the world who desperately wanted to change their sex [155].

6. Lesbian Types

Conspicuous neglect of the topic on the part of research workers, and a quite extraordinary dearth of factual information in published works, makes any statements about lesbianism peculiarly hazardous. Investigators of sexual behaviour in primitive societies have concentrated so much upon male deviance that one is often left guessing whether the women were uniformly conventional in their habits, or whether the observers simply failed to make the necessary inquiries. Imaginative literature, however, shows no such inhibition, and lesbian love themes appear in poems and stories of many periods and places. Jeannette Foster [105] sometime librarian to the Institute of Sex Research at Indiana University, has produced a scholarly survey of Western writing on the subject.

In classical Greek and Roman literature, references to female hermaphroditism and related topics occur plentifully in legend and mythology, but hardly at all in descriptions of ordinary life. although, as has been mentioned, male homosexuality was written about as quite an everyday matter. The lyric poems of Sappho, in the sixth century B.C., were exceptional. In later writings, such as Juvenal's well-known sixth *Satire*, lesbian practices are associated with courtesans, prostitutes and general debauchery. Some Renaissance fiction, such as Sir Philip Sidney's *Arcadia* (1580), depicts lesbian infatuations with surprising candour, and P. de B. de Brantome in his *Lives of Fair and Gallant Ladies* (1665) implies that at the French court of his day lesbian attachments were taken very much for granted.

In modern times, lesbian themes in novels have become

altogether commonplace, but it is interesting to notice that this development occurred later in England than on the Continent of Europe. In France, the great novelist Colette [62], published *Claudine a l'école*, which describes attachments between adolescent girls with their women teachers, as long ago as 1903. During the first decade of this century, another well-known French woman writer, Renée Vivien, produced a number of poems openly singing the praises of lesbian love. The authoress, a true eccentric, made no secret of her own interests, and even acquired a Greek villa near Mitylene, which she shared with a woman friend, in an attempt to recapture the spirit of Sappho. In contrast, when the English novelist Radclyffe Hall published her sad romantic novel *The Well of Loneliness* in 1928, the publishers, Jonathan Cape, withdrew it from circulation on a request from the Home Secretary, and a few months later a Bow Street magistrate declared the book obscene and ordered the destruction of all copies.

It has been suggested that men do not take lesbianism seriously, because it offends their masculine self-esteem. Since fact-finding research has been largely in the hands of men, this may partly account for the neglect of the lesbian question. Another reason is that homosexual practices are actually less frequent among women than among men, although still by no means uncommon. This came out quite clearly from the Kinsey surveys [208]. On the other hand, women seem more liable than are men to form emotional attachments to members of their own sex. They stop short of going to bed together, but their feelings often exceed in intensity the emotions they have with men. In Katharine Davis's survey of unmarried women graduates [75], a half of the 1,200 women questioned reported having intense emotional experiences with other women, whereas only a quarter admitted to physical contacts recognized as sexual. The increased emancipation of women in sexual matters since this material was collected may possibly have shifted the balance slightly from emotional to physical lesbianism. Nevertheless, the high incidence of unconsummated romantic attachments remains a feature that sharply distinguishes lesbian tendency from the homoeroticism of males, which usually manifests from the outset as a recognized sexual attraction calling for physical gratification. Of course such unconsummated attachments can be as powerful and as disruptive of normal marital adjustment as more overt love-making; but they may allow the participants to disassociate themselves from the taint of perversion and the guilt feeling that goes with it.

Physical contacts between lesbians most often arise out of strong friendships or protracted sentimental attachments, and for a long time they may be limited to kissing and caressing without any attempt at mutual masturbation or sexual orgasm. Like the majority of heterosexual women, most lesbians find sex without romance unattractive. Few are promiscuous, and very few go in for the restless searching for 'one night stands' after the manner so common among male homosexuals. It has been suggested that lesbians have less opportunity for such outlets, since specialized bars and meeting places are not so readily available to women; but it seems more likely that the absence of such facilities indicates a lack of demand. June Hopkins [184], a Cambridge psychologist, who has interviewed a hundred lesbian volunteers contacted through the Minorities Research Group (see p. 112), found that, even among a group who openly acknowledged their lesbianism and concerned themselves with a lesbian organization, many had had physical contacts with only one or two other women, only one was seriously promiscuous, and 95 per cent considered the impulsive 'one night stand' affair unthinkable.

Dr. Albertine Winner [386], while agreeing that promiscuous lesbians are comparatively rare birds, at least in England, refers to them as particularly dangerous because they are usually dominant, forceful personalities who may seduce weaker, more pliant woman. Occasionally, the 'butch' type, in pursuit of her masculine image, will deliberately aim to 'lay' as many women as possible in imitation of the male philanderer. However, as Dr. Winner points out, lesbians seem mercifully exempt from any counterpart of the 'choir-boy syndrome'; they never seem to be sexually interested in little girls. As a corollary to the female aversion to unromantic promiscuity, lesbian prostitution is almost non-existent.

Completely exclusive homosexual behaviour (Kinsey rating 6) appears to be comparatively unusual among lesbians. This does not necessarily indicate a higher incidence of bisexual feeling among women. A man has to be strongly attracted sexually to the point of sustained erection, before he can have intercourse, but a woman can remain passive and let a man satisfy himself while she remains unaroused. Being free from the masculine dread of impotence, lesbians can, and often do, experiment heterosexually even though they have little spontaneous erotic feeling towards men. This process is made easier by the social convention that requires the man to take the initiative and casts the woman in a passive role, waiting to be stimulated by the male's advances. Whereas the homosexual man does not usually get caught up in heterosexual love-making unless he starts it himself, an attractive-looking lesbian must take positive avoiding action if she does not wish to be seduced. Lesbians are under considerable pressure to marry. Whereas some people envy the care-free heterosexual bachelor, the spinster left on the shelf evokes only mild pity and condescension. Men tend to earn more, and to achieve executive positions more easily, and marriage brings the woman a share in these economic advantages. She also obtains the security of a settled home of her own, which further increases her personal and social standing. Moreover, many women who have no interest in sex for its own sake find the possibility of having children a powerful inducement. Finally, the lesbian woman can marry without exposing her inadequacy, since society tends to accept the notion that many women are naturally somewhat frigid.

Some of the women who enter into marriage for social more than sexual reasons nevertheless find fulfilment with their husband, and become completely weaned away from

68

their initial lesbian tendencies. On the other hand, others run into disaster. Since some women remain incompletely aroused sexually unless or until they experience the right style of love-making, there is always the danger, with a lesbian wife, that she will be swept off her feet by some passionate woman friend comparatively late in life. Diana Chapman [57] quotes one wife as saying she had been fairly happily married for six years until she met a woman. 'And it was as though I'd been sound asleep all my life'. Dr. Socarides [342], an American psycho-analyst, comments that in general, male homosexuals do not see marriage as a solution, but lesbians are particularly liable to enter into unsatisfying unions and to persist in them to the detriment of all concerned. He thinks lesbianism a frequent cause of frigidity, but it is hard to say how many marriages founder from this cause since wives may deceive themselves as to the reasons for their difficulties and complain of depression or other symptoms apparently unrelated to homosexuality.

In her novel *Winter Love* (1962, Jonathan Cape) Han Suyin sheds a cold, revealing light on the marital conduct of a wife pining for a lost lesbian love.

In spite of these points of contrast, lesbianism and male homosexuality have many features in common. The great majority of lesbians are of quite ordinary physique, with menstruation, breast size and other indications of female development all present and normal. Lesbian manners, dress and attitudes vary enormously. At one extreme the 'butch' or 'dyke' type, who swagger along in men's trousers and cropped hair and converse in gruff expletives, parody the normal male as grotesquely as the mincing, dyed, and powdered 'queens' parody the normal woman. The 'butch' lesbian usually takes the lead over her partner in social affairs (from opening doors to making decisions), and one expects her to take the active role also in love-making. This often happens, but it is by no means invariable. As with male homosexuals the love making of lesbians is very often a matter of mutual or alternating activity.

Again, as with male homosexuals the obtrusive, exhibitionistic, minority produces an unfavourable public image and earns the disapproval of the more discreet deviants. Apart from the butch grotesques, however, female dress offers no certain guide to sexual orientation, for custom allows women to choose masculine clothing styles, and this they often do to appear fashionable or to enhance feminine attractions rather than the reverse. Masculine dress styles can also signify (consciously or otherwise) the wearer's dissatisfaction with the soft, dependent or inferior roles assigned to women in our culture. Envy of male freedoms and privileges, or 'penis envy' and 'masculine protest' to use the psycho-analytic terminology, is said to play an important part in feminine psychology. While lesbians often have this masculine protest reaction particularly well developed, so do large numbers of heterosexual women. As Simone de Beauvoir points out [18], the heterosexual members of the feminist political movement were at one time as staunch as any lesbian in their devotion to severe tailor-made suits, felt hats and flat heels. In their case, refusal of feminine ornament arose from their unwillingness to appear before the eyes of men like decorative merchandise, rather than from any partiality towards forbidden sexual pleasures. All the same, the true female transvestite, that is the individual who goes to the lengths of deceptive masquerading as a man, is almost always lesbian, although the man who masquerades as a woman is not always homosexual (see page 63).

Attempts to delineate the personality characteristics of typical lesbians have met much the same obstacles as similar attempts in the case of male homosexuals. The main difficulty is that the characteristics revealed are often due to the method of selecting the sample. Lesbian prisoners naturally reflect the background and attitudes of the criminal classes, while lesbian psychiatric patients probably resemble other patients more than other lesbians. Bluestone and his collaborators [37], who compared young male homosexual prisoners at Rikers Island with lesbians in New York City's House of Detention for women, found that whereas the former were rather better educated and better behaved than their fellow prisoners, the lesbians were worse than ordinary women prisoners. Almost all were addicted to drugs and had never worked other than as prostitutes, many were also alcoholic, promiscuous or sadistic. In contrast Miller and Hannum [262], who gave a battery of personality tests (including the M.M.P.I. and the Kuder Preference Record) to women prisoners at another institution, failed to discover any systematic differences between those who were known participants in prison lesbianism and those who were not.

The most ambitious attempt so far published to demonstrate the peculiar personality characteristics of lesbians in the community is that of Virginia Armon [12]. She obtained women volunteers from a homosexual organization. None was receiving or seeking psychological treatment. She compared them with a group of happily married women with children who were similar in range of education, age and social class. Using the Rorschach and a Figure Drawing Test she found a 'general absence of dramatic differences between the performance of the homosexuals and the heterosexuals' which showed that female homosexuality was not necessarily associated with obvious limitations of personality. There were some slight differences however. For instance, the lesbians made disparaging comments about men rather more often than the heterosexual women, and their comments on the feminine role more often showed an anxious and aggressive quality. However, independent judges who rated the responses blindly could not tell to any reliable degree which were the lesbians' records and which the ones from heterosexuals. The conclusion that lesbian volunteers do not produce dramatically neurotic scores on personality tests seems likely to be confirmed by investigations now being conducted at Oxford [204] and at Cambridge [184]. Although lesbians may produce above-average 'neuroticism' scores on the Maudsley Personality Inventory, for instance, their scores remain well below what would be expected of neurotic clinic patients.

CHAPTER IV

SOME LEGAL PROBLEMS

1. The Letter of the Law

In many civilized countries homosexual behaviour does not contravene the law except in special circumstances of abuse, for instance if children are involved or if force is used to coerce an unwilling participant, but in other places, for instance in most parts of North America, including Canada, any kind of sexual contact between persons of the same sex counts as a serious crime. No comprehensive international survey of the various statutes governing sexual deviations has as yet been carried out. It would make an interesting project for legal research, but the difficulties would be formidable. For one thing, the peculiar legal terminology frequently employed, referring to such offences as 'crimes against nature', 'immoral conduct' and 'acts of indecency', prudishly avoids spelling out the details of the offences in question, but leaves the reader guessing as to what exactly the laws are intended to forbid. This vagueness gives the judiciary a great deal of latitude to interpret the law how they please. An even greater obstacle to understanding how the law works on these matters arises from the enormous variation in the frequency and stringency with which statutes are applied. In some places, where the laws may seem to be very fierce, homosexuals may in fact be allowed to live in comparative tranquillity, free from prosecution or harassment by police and civic authorities.

In many places in the East and in the Arab world, even today, male homosexual behaviour arouses little public concern, and even the presence of male brothels is treated with indifference or amusement, in spite of the fact that, in theory, very serious religious or legal crimes are being committed. However, so long as they exist, even half-forgotten laws may easily be invoked if the authorities feel the need for it. For example, in July 1966, in Yemen, a Moslem religious court convicted a sixty-year-old government worker, Ahmed el Osmay, of pederasty and sentenced him to death. According to newspaper reports, this was the first execution of a homosexual in the Yemen in modern times, and was all the more surprising in view of the traditional predilection of the Bedouins for homosexual pleasures. The convicted man was shot before a large crowd in the main square of San'a, the capital city.[1]

The laws governing sex conduct descend directly from ancient religious codes. In ancient times Jewish religious institutions included the *kadesh* or male homosexual temple prostitute (see II Kings xxiii. 7). In the earliest Jewish codes, therefore, and in Hittite and Chaldean writings, homosexuality is condemned only in special circumstances, for instance between blood relations. Horror of homosexual temptation is exemplified in the biblical story of the curse Ham brought upon himself through catching sight of his father, Noah, lying naked in his tent (Genesis ix). After their return from exile in Egypt the Jews came to regard all homosexual practices as foreign, pagan, and idolatrous. In Leviticus xx. 3 it is stated categorically that 'if a man lie with mankind as with womankind, both of them have committed an abomination: they shall surely be put to death'. The Old Testament makes no mention of lesbianism, but St. Paul (Romans i. 26) condemns women who lust after one another and give themselves up to vile passions [14].

The Christian Church adopted the ancient Jewish sex codes and formalized them into the Ecclesiastical Laws that governed medieval Europe and later provided the basis for English Common Law. In medieval times, when clerical preoccupation with sins of the flesh was at its height and sexual pleasure of any kind was considered almost damnable, many men and also a few women were sent to their deaths for homosexual offences. Even married persons were

[1] *New York Herald Tribune*, 2 Aug., 1966.

not immune from religious investigation, for confessors were supplied with manuals instructing them in questions to be addressed to married couples to ensure that sexual intercourse took place only in the approved position. Sexual perversions must have flourished in this repressive atmosphere, for the so-called penitential books of the period describe at great length and in the utmost detail every conceivable sexual aberration and give appropriate penalties for each sin [359].

In Europe, for many hundreds of years, homosexual offences remained a matter for the ecclesiastical courts, and were punishable by torture and death. Indeed, as late as the mid-eighteenth century, homosexuals were burnt at the stake in Paris. The great liberal change in the sex laws on the European continent came about with the French revolution of 1789. Under the influence of the famous rationalist philosophers, like Voltaire and Montesquieu, the penal code was limited to manifestly harmful acts, such as rape and violation of children, leaving questions of fornication and homosexuality to the private conscience of the individual citizen. Later systematized and widely promulgated in the Code Napoleon of 1810, this philosophy still provides the basis for the sex laws of many European countries.

In recent decades, French law has been slightly changed so as to discriminate against homosexual activity.[1] Whereas relations with a consenting teenager of the opposite sex are permitted, a penalty of from ten months to three years' imprisonment, plus a fine, is prescribed for any indecent or unnatural act with someone of the same sex aged under twenty-one.[2] (Owing to the system of suspended sentences those condemned, particularly first offenders, do not necessarily suffer the penalties pronounced upon them.) The statute covering sexual acts with children under fifteen prescribes severe penalties, but refers to children of either sex, and does not distinguish hetero-

---

[1] *Code Pénal* (1966) Paris, Dalloz.
[2] Ord. 8 Feb. 1945, 'quiquonque aura commis un acte impudique ou contre nature avec un individu de son sexe mineur de 21 ans'.

sexual and homosexual offences.[1] By an Act introduced in France in 1960, public indecency is more severely punished if the behaviour is homosexual rather than heterosexual. Article 330 of the penal code had long condemned 'un outrage public à la pudeur', but by an ordinance of 25 November 1960 it was specified that if the outrage consisted of an 'unnatural act' between persons of the same sex the penalty would be six months' to three years' imprisonment plus a fine, instead of merely three months to two years plus a smaller fine. Although prostitution, either heterosexual or homosexual, does not in itself constitute an offence against French law, importuning for immoral purposes carries a penalty of a few days' imprisonment.

In Belgium, the law has remained more purely Napoleonic. No mention is made of notions of pederasty, sodomy, or crimes against nature, and the laws concerning use of violence, indulgence with persons under age and public indecency, apply without discrimination to both heterosexual and homosexual behaviour [298].

In European countries where homosexual acts between consenting adults are not in themselves crimes, an age has to be fixed below which legal consent cannot be given. As has been remarked, this age has been set at 21 in France, and so it is in Holland, presumably on the assumption that youths are in greater need of protection from homosexual seduction than are young girls from heterosexual seduction. In Denmark and Sweden, however, the age is set at 18, in Greece at 17, and in Italy, Norway and Switzerland at 16 [54]. In some countries, where the age of consent is rather high, special provisions are made to exonerate or mitigate the offence if both parties are under age. Some European countries with a low age of consent (such as Switzerland) have provisions for protecting persons in dependent positions from homosexual seduction by rela-

[1] Art. 331. Ord. 2 July 1945. 'Toute attentat à la pudeur consommé ou tenté sans violence sur la personne d'un enfant de l'un et l'autre sexe agé de moins de 15 ans sera puni de la reclusion criminelle à temps de 5 à 10 ans.'

tives, employers, staff of residential institutions, etc. Another variation is that in some countries (such as Denmark, Holland and Sweden) where prostitution by females is not illegal, homosexual prostitution by young men is a crime.

The 1926 Penal Code of post-revolutionary Russia made no reference to homosexuality, but as in the case of divorce and abortion the law has since become more stringent. In March 1934 a Soviet decree was issued, without public discussion, instructing the republics of the U.S.S.R. to add to their codes an article making sex acts between males an offence. Homosexuality was designated a 'social crime', on a par with such crimes as banditism, sabotage, espionage, and counter-revolutionary activity, to be punished in lighter cases by three to five years' imprisonment. [249]. This is still in force, and if the offence is aggravated by violence, or by being perpetrated with a minor, or by taking advantage of a person in a dependent position, the penalty rises up to eight years' imprisonment [7]. Rather interestingly, the Czechoslovakian law has moved in the opposite direction, and in January 1962 consenting adult homosexuality ceased to be a crime, and the age of consent was fixed at 18. Prostitution, public indecency, and exploitation of a relationship of dependence remained punishable. In Polish law (as in Belgian) homosexual acts are subject only to the same limitations as heterosexual ones. In contrast, homosexuality remains a crime in both East and West Germany. In 1935, under the Nazi regime, the penalties were considerably increased, and under Paragraph 175 all types of indecent act were made punishable. In East Germany, since 1950, the law has been relaxed in so far as this statute is now held to cover only buggery and oral-genital contacts. A proposed new East German code would bring their law into line with that of Czechoslovakia [213].

American laws controlling sexual behaviour vary from one State to the next [27, 51, 123, 295]. Plain copulation between man and wife is the only sexual act which is nowhere a crime. Other forms of marital love-play, solitary masturbation, and pre-marital or adulterous sexual beha-

viour, are all crimes in one State or another. However, only
the anti-homosexual applications are at all widely enforced
by the police, or backed by public opinion, so many heterosexual Americans remain unaware that they too are technically criminals! Furthermore, though many statutes are
worded to apply equally to male homosexuals and to lesbians, in practice only the former are pursued. Kinsey
commented that 'in New York City we find three arrests of
females in the last ten years, but all of these cases were dismissed, although there were some tens of thousands of
arrests and convictions of males charged with homosexual
activity in that same period of time' [207].

Every state in the Union, except Illinois, makes some or all
homosexual acts a criminal offence, even when carried out
between consenting adults in private. The felony statutes
mostly refer to 'sodomy' or 'crime against nature', for
which the maximum penalty in seven of the States is life
imprisonment and in most States over ten years' imprisonment. South Carolina has a minimum punishment of five
years' imprisonment. In most of the States, legal precedent
or amended statutes have expanded the interpretation of
'sodomy' to include mouth-genital contacts and, in some
places, mutual masturbation as well.

Most of the States also have statutes covering homosexual misdemeanours, which carry lesser punishments,
but can be more easily held to apply to any and every sexual
act or gesture. Thus statutes covering 'outrages to public
decency' can be used for controlling male importuning, or
loitering round public lavatories, while homosexual conduct in private may be prosecuted as 'lewd', 'obscene' or
'indecent' behaviour. The police frequently choose to prosecute for these lesser offences, because homosexuals are
less easily persuaded to plead guilty to 'sodomy', and juries
may be reluctant to convict if the penalty seems dispro-
portionately harsh. However, in States where the misdemeanour statutes are specifically limited to nuisances in
public, acts in private can only be prosecuted under the
sodomy laws, and may therefore be punished more severely

than the same acts committed in public. Even more serious anomalies may arise from partners in marital disputes or divorce cases invoking, or threatening to invoke, the sodomy laws. Since many of the statutes apply equally to heterosexual and homosexual congress, erotic bedroom activities that once were a source of pleasure to both man and wife may suddenly become grounds for a charge of cruelty, or for unfitness to have custody of children. Since American journalists have more freedom than in England to report the details of divorce cases, these intimate particulars may be set out at length in the local newspaper, with disastrous consequences to all members of the family concerned, and especially the children. It can happen that a complaint lodged by a wife, much to her consternation, leads to the arrest and imprisonment of the husband, and results in the impoverishment of both parties. In short, the law puts a dangerous weapon at the disposal of any unscrupulous or vengeful spouse [336].

Finally, in some States homosexuals are liable to prosecution as vagrants, that is 'lewd, disorderly or dissolute persons'. Such ambigious definitions make possible the arrest of homosexuals whose conversation, mannerisms or style of dress appear to the police objectionable, even though they may not have been caught in any illicit sexual act.

A recent development in American law has been the somewhat hasty enactment of protective measures against sexual psychopaths. These laws, which were intended to safeguard the community from violent or dangerous sexual offenders, provide for committal to prison hospitals for indefinite periods, or until 'recovered'. Unfortunately, the definitions and procedures used are so wide that even relatively harmless persons, including homosexuals, who come before the courts on either a sexual or non-sexual charge, stand some risk of being dealt with in this way if the court decides they are sexually abnormal. Since the treatment facilities provided are sometimes inadequate, and the medical authorities' notions of fitness for discharge somewhat vague, these unfortunates may languish in institutions far longer than if they had been sent to prison in the ordinary way. The system has been subject to much criticism by both legal and psychiatric experts, and in a few instances the laws have been declared unconstitutional [39, 233]

Many times in recent years proposals have been put forward to reform the American sex laws. The *Model Penal Code* prepared by the American Law Institute provides (Article 213) that private sexual acts, whether heterosexual or homosexual, should be criminal only where minors are involved or some force or coercion is used. Since 1962 this reform has been put into effect in Illinois, but nowhere else. New York, however, has gone so far as to reduce the crime of consenting adult homosexuality from a felony to a misdemeanour.

Laws against sexual deviation are by no means confined to the Western Christian world. The Koran specifically condemns homosexual acts (Ch. IV, v. 20), and in the ancient Muslim religious code sodomy and adultery are both serious offences, punishable by death. In Pakistan, adultery is a criminal offence, and although some forms of homosexual behaviour are permitted sodomy is punishable with great severity [64]. It is interesting to note that in Morocco, when a modern legal code was drawn up after independence in 1956, the French code was largely copied, but some of the old religious offences were added, including the prohibitions against both homosexuality and extra-marital heterosexual intercourse (Sections 489 and 490). It does not follow from the adoption of such statutes that prosecutions based upon them become commonplace. Although adultery in Morocco is punishable by a minimum of one year's imprisonment, a complaint has to be lodged before a prosecution can be brought [44].

In England homosexual crimes first became a matter for the secular courts in 1533 when a statute was introduced (25 Henry VIII c.6) making sodomy punishable by death. So it remained until the nineteenth century, when the maximum penalty was reduced to life imprisonment. The

Some Legal Problems

Offences Against the Person Act, 1861, Section 61, which remained in force until 1956, read: 'Whoever shall be convicted of the abominable Crime of Buggery, committed either with mankind or with any Animal, shall be liable, at the Discretion of the Court, to [imprisonment] for Life.' In English law buggery of humans has always meant anal penetration; and both the active agent and the passive recipient who voluntarily participates in the act are guilty of this crime. The legal offence may equally well be committed by man and wife as by two men.

Short of buggery, homosexual activities appear to have been permissible in the nineteenth century, provided they did not involve children, violence, or public indecency. This gap was filled in the year 1885, when a Bill was introduced 'to make further provision for the protection of women and girls' and for 'the suppression of brothels'. One of the main provisions in the original draft was to raise the age of consent for girls from 13 to 16. Henry Labouchere, M.P., moved the introduction of a new clause making indecent acts between males in public or in private a criminal offence. Another Member asked if it was in order to introduce into the Bill an alien topic. The Speaker ruled that it was for the House to decide, and the new clause was accordingly accepted without any discussion.[1] From then on all sexual acts between males of any age became offences of 'gross indecency' [315], punishable by two years' imprisonment under the Criminal Law Amendment Act of 1885. The change in the law thus unobtrusively introduced did not pass without comment. One Recorder at the time called it scathingly 'the blackmailers' charter'.

The contemporary English law on sex matters is mostly governed by the Sexual Offences Act of 1956 [193, 303]. This Act brought together offences previously dealt with under different statutes of various dates, but did not change the substance of the English law. Any sexual touching of a child of either sex under the age of sixteen is defined and punished as 'indecent assault', regardless of

[1] Hansard 6 August 1885. Col. 1397–8.

whether the child resists or encourages the offence. However, the maximum penalties differ, being two years' imprisonment if the victim is a girl (Section 14) and ten years if a boy (Section 15). When sexual intercourse takes place with a girl under age, the law makes a sensible distinction between child victims of twelve or under (maximum penalty life imprisonment) and adolescent victims under sixteen (maximum penalty two years). No such distinction occurs in the case of homosexual activities with boys; indeed the maximum penalty for buggery is life imprisonment, regardless whether the 'victim' solicited, consented to, or resisted the behaviour.

The Sexual Offences Act fails to define 'gross indecency' (Section 13), the charge which is used to cover any kind of sex activity between males of sixteen or more years. However, the Court of Criminal Appeal has held that it is not even necessary for the men to touch each other; indecently exhibiting the genitals suffices.[1] Usually, however, the offence involves touching the private parts, or mutual masturbation.

Under Section 32 it is an offence for a man 'persistently to solicit or importune in a public place for immoral purposes'. This is the law generally used to prosecute men who loiter around public lavatories trying to make contact with other homosexuals. In this context it appears that lingering is sufficient to constitute persistence. Furthermore, the offence does not require any physical act of indecency, or anyone to be annoyed by an immoral proposition. It has been held that smiles or suggestive gestures observed by the police are sufficient to constitute solicitation, even though the men to whom they were directed may not have noticed them.

Another homosexual offence of an indirect character is the 'attempt to procure' an act of gross indecency between men. If a letter containing an immoral proposition were intercepted, or if one man were overheard asking another how to find a boy prostitute, these circumstances would

[1] Rex *v.* Hunt (1950) *Criminal Appeal Reports, 34,* p. 137.

provide *prima facie* evidence of this offence, for which the penalty is up to two years' imprisonment.

Finally, homosexual acts in public, for instance in parks, are sometimes prosecuted under local bye-laws directed against indecent or offensive behaviour. In London, the Hyde Park Regulations, 1932, provide that no person in the park shall 'behave in any manner reasonably likely to offend against public decency. Penalty £5'. Homosexuals prosecuted under bye-laws may consider themselves to have had a lucky escape, and will be under some pressure to plead guilty if they think that by so doing they can avoid a more serious charge. Not only are the penalties less, but the conviction is not so likely to attract publicity since it does not distinguish between homosexual acts and such things as urinating out of doors or appearing inadequately clad. However, for that very reason these procedures also conceal the true incidence of homosexual prosecutions from readers of the official *Criminal Statistics*.

Since 1958, when the Departmental (Wolfenden) Committee reported in favour of a relaxation of the laws against adult homosexuality, the campaign for reform of the English law has gathered momentum. After endless Parliamentary debates and many procedural delays the new Sexual Offences Act, 1967, finally removed the legal penalties for homosexual acts in private between men over twenty-one. Except for offences with boys under sixteen, the Act abolishes the anomaly, once referred to by Lady Wootton as 'queer geography', whereby anal contacts carry much severer penalties than other kinds of sexual congress. As with female prostitution, the individual private transaction is not now illegal, but in addition to existing law against importuning the Act prescribes penalties for benefiting from the earnings of male prostitution and for procuring men for homosexual acts.

The argument, which has raged so long, and must have cost the tax payer a considerable sum, is important in principle, but the outcome cannot have any great effect on the statistics of convictions for homosexuality. The great bulk of prosecutions have always been for importuning, indecency in lavatories or public places, and offences with minors. In later years, especially since the Director of Public Prosecutions announced that he would like to be notified before any proceedings were taken in connection with behaviour by consenting adults in private, prosecutions of this kind had dwindled away—although, of course, the threat of them remained. As for the very severe penalties for buggery, these were not usually invoked by the judges, except where child victims were involved, or there was a history of previous convictions, but their continued existence allows the occasional injustice. In 1964, in a survey of men in prison for homosexuality, Michael Schofield [326] found that some of those serving the longest sentences were men convicted for the first time, whose offences were with consenting adults in private, but who had unwisely confessed to acts of buggery.

The Sexual Offences Act, 1967, although faithful to the Wolfenden proposals, deals gingerly with the reformers' points. All homosexual acts, whether buggery, gross indecency, or attempts to procure gross indecency, committed by men over 21 with youths of 16 up to 21, even though the youth willingly participates, are to incur penalties of up to five years' imprisonment for the older man. For buggery or indecency with boys under sixteen the existing penalties, including life imprisonment, are to remain unchanged. Homosexual acts, whether of gross indecency or buggery, committed by a youth under twenty-one with a consenting partner of any age over sixteen, now incur a penalty up to two years' imprisonment; but youths under twenty-one are not to be proceeded against without the consent of the Director of Public Prosecutions. The freedom of those over twenty-one to indulge homosexually in private are to be hedged by several precautions. The provisions against soliciting or importuning are to remain in force, and however secluded the room the acts will not be legally private if more than two persons are present. The crew of merchant ships at sea and men in the Forces

83

will be excluded from the new freedom, since the Army, Air Force and Naval Discipline Acts will remain in operation. In most countries where consenting homosexuality is not criminal, if such conduct appears prejudicial to good military order it is dealt with as an internal disciplinary matter, as happens at present in England in connection with lesbianism in the Women's Services. In England, however, the male military authorities unanimously disapprove of the removal of criminal sanctions in this sphere.

2. *Enforcing the Law*

For the most part sexual misconduct takes place privately, or at least stealthily, leaving behind no damage and no complaining victim. Convictions have often to be secured either by persuading one of the participants to confess, or by the unsupported testimony of police officers describing what they saw. This puts an unusually heavy responsibility upon the police.

As with other hidden crimes, like espionage or drug-peddling or abortion, detection is easiest by clandestine methods, such as paid informers, plain clothes decoys, the agent provocateur, interception of mail and telephone calls, scrutiny of bank accounts and other private records, etc., etc. Where the safety of the state is at stake, ordinary rules of police procedure may be waived without too much fuss, but in matters of sexual morality public attitudes are highly ambivalent, many people consider the law should not interfere at all, and so the police must tread more warily. In the conflict of interest between the needs of detection and the rights of the citizen to enjoy reasonable privacy and freedom from harassment, citizens' rights come before police convenience in all democratic countries. In the United States, a number of small but vocal organizations (such as The Mattachine Society of Washington, which publishes *The Homosexual Citizen*[1]) watch over the interests of homosexuals and expose instances of

[1] P.O. Box 1032, Washington D.C., 20013.

questionable police methods or infringements of constitutional rights.

Where offences occur in private houses they rarely come to the notice of the police, and homosexuals may regard prosecution as a remote possibility which, like an earthquake, nothing will prevent. Indeed, many such prosecutions have come about through the operation of accidental or extraneous circumstances, such as the discovery by the police of an address book in the possession of a man arrested for importuning, denunciation by a spiteful neighbour or a jealous lover, or the activities of blackmailers.

A few examples from the newspapers will illustrate what happens. In 1965, Michael, a youth of nineteen, lost a wallet containing addresses and letters from homosexual friends, some of them from adolescent boys. The police took action, and on this, his first conviction, the youth was sentenced to imprisonment for three years.[1] He had no other delinquent tendencies, he came from a religious background, and he gave the authorities full and frank statements about his sex life. It transpired that, having lost his own father, he had formed at puberty a close attachment to a priest who introduced him to homosexual life and taught him that there was nothing particularly wrong about it. On appeal, the Lord Chief Justice described the case as tragic, but since the young man was now definitely homosexual and perhaps unresponsive to a psychiatric approach, he saw no alternative to prison, and the sentence was confirmed.[2]

The practice of allowing immunity to prosecution to those prepared to testify for the Crown has given rise to adverse public comment. In 1953, a young peer was sent to prison, while two young airmen who admitted improper conduct, but gave evidence for the prosecution, were allowed to go free. The case led to widespread discussion

[1] Monica Furlong. 'Can such a sentence on this boy be justified?' *Daily Mail* 20 Nov. 1965.

[2] Editorial (1965) *The New Law Journal, 116,* 115–116. *The Times,* 9 Nov. 1965.

and eventually to the appointment of the Wolfenden Committee of inquiry. Incidentally, this was another example of a prosecution coming about almost by accident. The process began when, in the course of a routine search unconnected with homosexuality, military police discovered letters in an airman's kit bag.

The dangers that may follow from the ending of a homosexual love affair are illustrated by a case at Croydon in 1966.[1] A young man was accused of demanding £50 from Mr. X before he would return some incriminating photographs showing Mr. X engaged in homosexual activity. The young man admitted that both he and Mr. X were homosexuals, and had lived together as 'man and wife', until he left after a row. In one recent case notified to the Homosexual Law Reform Society,[2] a man who had given up homosexual practice in favour of heterosexual life was threatened by his former man-friend with denunciation unless he returned. The threats continued until the blackmailer, himself emotionally overwrought, finally committed suicide.

Sometimes relatively harmless homosexuals get caught up in police purges. Dr. G. W. Henry [167] has told of the personal tragedies that often follow from the American vice squads' habit of 'persuading' arrested men to give away the names of all their homosexual friends. He described the case of a socially prominent man who returned to his home in an American town after an absence. Unaware that a vice crusade, accompanied by much newspaper publicity, was in full swing, he readily accepted an invitation to call at the police station. When he got there the police told him that they had a sworn statement from a man who said he had had sexual relations with him. After the police had assured him that anything he said would be strictly confidential, he naïvely admitted having had occasional homosexual experiences when away from his wife. He was at once arrested and put into jail. Five days later he appeared on a charge of

[1] *Croydon Advertiser*, 1 July, 1966.
[2] *Homosexuality—The Law in Action.* May, 1965.

being 'an idle, lewd, and dissolute person'. The lawyer who tried to plead for him was told by the judge, 'these men are wanton, all of them, young or old . . . these pleadings . . . have not affected me one iota'. The purge went on. More and more men were arrested, among them one of the city's leading physicians, who promptly killed himself. Finally the situation became so embarrassing to all concerned that the crusade was dropped.

Mass purges of homosexuals are now uncommon in England, although on occasions a whole group of men are prosecuted. For example, in July 1954, twenty-eight men came before the Birmingham Assizes on charges of homosexuality. The judge spoke of 'these disgusting practices which corrupt the life of the community' and awarded prison sentences totalling thirty-six years. The exposure of the men was reported to have come about through one man giving up to the police an address book containing the names of 213 homosexuals with whom he had associated over a period of years.[1] Such proceedings, or the threat of them, have been responsible for many suicides. When nine men and two youths of seventeen were brought before Evesham Magistrates' Court in April 1956 on charges of indecency a defending solicitor commented that three others who might have been before the Court were facing a higher tribunal.[2] Following questioning one man had gassed himself and another, a married man with three children, lay down on a railway line and was killed. Of those actually summoned one old man of eighty-one was taken to hospital with cerebral haemorrhage before a verdict could be given. Mostly these incidents escape public attention because suicides evade Court appearances. Sometimes a short notice of an inquest indicates what has happened, as for instance when it was reported that two men, aged sixty-six and forty-one, gassed themselves in their home following police inquiries about indecency.[3] More recently, in 1965,

[1] *News of the World*, 1 August 1954.
[2] *Evesham Standard*, 13 April 1956.
[3] *Daily Telegraph*, 16 December 1958.

at Pembrokeshire Winter Assizes, six men pleaded guilty to homosexual offences with a labourer aged twenty-four. The case arose as a result of the labourer, who was mentally subnormal, being questioned by the police on another matter, and then confessing to homosexuality with various men, most of whom confessed in turn when interviewed by the police. The labourer was committed to hospital under the Mental Health Act, Section 60.

In 1958, following correspondence in the press about large-scale arrests in Wells, and a general concern about suicides and other undesirable effects from this kind of police activity, the Homosexual Law Reform Society[1] was established in London in order to press for modification of the law and try to alleviate some of the social difficulties experienced by homosexuals. The Society has built up an impressive list of distinguished supporters.

Men apprehended in urinals, parks, baths and other public places sometimes complain of the tactics of young policemen in plain clothes who dress, talk and act in a deliberately provocative manner in order to trap unwary homosexuals into revealing themselves. In the United States especially, arguments rage over the distinction between legitimate decoys and illegitimate entrapment. A study by the University of California Law School has described the police practices allowable in parts of that State [122]. Decoys may wear tight pants, act effeminately, jingle coins in their pockets, eye men suggestively and enter into conversations, while loitering around toilets or using the urinals. If a man responds with an immoral proposition or lewd gesture, the decoy usually suggests going elsewhere. If the man agrees to this, a second police officer moves in to make the arrest when they leave the toilet. The policeman may provoke the offending sex act, but is not supposed to initiate it himself. In New York the police stopped entrapment in 1966 when the mayor ruled that charges of soliciting could be brought only on the complaint of a citizen.

[1] 32 Shaftesbury Avenue, London, W.1.

Without the use of decoys, a clandestine watch on public toilets and parks often suffices to provide eye-witness testimony sufficient to secure conviction. Some men will take any risk to satisfy their sexual needs. In England, in 1953, a detective who had served twenty years in the police force was sent to prison for indecency observed at a Turkish bath. He had gone to the bath knowing full well that others had been arrested there by police officers who spied upon the occupants through peepholes.[1]

Sexual misconduct is more easily alleged than disproved, but in one celebrated English case the evidence of the psychologist Dr. L. R. C. Haward secured the release of two men said to have been caught in *flagrante delecto* in a public urinal [163]. The stalls were watched surreptitiously by two policemen looking through the fanlight above the door of a broom cupboard. They sprang out of their hiding place to secure an arrest when the two men were 'seen' to engage in mutual masturbation. Measurements and experiments at the scene served to establish that the dim lighting, and the distance of the accused and their position relative to the watchers' line of sight, were sufficient to cast doubt upon the accuracy of observations made under such conditions. In order to avoid disputes, clandestine observation by cine camera has been employed in Mansfield, Ohio. Police, concealed behind a two-way mirror in a park lavatory and equipped with a 16 mm. cine camera, recorded, in the space of two weeks, indecencies by sixty-five different men. A radio transmitter enabled the watching police to signal to colleagues waiting outside, prepared to identify and arrest the offenders as they emerged [220]. Technical difficulties of lighting, whirring noise, and expense would probably preclude the use of this technique in the murkier English conveniences.

Considering the opportunities for abuse, the English police exercise surprising restraint and integrity. Of course policy varies from one town to another. Ben Whitaker commented on the extraordinary rise in the incidence of

[1] *News of the World*, 19 July, 1953.

convictions for importuning in Manchester, from less than one to over two hundred per year, which coincided with the appointment of a new chief constable [381]. Now and then, some exceptional example of police malpractice hits the headlines. For example, in October 1964, a constable from Bexley Heath was convicted at the Old Bailey for demanding money from a man in a public urinal whom he had threatened to charge with importuning.[1] In March 1966 at Manchester Crown Court a detective was convicted for having tried to blackmail a married man who had spent an afternoon in a hotel room with a youth of eighteen. The youth had said nothing, but the detective pretended that a statement had been made, and asked for money to buy the young man's silence.[2]

The occasional English scandal pales into insignificance compared with what happens in the United States. Albert Deutch, in an article on vice squads,[3] alleged that American policemen have made small fortunes by accepting bribes and protection money from homosexuals. Others have made fortunes by merely pretending to be policemen. According to a statement to the press in 1966 by F. S. Hogan, a District Attorney in New York, a gang of extortionists had been operating for some ten years in the United States, battening upon men in established positions known to be homosexuals and extorting from them hundreds of thousands of dollars. In one instance, two gang members posing as New York City detectives walked into the Pentagon and took away a high-ranking officer from whom they extorted several thousand dollars. The officer committed suicide just before he was due to testify before a grand jury. Another homosexual victim, a New York businessman, who had been beaten up and robbed of his wallet and identity card in Chicago, was later apprehended in New York by bogus police from Chicago who extracted

[1] Homosexual Law Reform Society. *Homosexuality: The Law in Action*, May 1965.

[2] *Sunday Express*, 28 Nov. 1965 and *Manchester Evening News*, 21 Mar. 1966.

[3] *Collier's Magazine*, 28 May 1954.

two thousand dollars. The matter having at last come to light, seventeen persons were indicted on charges of extortion.[1]

In case it should be thought that law reform will do away entirely with these troubles, it needs to be pointed out that most of the situations cited in this section involved offences in public places or men aged under twenty-one.

3. Civil Disabilities

Once convicted, or once their condition becomes known to the relevant authorities, male sex deviants (like the leprous or the insane) must expect some legal and social restrictions. If they work in certain fields, such as teaching, or government posts involving security risk, they will lose their jobs. If they belong to a profession with strict disciplinary rules, like solicitors and medical men, they may have their licence to practice taken away. They will not be accepted for admission to the armed forces or the merchant navy, they will be found unsuitable for a wide range of employments such as police, prison service, youth workers and so forth. They will never be considered for important posts in politics or public life. They may even encounter difficulties if they want to enter as students at a university. They will be rejected if they apply to immigrate to another country.

These disabilities weigh more heavily upon many homosexuals than the comparatively light penalties of the criminal law. They also arouse much resentment, since they underline the deviant's inferior social status. They often seem to operate unjustly, penalizing the comparatively well-behaved man whose condition happens to have come to official notice, while leaving other more obvious homosexuals unmolested. They also place a heavy burden upon those responsible for advising on or administering the regulations. For example, I was lately asked to see a schoolteacher who had been suspended from work pending a psychiatric report to the Department of Education and

[1] *West Australian* (Perth), 4 Mar. 1966.

Science. Somehow or other a conviction for importuning many years previously had just come to the notice of the Department. The man was a confirmed homosexual, but he had a stable relationship with a friend of his own age, no sexual inclination towards children, and he was leading a perfectly orderly life. He was an efficient teacher who liked his job, and presented no more threat to his pupils, either morally or physically, than many of his colleagues. Because he had been truthful about his condition, it was not possible to say he was heterosexual, and I knew that any other report would risk his dismissal.

Discriminatory sanctions against homosexuals have been a source of great public controversy in the United States. In the decade that has since become known as the McCarthy witch hunting era, certain politicians tried to gain advantage by accusing their opponents of un-American activities, namely communist sympathies or homosexual tendencies— the two types of deviation being thought to go together. Government agencies were accused of harbouring dangerous perverts [368]. Naturally the administration became more cautious in the screening of their employees, and the risks involved in having homosexuals in the foreign service, or engaged upon secret work, were widely publicized [148]. It was realized that homosexuals find foreign service attractive, since they have no family ties, and they like to travel and meet new faces. However, if they indulge in amorous encounters with foreigners, they may find themselves in compromising situations, and forced to co-operate with enemy agents under threat of their homosexual deviation being exposed.

Since the McCarthy era the political and security risks arising from homosexuality have been emphasized less often in political debates. Nevertheless the argument continues. A Senate fact-finding committee on un-American activities, which reported in May 1966, charged the President of the University of California at Berkley, not only with allowing the campus to become a hot-bed of communist activity, and a base for the campaign against war in Vietnam, but also with letting it develop into a centre of homosexual vice among students.[1]

From time to time, cases are brought before the American Courts in an effort to get discrimination declared invalid. For example, Clive Boutilier, aged 32, who was born in Canada, but had worked for eight years in America, applied for United States citizenship, and in answer to the customary questions reported that he had once been arrested for a homosexual act, although the charge had been dismissed. He was ordered to be deported on grounds of 'psychopathic personality'. In 1966, supported by psychiatric evidence that he was not a psychopath, he took the case to the U.S. Court of Appeals, 2nd Circuit, but it was rejected. In his ruling, Judge I. R. Kaufman described psychopathy as a vague rubric covering Congress's intent to bar all perverts.[2] The U.S. Supreme Court, on 22 May, 1967, upheld the legality of deportation of alien homosexuals as psychopaths.

Another sore point is that if, under medical examination, an American serviceman admits to or is diagnosed as having homosexual tendencies, even though he may have committed no offence, he is promptly discharged 'without honor', which means that he forfeits veterans' rights and financial benefits, and may have trouble finding employment [66]. The Department of Defense has issued specific instructions (Memo. 11 Oct. 1949) that all known homosexuals must be eliminated from the services. Commanding Officers who receive information suggesting that a man has such tendencies, or has ever engaged in homosexual acts, must report the matter to the Office of Special Investigations. Although it may seem unfair to penalize men for what is admittedly a psychiatric condition, it is argued that to give 'honorable discharges' might encourage some heterosexuals to make false admissions of deviancy in order to get out of the service. And anyway these men must have

[1] *The Times*, 7 May 1966.
[2] *Medical News* (London), 15 July 1966. *Time* (New York), 22 July 1966.

93

enlisted fraudulently by concealing their tendencies on induction. Psychiatrists have pointed out that this harsh in approach defeats its own purpose, since it ensures that homosexual servicemen take care to conceal their condition. That they can generally do so successfully was demonstrated by Fry and Rostow [376], who followed the service careers of 132 former students known from pre-war studies to be homosexual. Of these, 118 served successfully, 58 per cent as officers, achieving creditable records, and hiding their disability. The total number who received premature discharges, for any reason whatsoever amounted to only 14.

A point of theoretical interest is that apart from the sexual psychopath laws, which apply only to persons brought to court on criminal charges, the mere fact of being homosexual might, in some States, render a man liable to compulsory committal to a mental hospital. In Massachusetts, the relevant clause defining such liability refers to any person who conducts himself 'in a manner which clearly violates the established laws, ordinances, conventions or morals of the community.' [354] In England, sexual immorality is specifically excluded from the anti-social behaviour which may be used as grounds for committing a person to hospital with a diagnosis of psychopathy.

Awareness of their vulnerability to discriminatory sanctions makes homosexuals specially sensitive to the threat of investigations into the private affairs of present or prospective employees. An article on this topic by Richard Harwood, entitled 'There's a Dossier on You', which appeared in the *Washington Post*, 29 May 1966, was reprinted in *The Homosexual Citizen*. The article drew attention to the millions of dollars spent on these inquiries by the Federal Government, the F.B.I., the Atomic Energy Commission and similar agencies. The Civil Service Commission were said to hold secret dossiers on millions of persons, including thousands of allegations of immoral conduct. Applicants for entry into some government departments were asked to undergo lie detector tests, or to answer such questions as: 'Have you ever engaged in homosexual acts since the age of sixteen?' In a recent six months' period, the Defense Department had unearthed 22 perverts and 10 psychiatric cases among persons coming under scrutiny because the companies they worked for had accepted defence contracts. Even the Federal Housing Authority kept confidential reports from private investigation agencies, since information about marital stability had a bearing upon the granting of mortgages. A recent book by Vance Packard [287] describes a host of similar examples that have become commonplace in America. For instance, large business concerns, as well as government agencies, employ professional workers (using subtle interview techniques, lie detectors and personality tests) to probe into the private lives of prospective employees, particularly as regards homosexual interests, even when this seems to have no relevance to the job under offer. Missouri police have a psychiatrist, Dr. G. H. Lawrence [228], helping with the selection of candidates for entry into the force. He has published an article arguing in favour of the polygraph as being a more effective means than straight interviews for detecting lies and evasions, and hence for identifying homosexuality and incipient alcoholism, which are considered the two commonest disqualifying conditions.

In England, the government has never been quite so sensitive to the supposed menace of sexual deviants. In the Radcliffe Report on security in the public service, it was stated that every candidate for a post involving access to highly secret information goes through a positive vetting procedure, which includes a check with the Security Service and 'a field investigation into his character and circumstances'. Occasionally these investigations reveal insobriety, financial instability, untruthfulness or irregular marital or sexual relations. The report commented: 'While it can be said that in theory such defects constitute vulnerability to temptation or pressure, they do not present themselves as necessarily the most dangerous traits from a security point of view . . .' The report strongly advised transfer to a more innocuous post rather than discharge for staff who fail to obtain clearance [301].

Faint echoes of American polemics made themselves heard for a time in England in 1962 when William Vassall, an Admiralty employee, was convicted for giving away state secrets. It emerged that, unknown to his superiors, Vassall was a practising homosexual, and during his period of service as clerk to the Naval Attaché in Moscow he made friends with a local employee, who was also homosexual. This led to his seducibility becoming known to the Russian Secret Service, who engineered other encounters, and finally had him enticed to a party where he was photographed during acts of indecency. Menaced with exposure and prosecution, he was persuaded to buy his continued freedom by working for the Russians, which he did off and on for eight years. The subsequent Tribunal of Inquiry, which was set up to look into the circumstances of this breach of security, commented on the variety of pressures brought to bear upon embassy officials. The manufacture of compromising situations was a regular secret service technique, 'attempted again and again in various forms, through black market operations, through currency offences, through involving men with women, women with men, and, as in Vassall's case, men with men'. [178]. Clearly, homosexuals are not the only people at risk in the espionage business, although, in their case, great pressures can be brought to bear because the penalties of exposure are so heavy. The Tribunal emphasized that Vassall's homosexual friendships over many years were essentially private, and unconnected with his work, and would have been unlikely to come to the notice of the authorities if he had not fallen into the Russian trap.

4. *Ethical and Religious Issues*

Christian dogma has long considered homosexual behaviour in all circumstances utterly immoral and inexcusable. In 1953, Dr. Fisher, then Archbishop of Canterbury, declared categorically: 'Let it be understood that homosexual indulgence is a shameful vice and a grievous sin from which deliverance is to be sought by every means.'[1] And a year later, the Bishop of Rochester, writing for a medical audience, declared: 'Homosexual practice is always a grievous sin and perversion. Defective sexual intercourse between two persons of the same sex can only be gross indecency under the guise of expressing affection. Even if safeguards could eliminate the corruption of youth, and the practice be confined to inverts of mature age, it would remain the perversion of a wholesome instinct to an unnatural and loathsome end. For all such inverts continence is demanded.'[2]

In recent years, the thinking of some of the more radical churchmen has undergone a subtle change. In 1955, the Rev. Sherwin Bailey [14], an Anglican priest, published a book questioning the scriptural authority for singling out homosexual vice for special condemnation. He contested the interpretation put upon some of the words in the old biblical texts, and doubted whether the sins of Sodom had any connection with homosexuality. Some theologians, while not questioning the sinfulness of homosexual activity, recognize that a blanket rejection of all those who succumb to temptation may be not only uncharitable but perhaps un-Christian. As long ago as 1952, a French Catholic doctor and priest, Father Marc Oraison [284], published a book in which he pleaded against the automatic rejection of homosexuals as monsters condemned to eternal damnation, and suggested that their sexual lapses should be considered acts of weakness rather than mortal sins. At the time these views were too advanced, and the book was condemned by the Holy Office and withdrawn. A still more advanced view was put forward by an English Quaker group in 1964 [169]. They questioned whether the physical nature of a sex act, either heterosexual or homosexual, should be the criterion by which the morality of the behaviour is decided. They pointed out that homosexual affection could sometimes be

[1] *The Times*, 25 Nov. 1953.
[2] *The Practitioner*, April 1954.

as selfless as heterosexual affection, and they failed to see why it must always be morally worse.

These views come close to acceptance of homosexual love, and its physical expression, as right and proper for certain persons in certain circumstances. Father J. Gottschalk (cited by Antony Grey), a Dutch Catholic priest, is one of the few religious authorities to go the whole way. He has suggested that Christians should accept homosexuals not just as persons, but as persons with sexual lives, for whom the virtues of fidelity and self-discipline may be more appropriate than the loneliness and mental stultification of absolute continence [142, 147].

This new-found religious freedom from the absolute proscriptions of Revealed or Natural Law tends to be hedged about with a great many ifs and buts and warnings about the dangers involved in making personal moral decisions. A recent pronouncement by a working party of the British Council of Churches [43] emphasizes that such decisions may be more far-reaching than the individual realizes, that 'every action, however private, has some repercussions on society sooner or later', and that 'it is a fallacy that what goes on between two people in the sexual sphere is no one's business but their own'. 'We cannot excuse e.g. homosexual seduction of the young, just because it is in private'. Characteristically, the report avoids saying whether private homosexual acts between adults could ever be 'excused'.

Notwithstanding the questionings of these advanced churchmen, orthodox Church teaching remains clear on the point that homosexual acts are always wrong. The position has been set out at some length by the modern Catholic writer, Rev. Michael Buckley [46]. While taking careful note of the available scientific information, he rejects the idea that Christians could ever tolerate sexual deviancy, and describes at length the scriptural and church authorities for defining homosexual acts as crimes against Natural Law.

Although the orthodox Christian cannot regard homosexual acts as other than sinful, representatives of the major Christian sects in England, in their evidence before the Wolfenden Committee and elsewhere, have made clear that in their view adult behaviour should be a question for the individual conscience and not a matter for the criminal law. The Archbishop of Canterbury put this point of view most forcibly in the course of one of the House of Lords debates.[1]

In marked contrast to the aid given by the churches to ladies with illegitimate babies, male sex sinners are talked about in the abstract rather than helped in practice. A few American ministers of religion have proved an exception to this rule and founded a Council on Religion and the Homosexual, with the object of befriending the troubled and pleading for greater social justice. A report by this Council published in 1965 [244] not only took up the usual points about unjustifiable harassment of homosexuals, but complained that the police were unsympathetic and intimidating towards priests wanting to help. At a fund-raising dance arranged by the Council, police stood around taking photographs of the guests as they entered, and when some of the organizers protested they were arrested for obstruction.

Eminent jurists are rather less decided than churchmen where to draw the line between law and morals. Professor Hart of Oxford [161] follows John Stuart Mill in believing that the power of the criminal law should be invoked only against actions which do harm to others, and not against actions which merely violate the conventional Christian version of morality. He therefore welcomed the Suicide Act, 1961, by which attempted suicide ceased to be a criminal offence, and he supported the proposals of the Wolfenden Report and the American Law Institute [6] that deviant sexual practices between consenting adults, which do not harm others, should not be punishable by law.

Lord Devlin, a leading opponent of this legal laisser faire, takes issue both on the principle and on the premises on which the argument rests [80]. In his view, by helping

[1] 12 May 1965.

to define the limits of permissible conduct, the law con-
tributes to the discouragement of immoral behaviour and
the prevention of the spread of habits which could eventually harm society. He draws an analogy with non-inter-
ference with the individual who chooses to get drunk in
privacy. This policy seems eminently proper until one
wonders what would be the right attitude to take if half the
population began to get drunk nightly. In his view, if
society feels homosexuality an abominable vice, so that its
presence is an outrage, and a threat to the moral basis on
which the community is organized, this amply justifies
legislation against it. Apparently, Lord Devlin does not
himself subscribe to the view that homosexuality in England presents this kind of threat at the moment (in fact he
signed a joint letter to *The Times*, 12 May 1965, supporting
the Wolfenden proposals), but he wishes to preserve the
principle that the law should sometimes be able to intervene
in matters of private morals.

Among the many criticisms of these views by legal
experts, the one which seems to me to have most force is
the argument that, if one follows the Devlin line to its
ultimate conclusion, the principles of justice would be
sacrificed to popular clamour. The moral views of the man-
in-the-street do not provide a safe criterion for legislation;
they may stem from prejudices or aversion (e.g. homosexuals, Jews, negroes, etc., are 'not real men' or 'they
make me sick'), or they may be copied parrot fashion from
one person to another, or they may stem from preconcep-
tions that have long since been disproved [86].

The outcome of these legal wrangles may not have a
great influence on how people react in everyday life. All the
same, it seems equally unrealistic to argue, as some do, that
the state of the law has no effect at all upon sexual behaviour, as to imagine that tinkering with statutes will
bring about profound changes in the attitudes and conduct
of the masses. In the long run, the controversies about
social policy will probably be settled by practical considerations, and by increasing scientific knowledge of the

causes of homosexuality, rather than by further mulling over the finer points of theological or legal philosophy.

Are homosexual practices in fact spread to any significant degree by example or by seduction? What are the effects of trying to stifle or repress homosexual desires? Would an increase in incidence produce some social disaster? In what proportion of cases can self-determination or medical aid produce a satisfactory conversion to heterosexuality? To those who believe that divine revelation has already settled the moral issue, these questions will seem irrelevant, but for the rationalist the morality of homosexual acts depends upon the answers.

CHAPTER V

SOME SOCIAL PROBLEMS

1. Intolerance and its Effects

In many Arab and Asian countries where homosexual practices are commonplace, and regarded by most people with easy-going indifference, no great trouble arises. But the situation is changing rapidly as American influence spreads over the globe. In the developing countries persons of advanced ideas are becoming sensitive about behaviour that might be stigmatized as primitive. This may partly account for the presence of anti-homosexual legislation in the modern penal codes of places like Lebanon and Morocco, at a time when the trend among American intellectuals is towards liberalizing the law. It may also account for the curious contradiction that travellers in the past have commented on the homosexual vice of the Orient, and homosexual tourists today return home with tales of sex adventures in an atmosphere of comparative freedom, whereas officials in the developing countries tend to blame visiting Europeans or American troops for introducing a homosexual problem. Perhaps a more accurate version would be that homosexual behaviour has always been prevalent, but that the social problems began when people started to think about it along Western lines.

The intense and irrationally motivated hostility of Anglo-American culture towards homosexuals is to blame for many of the attendant social evils. Were it not for their sense of sinfulness and rejection, and their heavy burden of guilt, many homosexuals would function better in society, work more efficiently, and have less tendency towards escapist behaviour, neurotic breakdowns, despondency and suicide. So long as public exposure of their condition means family disgrace, social ostracism, loss of employment and, above all, criminal prosecution, homosexuals will remain easy targets for blackmail, extortion, robbery and other more subtle pressures. The factual writings of Peter Wildeblood in England [383, 384], and D. W. Cory in America [66], have portrayed most vividly the difficulties and discomforts of the homosexual way of life.

This state of affairs forces thousands of seemingly solid citizens to lead a Jekyll-and-Hyde existence, posing among their work-mates as 'normal', perhaps dating girls for the sake of appearances, while at other times sinking into a twilight world of secret assignations, parties and dubious drinking haunts. For those in respectable professional positions every fresh stranger they meet in their clandestine wanderings exposes them to added risk. In a lecture published in 1954, the Rt. Hon. Earl Jowitt, Lord Chancellor of England from 1945 to 1952, made the surprising declaration that when he became Attorney-General in 1929 he was impressed with the fact that 'A very large percentage of blackmail cases—nearly 90 per cent of them—were cases in which the person blackmailed had been guilty of homosexual practices with an adult person' [199]. The Wolfenden Report stated that of 71 cases of blackmail reported to the police in the years 1950–3, 32 were connected with homosexual activities. Contrary to popular belief, the homosexual who denounced a blackmailer did not enjoy immunity from prosecution. The Wolfenden Report quoted one example of a man who complained to the police he was being blackmailed by a homosexual partner. Although he had no previous convictions, when the case came to Court he got nine months' imprisonment, the same as his blackmailer. The new Sexual Offences Act will prevent such injustices in future, except where the blackmailer is under twenty-one. Countries with a legitimate age of consent for homosexuality seem to have much less of this kind of blackmail.

In some ways, the move towards more open recognition of the deviant's predicament makes matters worse, for the young homosexual may not realize just where he stands, and may feel rejections all the more acutely if he has been led to expect a certain tolerance. Furthermore, increasing awareness on the part of ordinary people means that deviancy becomes more difficult to conceal, especially from prying relatives. Young people who have had a few homosexual experiences in the natural course of events may hear about the frightful problems of deviants, and imagine themselves for ever tainted or disabled [292].

Contributors to the intellectual weeklies may affect a fashionable tolerance in their writings (although perhaps not in their actions if they thought their own son or daughter were involved), but the popular press remains on the whole unsympathetic. The topic gets most coverage when sordid cases of child molestation or lust murder come to light. This constant harping upon demoralized and dangerous characters must help to form an adverse climate of opinion. For example, the widely read American magazine *Life International* for 24 January 1966 carried a long article about police work on Broadway, New York. This famous avenue was described as the haunt of 'The worst America has to offer in the way of degenerates, perverts and law breakers'. The article, which dealt with confidence tricksters, car thieves and armed robbers, was illustrated with pictures of Lesbians in trousers. It was explained that the 'butch' women were giving heroin to their 'fem' girl friends to make them dependently addicted, in preparation for exploiting them as prostitutes for men. Other pictures showed boy prostitutes, some dressed in wigs and skirts, posturing on the kerbside, and soliciting men. These may be the sort the public likes to read about, but they no more represent homosexuality than pimps typify heterosexuality. In contrast, the more exclusive English magazine *Nova*, for February 1967, featured a lead article on homosexuality illustrated with middle-class male couples at home in tasteful apartments in Holland. The writer, Irma Kurty, took pains to point out that legal discrimination creates 'a breed of pimps and prostitutes, a set of professional blackmailers, a whole race of twilight people'. She also quoted the theory that Dutch homosexuals are more optimistic about and more successful at maintaining pseudo-marital relationships because the law and the moral climate in Holland is comparatively tolerant.

Modern fiction and drama, by its preoccupation with themes of violence, sexual licence, and anti-social behaviour, adds a further quota of unsavouriness to the popular image of the homosexual. Readers can discount something for artistic licence when it comes to descriptions of wild behaviour by heterosexuals, and they don't expect the man next door to behave like a sex criminal or a character in problem fiction, but their experience of homosexuals in real life may be insufficient for them to realize that novels like *Last Exit to Brooklyn* by the American author Hubert Selby—(London, Calder and Boyars 1966),[1] or *The Pole and Whistle* by George Moor (London, New English Library, 1966), are not in the least representative of the humdrum existence and essential ordinariness of the average homosexual. In the former book, the chief character in one of the stories is a drug addicted 'queen' called Georgette, who hangs around a gang of hoodlums, and delights in arranging parties for them at which, after all present have got drunk on a mixture of alcohol and drugs, Georgette and her friends of similar tastes are likely to undergo communal rape. In the second novel, the homosexual hero falls for a masculine-looking young delinquent. During this lover's absence in prison, some of his more aggressive criminal acquaintances force their way into the hero's flat and indulge themselves in a sadistic orgy. The homosexual is raped repeatedly, burned with cigarette ends and hot fat, beaten mercilessly, robbed, and then denounced to the police by a neighbour who has overheard the noise. Nevertheless, the story ends happily, because the hero gets the chance to emigrate to Japan, where he finds another lover and greater social tolerance.

Even the more serious literary works, by dwelling upon

[1] Declared obscene at Marlborough Street Magistrates' Court, London, December 1966.

horrific situations, contribute further to this image of misery. In the novel *Radcliffe*, by David Storey (Longmans, 1963), the chief character, a highly introspective, neurotic weakling, falls in love with a powerful, bullying working man of bisexual inclinations. The tortured relationship that develops ends in him battering the bully to death with a hammer, after which a former male lover of the murdered man attacks the hero and then kills himself and his whole family. Following his trial, the hero lapses into complete insanity and dies in a mental institution. Against these more lurid themes one must set the sensitive but comparatively realistic stories by writers like Christopher Isherwood, Julien Green and Mary Renault, who manage to portray credible homosexual characters behaving in familiar situations.

Criminologists such as Leslie Wilkins [385] have argued that society's intolerance of mental patients, detected lawbreakers, drug addicts, homosexuals and social deviants generally makes matters worse than need be. Due to fear and ignorance, fostered by sensational stories in the newspapers, most people harbour exaggerated notions of the peculiarities and viciousness of deviants. Wrongly perceiving relatively mild nuisances as a serious threat, they react with severe condemnation. Feeling themselves under attack, the deviants' own attitudes harden, and they start to reject the values of the society they now perceive as oppressive. A bogey that first existed only in anticipation may be brought into reality by this vicious circle of rejection and counter rejection. The manners and morals of the more outlandish homosexual groups, their 'camp' tastes, their addiction to 'gay' life, and their contempt for the dull, conventional outlook of the 'normal' world, might well be in part a counter-rejection phenomenon. In individual cases one can observe how some homosexuals, who feel themselves continually spurned, finally contract out of the whole business of trying to keep up with normal society. They throw discretion to the winds, begin to dress and talk in a manner calculated to cause offence, give up contacts with normal people in favour of the company of other blatant deviants, and fling themselves into a reckless routine of sexual display and promiscuity that crowds out all other concerns. It has been suggested that society gets the criminals it deserves. Sometimes it certainly gets the kind of homosexuals it deserves.

2. *Homosexual Society*

In the last few years many books, novels and plays have appeared, giving lurid accounts of the 'gay world' of homosexual society, but it would be wrong to suppose that the average deviant either feels himself part of a secret brotherhood, or enjoys the glamour of an exciting and unusual way of life. As Gordon Westwood's English survey made clear [378], many homosexuals, especially in the provinces, live in isolated and unobtrusive fashion, scared to mingle too obviously for fear of calling attention to themselves, and far removed from the Bohemian groups who frequent the big cities.

All the same, where possible, homosexuals, like other unpopular minorities, do tend to retreat from the unfriendliness of the large community into protective ingroups of their own. Like heterosexual groups, they vary in character according to the locality and depending on the social class and educational backgrounds of their members. The most noticeable groups are not the most typical. It is probably the better-adjusted among homosexuals who succeed in joining the small cliques of friends of longstanding who visit each others' homes, patronize the same bars and cafés, and meet at each others' parties. The entertainment at such gatherings consists of gossip and gramophone rather than sex, in fact the homosexual mores in some places discourage sexual affairs between members of these little coteries [229]. Nevertheless, their social activities fill a great need. In ordinary company, many homosexuals, even those who put up a front of normality quite successfully, feel themselves outsiders, merely pretending to share the lives and interests of the majority. Among their own kind they can drop the mask, feel completely at ease, and enjoy the morale-boosting effect of being accepted for what they are.

Unlike some other minorities, for example negroes, who cannot change their skin to suit the occasion, homosexuals will drop their masks and mix together when they feel the need, whereas at other times, when at home with relatives, or when dealing with colleagues at work, they function as part of the normal world. In this respect they resemble some members of the 'bent' criminal fraternity who know where to go to find accomplices, but otherwise keep out of sight. From both necessity and preference, the majority of homosexuals try to conceal their condition from employers and work-mates. They keep their private lives as detached as possible and usually avoid making sexual contacts with persons they meet at work.

In all large centres of population male homosexuals have a certain social organization to fall back upon. There are always certain notorious resorts—bars, clubs, cafés, baths, hotels, beaches, even cinemas—where they can go to pick up new partners [165]. Depending upon the prevailing community attitudes, police policy and local laws, these meeting places may stay in the same spot for generations, or change around from month to month, and what happens there may be either disguised and furtive, or fairly obvious to outsiders. In one European capital, a well-known park, crowded by day with innocent visitors and schoolchildren, comes alive again with mysterious rustlings after nightfall. Men hidden under the trees wait patiently, puffing at a glowing cigarette when they want to attract the notice of the lone searchers who meander slowly along the paths, then moving off to still deeper shadows when they have found the company they seek.[1] In Paris, certain fashionable cafés, their reputation enshrined for ever in the writings of some famous homosexual novelists, continue to function as discreet meeting-places of the sophisticated, who conglomerate inconspicuously among the crowds of more ordinary

[1] Described in *Le Guide Gris*, 6th Ed. San Francisco, 1965, p. 10.

patrons [316]. At the 'gay' bars which exist, blatantly or discreetly, in most cosmopolitan cities, homosexuals can quickly find the practical information they need. Some of these places provide copies of one or other of the notorious directories (e.g. *The Grey Guide, The Lavender Baedeker*) which list, country by country, the bars, hotels, Turkish baths and picking up spots where the 'cruising' homosexual may expect to find solace and tolerance.

Some meeting places, such as public toilets, serve only for picking up, or perhaps for swift, furtive, and impersonal sexual release on the spot. (Indeed, where masturbation occurs via a hole in a lavatory partition, the participants may never even see each other.) At bars and clubs, however, homosexuals may come together for the sake of company as much as for the chance of a 'one-night-stand'. This can give rise to nuisance if the place becomes too popular among clients who like to make a public exhibition of themselves. Some of these may arrive looking like grotesque caricatures of women, or actually 'in drag' (i.e. in female dress), 'swishing' about demonstratively, calling out to each other loudly in 'queers' argot,[1] and generally making sure that no one remains unaware of their presence or their interests. These 'screaming bitches' are not the only obvious types. Others may come along draped from head to toe in black leather, complete with jackboots and studded belts, all in aid of their 'butch' image. The atmosphere can deteriorate in other ways if the 'rent boys' and their 'cruising' patrons take over. Such developments scare off the ones who like to keep up some semblance of propriety, endanger the owner's licence, and give the public a strange idea of what homosexuals are like.

The drinking clubs in London that are patronized by homosexuals (described by Westwood, McGee [242], Plummer [296] and others) are not allowed to run to these extremes. The proprietors may be quite uninterested in homosexuals —except as paying customers; the clients are not allowed

---

[1] A glossary of homosexual slang is given by G. Westwood (1960): *A Minority*, Appendix C. (Longman's).

to dance or kiss, visits by plain-clothes police ensure decorum, and often there are women present. These may be either lesbians, or that special type who finds the company of male homosexuals congenial, perhaps because they can enjoy free drinks and polite attentions without personal commitment. A casual caller at these clubs might hardly notice anything amiss until he began listening to the conversations.

Entry into this camaraderie is a matter of visiting the right places in the right clothes and knowing the right conversational gambits. In some West End clubs, the elegant informality of attire, the 'young' look, and the carefully groomed appearance assumed by most of the men present obscures the wide social class differences between them. In the public bars, where the clientele is mixed, men on the look-out for others of similar states have to be circumspect in their approach. They throw out little hints or *double entendres*, which might escape the attention of the unsuspecting, but if these are taken up or reciprocated then gradually broader and broader hints get passed back and forth until open declarations of sexual preferences are exchanged.

Many homosexuals use these resorts sparingly, and then only when they are out for sex, or if they have just moved into town and need to establish contacts. Others, however, are veritable addicts, their whole lives revolving around the gay spots, where they may be seen, night after night, enclosed by their own tight little circle, insulated from the outside world almost as effectively as monks in a monastery.

Although quite well known to the police and to all interested members of the public, these special bars have no official status in England and cannot advertise themselves as rendezvous for homosexuals. In other countries, where law and public opinion permits, one finds clubs in the true sense of the word, places openly set up to provide a social forum for the homosexual minority. The most famous of these, the C.O.C.,[1] was started in Amsterdam in

[1] Cultur- en Ontspanningcentrum, Korte Leidsedwarsstraat 49a, (Postbus 542) Amsterdam.

1947 by Bob Angelo. Besides providing rooms where homosexuals and lesbians can meet and have discussions, it runs a restaurant and a night club where men (as well as women) are permitted to dance with each other. The organization, which is openly run by homosexuals for homosexuals, has some four thousand members. It campaigns for social, religious and legal tolerance. For instance, the society advocates changing the Dutch age of consent from 21 to 18, as it used to be up to 1911, so that homosexual youths over 18 who now frequent the streets and public bars, with all the temptations that involves, may be admitted as members of the C.O.C. and have the benefit of some responsible guidance. Members of the club are expected to behave decently, are encouraged to form stable relationships, and may be put in touch with the right lawyer, priest or doctor if the need arises.

The other well-known homosexual night-club in Amsterdam, the D.O.K. (De Odeon Kring), is more of a commercial pleasure-spot, free from do-gooding social workers, and a favourite resort of tourists from less tolerant lands (e.g. America, Germany and England), who are eligible for temporary membership on showing a passport. Apart from the fact that the dancing and occasionally kissing couples are all of the same sex, the atmosphere remains quite controlled, free from rowdiness, drunken disturbance or obscenity. Of course the liberty is circumscribed. The entrance door is so discreet as to be almost camouflaged, and most of the members would hate their families to know where they were [242].

One feature of homosexual society which particularly shocks the susceptibilities of moralists is the predilection of some males for orgiastic parties at which numbers of couples, or groups of three or four or even more, may have sex together in the same room, changing roles and swapping partners as the mood takes them. As has been remarked previously, many homosexual parties are, if anything, more restrained than modern gatherings of young people of heterosexual inclinations; but nevertheless, some homosexuals of otherwise socially conformist tastes and respectable status will participate in orgies on a scale that would be rather unusual among middle-class heterosexuals. The fact that homosexuals incur no risk of pregnancy however abandoned their conduct scarcely accounts fully for this phenomenon. Perhaps it is an indication that in some homosexual persons the emotional concomitants of sexuality have never matured further than the stage of adolescent dormitory games. Further evidence of the prevalence of orgiastic fantasies at this level is provided by homosexual pin-up magazines, which frequently depict groups of men engaged in thinly disguised sexual games, fooling about in showers or changing rooms, or, in one example, forcibly undressing the loser in a game of strip poker.

In California, where a supreme Court decision has upheld the homosexual's right to peaceful assembly, similar clubs exist (e.g. Society for Individual Rights, Box 5526, San Francisco), but elsewhere in the U.S. homophile organizations work through conferences and magazines. The Mattachine Society of Washington (P.O. Box 1032, Washington D.C., 20013) publishes *The Homosexual Citizen*, while the *Mattachine Newsletter* is published by the Mattachine Society of New York, (1133 Broadway, New York, N.Y. 10010). *The Ladder: A Lesbian Review*, is published monthly by the Daughters of Bilitis, Inc., founded in 1955 (3470 Mission Street, San Francisco). Similar European publications include *Der Kreis* (Postfach 547, Fraumünster, Zurich 22, Switzerland), *Arcadie* (74 Boulevard de Neuilly, Paris 12e) and *Vennen* (P.O. Box 183 Copenhagen K.). In England, the Albany Trust publishes *Man and Society* (32, Shaftesbury Avenue, London, W.1.) and there is also a lesbians' periodical *Arena Three* (44, Platt's Lane, London, N.W.3) linked with the Minorities Research Group.

The magazine articles are mainly devoted to social issues of concern to homosexuals (e.g. church pronouncements, civil discrimination, police practices, law reform, psychological theories). They also have reviews of books and of the many new plays and novels with homosexual themes. The more popular magazines print love stories, have agony columns carrying personal advertisements for flat-mates and holiday companions,[1] and somewhat provocative illustrations. Even so, they must not be confused with the purely pin-up type magazines that flourish in the United States and consist entirely of photos and drawings of nude or semi-nude men in suggestive poses.[2] It is a strange commentary on the ambivalence of American society concerning the legitimacy or practicability of suppressing homosexual interests that specialist magazine shops in big cities like San Francisco and New York are allowed to purvey vast quantities of homosexual erotica. Walking towards the rear of these shops, into the sections marked adults only, one comes across shelf upon shelf of lurid picture books. Overt sexual activity or visible erections are not openly displayed (since these would be classed as hard pornography), but sadistic interests are amply catered for by drawings of naked youths tied up. Rows of shelves are stacked with homosexual novels and pseudo-scientific texts with titillating case histories.

R. E. L. Masters [250] thinks that homosexual propagandists lose sympathy for their cause by seeming to claim that homosexuals are somehow superior to the rest of humanity, or by demanding liberties beyond the limits of reasonable tolerance. One certainly runs across a good deal of sniping back at the sick society that presumes to criticize them [28], and although this may be an understandable underdog reaction, it helps spread the impression that homosexuals are politically subversive. The homosexual magazines, in particular, provide a forum for the most militant minority. The articles are of uneven quality (perhaps unavoidably so in view of the limited range of topics

---

[1] In England, the publication of addresses of admitted homosexuals might possibly lead to prosecution for conspiracy to corrupt public morals, as in the case of the *Ladies Directory*, which listed women prostitutes. R. *v.* Shaw (1961) *All England Reports* 330; Shaw *v.* Director of Public Prosecutions (1961) *All England Reports*, 2, 446.

[2] e.g. *Boys' Art Quarterly*, New York 21.
Physique Art Special, Male Classics Ltd., London, W.8.

and contributions) and some pretty strange ideas get aired occasionally. For instance, it has been suggested in all seriousness that homosexual marriages should have legal status, and that homosexual couples should be allowed to adopt children.

3. Child Molestation

Most people, heterosexuals and homosexuals alike, find mature adolescents, roughly speaking the 'teen age group, physically attractive. Females of this age are much appreciated as chorus girls, in strip shows, in beauty contests, and as film performers. Although at present a legal and social taboo protects girls under sixteen, however fully developed they may be, their attractiveness is tacitly recognized in the care taken to shield them from premature heterosexual seduction. In Eastern countries, however, marriages of girls under sixteen were, until recently, quite respectable, and in Victorian England, up to the time of the Criminal Law Amendment Act of 1885, girl prostitutes of less than sixteen years were commonplace. For older heterosexuals to yield to their impulses with adolescents many years younger than themselves may be unwise, unseemly and immoral; but it can hardly be called a perversion. It seems somewhat hypocritical, therefore, to condemn homosexuals as doubly perverse when they show an interest in youth, although of course, in their case, indulgence may be thought of as particularly immoral, on the grounds that seduction might affect a young person's sexual orientation.

Child molestation (or paedophilia, to use the technical name) means making sexual approaches to immature, prepubertal children. Since this represents the acting out of an impulse few people admit to sharing, it can properly be classed as a perversion—or a double perversion if the assailant chooses a child of his own sex. The legal classification of indecent assault on children does not correspond exactly with child molestation, since it is defined by the chronological age of the victim, regardless of the stage of actual development. Furthermore, assault is a misnomer, since the molester's approaches are usually gentle and tentative.

The criminal statistics show that the assailants are practically always males, although the children may be of either sex. Indecent fondling of children is not completely unknown among women, especially when adolescent servant girls worked as nursemaids, but it is comparatively rare, and when it does happen it tends to be concealed under the guise of maternal solicitude. For practical purposes, however, paedophiliac perversion does not affect either lesbians or heterosexual women.

Sexual fondling of children is not in itself harmful. In some primitive communities adults do this as easily as we might stroke the child's hair, and in some places parents masturbate their children to pacify them [74]. But our own strong taboos against children coming into contact with adult sexuality ensure that, however much they enjoy among themselves sex games like doctors and patients, they will often take fright if approached by an adult. Although the typical paedophile is a timorous, inhibited male who solicits with pathetic gentleness, with a view to no more than the sort of mutual fondling and inspection that children often indulge in with each other, the child may well be scared to perceive the intensity of an adult's passion. If, as is the case in the majority of the indecencies which come to the notice of authorities, the assailant is a relative or family friend familiar to the victim, the episode tends to be repeated, and the child to be frightened or cajoled into a conspiracy of silence. This can provoke strong guilt feelings, all the more so perhaps if the child finds the fondling pleasurable and the sweets or attentions earned by co-operation highly gratifying. If, finally, the child lets out the secret, or the situation otherwise comes to light, the bitterest family disputes may follow, to say nothing of police interrogations and court appearances, all of which help to convert what might have been a casual childish experience into a ghastly nightmare. In Israel, the law recognizes the danger of making children testify in public about their sexual experiences, and allows private interrogations by a special children's worker [311].

Many of the children who fall victim to sexual offences have laid themselves open to advances by their coy provocative behaviour. Dr. Trevor Gibbens [129] found that in a London sample two-thirds of the child victims had participated in indecencies on more than one occasion or with more than one assailant. In a California State study of sexual offences against children [50], two-thirds were considered to have been actively participating victims, as opposed to the one-third who had a more or less accidental contact with an assailant. Some of these participating children are both sexually precocious and emotionally unsettled, in difficulties with their own parents, and rather obviously looking to other adults to satisfy their craving for attention and affection. Casual encounters with strangers at cinemas and elsewhere account for a higher proportion of the experiences of boy victims, perhaps because even at this tender age boys are more boldly exploratory and uninhibited than girls. For this reason, the boys' experiences often carry less emotional significance. Where instances of paedophilia have been exposed at boys' boarding schools, it sometimes emerges that the whole class has long been aware of the schoolmaster's interests, and that a high proportion of the boys have allowed some sex play to take place, perhaps joking about it afterwards. This lighthearted openness to adult homosexual advances is a characteristic of boys at or approaching puberty, especially where the social setting or the influence of a delinquent subculture counteracts the usual taboos. It is perhaps as much a reflection of the sexual psychology of growing children, as of the ways of sex offenders, that the girl victims of sexual indecency are most often either definitely immature or definitely post-pubertal, whereas boy victims steadily increase in number with the approach of puberty and beyond. Of course, in this, as all other matters, the official statistics are also much influenced by prosecution policy, and by the varying tendency of parents and others to report or to conceal sexual incidents with children.

Questioning adults about their sexual preferences for younger or older persons may not yield truthful answers, but the Czechoslovakian psychiatrist, Dr. K. Freund [117, 118, 120] has developed a beautifully direct method. Using an instrument for registering small volume changes in the penis, Dr. Freund found that the responses of a series of male patients to the sight of pictures of male and female nudes of different ages reliably distinguished between homosexuals and heterosexuals and also between men attracted primarily to adults and those attracted primarily to children. In addition to their consistent preference for the same or the opposite sex, the majority of subjects tested also showed a consistent preference for adults, adolescents, or children. Of both the homosexuals and the heterosexuals only a small minority preferred children, but those who did were consistent in their reactions [117]. Freund also showed that, except in the case of paedophiles, an evenly balanced attractiveness towards both sexes (bisexuality), was distinctly rare.

Gordon Westwood [379], in his survey of a sample of male homosexual volunteers, came across only three paedophiles out of a total of 127 men interviewed. All three were exclusively or predominantly attracted by young boys. One of them remarked that he understood how homosexuals generally despise men who go with young boys, but he felt just the same disgust for the men who go with other men, and the thought of an act of buggery appalled him. Two other men in Westwood's sample admitted to isolated incidents with boys under thirteen, although they actually preferred and normally obtained for themselves adult partners. They were both persons who showed a complete disregard for the consequences of their actions. A further seven per cent of the interviewees confessed, usually with shame, to occasional experiences with adolescents of fourteen or fifteen.

In a massive study based on thousands of convicted sex

offenders carried out by the Institute for Sex Research at Indiana University [124] it was found that only 9 per cent of men convicted for homosexual offences with adults had ever had contact with children, and only 1 per cent admitted to a preference for children, but as many as one-third had had some experiences with sexually mature youths under sixteen.

It seems beyond dispute that a significant minority of male homosexuals shares with heterosexuals a predilection for adolescents who have only recently reached puberty. While some homosexuals will indulge these desires frequently and shamelessly, others will do so only occasionally and perhaps with severe guilt feelings. Men strongly attracted by *prepubertal* children, the true paedophiles, are much less common. Offenders of this kind have been closely studied in a number of countries [326, 124, 264, 367, 253, 50, 303, 224]. They seem everywhere to run very much to type, and to differ considerably in background and personality from ordinary heterosexuals or homosexuals.

The public image of sex offenders is much influenced by the newspaper publicity given to cases of murder of children motivated by sexual lust or by an attempt to conceal an act of paedophilia. In a series of over 200 murders in the London area, the records of which I had occasion to examine for purposes of criminological research [374], only three were sex murders of children; this corresponded to a rate of about two per annum in a population of fifty millions.

The essentially non-violent nature of the typical paedophiliac offence has emerged in all systematic sex offender surveys, including the Cambridge Study, the California Study, the Canadian Study by Mohr and others, and the Indiana Institute Study. In this last, which included over two hundred men who had committed homosexual offences against children or minors, no instance of serious physical violence was recorded. This was not true of the offenders who assaulted girl children, a few of whom used frightening violence. These aggressive heterosexual paedophiles were the most persistently criminal of all the sex offenders; many were ruthless and dangerous characters in other respects, and 88 per cent of them had also been convicted for non-sexual offences.

Some paedophiles show little discrimination about the sex of the child chosen. In Schofield's series, a quarter of the men imprisoned for offences with small boys had also committed offences against young girls, and less than a quarter were exclusively attracted to boys. A substantial proportion of paedophile offenders are married, but these are generally men who have attained a precarious hetero-sexual adjustment only after a considerable struggle. Later in life, having become depressed or disillusioned with their unsatisfying social or sexual performance as husbands, they find themselves overcome by homosexual or paedophiliac desires. (Incidentally, this point suggests that where a man lacks genuine wish or capacity to undertake matrimony, it can be unwise to push him into it.) The prospects of attaining a more normal adjustment with psychiatric help, however, are better for married paedophiles than for men who have never had any sexual experience other than with young boys.

Ordinary homosexuals do not share, do not approve, and fear to be associated with paedophiliac interests. The paedophiles' sexual outlets are comparatively infrequent, unsatisfying and guilt-ridden; remaining secret episodes known only to themselves, and out of keeping with the general tenor of their lives. Whereas many homosexuals question the assumptions of conventional morality, homosexual paedophiles tend to compartmentalize their thinking, assuming attitudes of impregnable respectability and sexual purity, hardly admitting their real interests and motives even to themselves. One self-righteous head-master of a private school, already convicted and shortly to be re-arrested for molesting small boys, asked me to interview a member of his staff because he suspected the man of having homosexual tendencies. In contrast to their generally circumspect behaviour, child molesters often show a reckless disregard for the risks of discovery when they come to indulging their impulses or planning future opportunities to do so. One finds men with several convictions still volunteering for posts in boys' clubs or Sunday schools, and sometimes being accepted on account of their thoroughly respectable demeanour.

The long-term effects of sexual molestation upon children are probably much less serious than generally supposed [307], but they are difficult to assess, especially as children with some antecedent emotional disturbance are specially prone to become victims. Lauretta Bender [20] who followed a number of such children for many years, suggested that the experience does not necessarily have any directly adverse effects upon sexual development. However, where a boy has been unwillingly molested by some stranger, Halleck thinks he is very likely to be confused and frightened and to stand in need of reassurance [154]. Psychiatric opinions on this point are often purely speculative.

4. Seduction of Youths

Physical maturity arrives much sooner than is socially convenient, and with the improvement in health and nutrition of children pubertal changes occur earlier than ever. Boys have strong erections, ejaculations and irresistible urges to masturbate to orgasm long before parents and teachers are willing to encourage them in heterosexual pursuits. Furthermore, boys approaching puberty are not only segregated from girls in many educational and social situations (especially sleeping arrangements), they are also directed into games and practical interests that exclude girls as creatures of inferior accomplishments. This setting makes it inevitable that boys' first sexual contacts are likely to consist of masturbation with each other. If this is less true of girls, it is probably only because their physical needs are more often suppressed. The homosexual stage of adolescence, now widely accepted among psychologists as a natural phase, is obviously encouraged if not entirely generated by cultural factors.

The supposed dangers of homosexual corruption of

youths by older males is almost an article of faith among some judges and politicians. Ollendorff [282] has suggested that if the first orgasms shared with another person are obtained homosexually, this may condition the adolescent towards deviant sexuality for the rest of his life. If this were so, then obviously youths would stand in much greater danger from each other, by their mutually seductive influence, than from adult strangers. The importance of crude physical initiation in the determination of human sexuality is surely over-rated. A first attempt at heterosexual intercourse rarely produces much satisfaction, but it soon gets repeated. The first experiences of orgasm in solitary masturbation do not prevent the adolescent reaching out for sexual contact with others.

The suggestion that some powerful erotic stimulus at a critical phase of development may condition a person's sexual preference ever after receives some support from case histories of fetishists. The story of the shoe-fetishist who had once been tickled by a nursemaid with the toe of her shoe is well established in psychiatric folk-lore. Paul Gebhard [125] relates a similar case of a boy in the full flush of normal pubertal sexual excitability who had a fracture set without anaesthesia while being caressed and comforted by a brunette nurse. As an adult, he developed a strong attraction to brunettes with the same hair style as this nurse, and also had some sado-masochistic interests. The analogy between such cases and stories of homosexuality arising from seduction is probably more apparent than real. Clinical experience suggests that fetishistic interests remain harmless, and do not become exclusive or troublesome perversions in the absence of inhibitions against ordinary sexual outlets. The same may be said of homosexual interests.

Homosexual experiments by adolescents, especially if this happens to be the only readily available outlet, do not necessarily signify any strong preference for or emotional commitment to this form of sexual expression. Except for the minority who have become unhealthily scared or repressed, the fantasy life at puberty is at least bisexual, and the mystery surrounding the female genitals titillates rather than diverts the boy's interest. Furthermore the normal adolescent's gender identity and expected sex role has been established in his intellect, imagination and attitudes since infancy. Hence, for many youths homosexual play represents no more than an extension of masturbatory techniques, and perhaps even facilitates their aptitude for love-making when they find partners of the opposite sex. As will be seen later, the minority who remain stuck with this as their only outlet have generally arrived at adolescence with an already established fear of heterosexual development. Moreover, many confirmed homosexual adults recall erotic longings for friends of their own sex during adolescence, but no actual physical experiences until much later. They also often state that schoolmates who they recall as being particularly active homosexually have since married and made good heterosexual adjustment. Boys who avoid overt homosexual conduct at adolescence because they are inhibited, probably stand a greater chance of becoming chronically homosexual as adults than the boys who go in for sexual romps and commit 'gross indecency' without a second thought. Research does in fact suggest that persistent homosexuals tend to be relatively late starters as regards overt sexual acts [166].

Factual evidence of the after-effects of homosexual seduction is conspicuously lacking, in spite of strongly held opinions. Calder, giving 'a prison medical officer's viewpoint' notes that men in prison for sex offences often complain bitterly of seduction in youth and say that is what perverted them [49]. On the other hand Gibbens investigated 100 Borstal lads of 16 to 21, asking if any stranger or adult had ever made a pass at them or tried to interfere with them [128]. Of the lads with known homosexual trends 32 per cent reported such experiences, of those without known homosexual tendencies 33 per cent reported the same experience. The majority of the lads looked upon the experiences they had had with older men as trivial and not worth mentioning when describing their sexual experiences with other youths.

Doshay [83] followed up 108 boy sex offenders aged from seven to sixteen. None had been convicted for other kinds of crime, but over a half of them had been involved in homosexual offences, either with older males or with other boys. In the whole group there was not a single instance of a sex violation in adult life. Furthermore, individual case studies showed no evidence of homosexual interests being continued into adult life. Tolsma [366] followed 133 boys who had had homosexual experiences with adults. All but 8 were married and had not continued homosexual practices. Westwood [378], who interviewed adult homosexuals living in the community, found that their interests were usually established before their first actual experience took place.

Many admitted that when they were boys they used to go out of their way to tempt older men. Contrary to the impression produced by prosecuted offenders, this group, who had no particular axe to grind, gave the impression that seduction had played no significant part in the development of their homosexual propensities. The fact that young male prostitutes can satisfy homosexual clients on innumerable occasions without affecting their own heterosexual adjustment (see page 138) provides yet another piece of evidence against the motion that casual homosexual contacts produce permanent perversion.

Belief in the spread of perversion by example and seduction provides one of the strongest arguments against any reduction in the penalties for homosexual crime. Legal authorities have often opposed toleration of acts in private on the grounds that this is merely a prelude to wider social acceptance of deviation, and hence to a greater likelihood of young persons coming into contact with and being permanently contaminated by the proselytizing homosexual [61]. In view of the widespread acceptance of this argument, it cannot be emphasized too often or too strongly that a positive aversion to heterosexuality is the crux of the chronic deviant's difficulties, and this has nothing to do with a history of seduction.

5. *Imprisonment and its Effects*

If one wanted to perform a cruel experiment to find out how readily perversion spreads by seduction and contamination one could hardly imagine a more effective method than the present penal system, in which inmates are confined for long periods in one-sex institutions with no heterosexual contacts allowed. Unfortunately the results of the penal 'experiment' have been little studied owing to the understandable reluctance of Prison Departments to probe into matters so embarrassing. Douglas Gibson, himself a former prison governor, has pointed out that prison staffs rarely discuss the homosexual behaviour that takes place in their institutions, they don't like it, they can do little to control it, and they would rather not know about it [131]. Sir Lionel Fox, former chairman of the Prison Commissioners, and author of a standard text-book on the subject, wrote: 'The problems of homosexuality in prisons are patent to all familiar with prison life' [106]. But he did not go into detail.

Books by ex-prisoners give a more frank and vivid picture. Autobiographical reminiscences by literary lions[1] arouse suspicion of artistic exaggeration, but one need look no further than the sober factual account by Anthony Heckstall Smith [341] to understand the impact of an English prison upon sexually normal men. He paints a particularly dismal picture of the sexual habits of youths in borstals and of their addiction to dormitory orgies.

These revelations are not very surprising, since most prison inmates are fit young men with pressing sexual urges which they are not accustomed to suppress, and their only possible outlets during confinement are solitary mas-

---

[1] For example:
Jean Genet (1965) *Miracle of the Rose* (translated B. Frechtman). London, Blond.
Brendan Behan (1961) *Borstal Boy*. London, Corgi Books.

turbation or homosexuality. As one ex-prisoner put it: 'To the man dying of hunger and thirst it makes little difference that the available food and water are tainted. Likewise it makes no difference to the average prisoner that the only means of sexual gratification are abnormal' [275].

Most studied accounts of homosexuality in prisons come from the United States. One of the earliest and best was written by J. F. Fishman, a one-time Inspector of Prisons [99]. He explains how the impersonal discipline with no outlet for affection, the bar on all contact with women, the enforced idleness, the perpetual salacious talk, and the loss of self-respect and normal social standards, all conspire to create sexual tension and to foster homosexual habits. Men who were homosexual before they came to prison, especially the 'pansy' street nuisances who so often find their way to gaol, aggravate the situation by proffering themselves shamelessly to all and sundry. Good-looking young men find they can take advantage of the situation and gain money or favours in return for sex. They may not at first do this for pleasure, but the habit may grow into a need. The active type of homosexual tends to court any newcomer who takes his fancy, pursuing his object with the frightful pertinacity of one who has literally nothing else to think about. If the newcomer cannot be seduced by ingratiating tactics he may take to threats. Fishman quotes one prisoner who described how he had been forced into sodomy at the point of a knife. A youth molested by an old lag has, unfortunately, no redress. He dared not give away the offender for fear of reprisals. The whole prison population bands together to make life hell for any inmate suspected of being a 'stool pigeon'. Fishman refers to the numerous allegations by prisoners that they have been forced into sexual practices by warders, and he thinks it quite possible that some of their statements are true. Some individuals may take on the job of prison guard, just as some become rubbers in Turkish baths, for the opportunities of intimacies with men.

More recent American accounts have elaborated this

theme, occasionally documenting with statistics the actual incidence of deviant practices [124]. In a survey of 2,300 men in prison Clemmer [60] estimated that ten per cent were true or habitual deviants, while a further thirty per cent participated in abnormal practices from time to time during their confinement. Sociologists have been struck by the way homosexuality becomes incorporated in the inmates' culture, to the extent that different sexual roles, identified by slang labels, are allocated according to the prisoner's status in the inmate hierarchy [352]. The tough, aggressive leaders of the criminal social system must preserve their image as super-men in order to maintain the respect of their underlings. In a world without women they can do this by becoming 'wolves'. These are predatory homosexuals who always take the active or 'husband's' role, subduing the weaker brothers by bribery, intimidation (e.g. extorting sexual submission in repayment of 'debts') or by actual force. So long as they show no softness towards their sex objects, using them as masturbatory machines rather than sexual partners, they risk no loss of face. Their status as men and heterosexuals remains unchallenged in their own estimation and in that of their fellow prisoners. Indeed, sometimes in fact, and often in pretence, the fantasies which accompany these activities remain essentially heterosexual [36].

Reality rarely conforms fully to a society's ideal, whether in prison or outside, and in practice, though wolves may treat their partners like slaves, they may also display fierce jealousies and possessiveness. The discovery of seductive letters or proposals addressed to one already 'married' may occasion serious fights. But even these events can be interpreted on the masculine model of a 'husband' standing up for his rights.

The men who yield to pressure from the stronger and more experienced prisoners, and passively submit to the sexual requirements of the 'wolves', thereby lose status and become type-cast as 'punks'. Huffman [188], describing a similar social organization among prisoners in New Jersey, notes the rigidity of the caste system. Once a man has been labelled a 'punk', he can rarely break into the higher ranks of 'jockers' or 'wolves'. Lowest of all on the inmate social scale come the 'fagots', natural homosexuals of passive inclinations, who proffer themselves spontaneously. As with women who are 'too easy', the prize in this case has little value. Finally, in prison as elsewhere, some just won't fit into the system. One example is the opportunist who will, on the quiet, perform without trouble whatever sexual role is required provided the reward is sufficient. Of course the authorities try to reduce the problem by keeping a special watch upon or segregating known deviants, but since the majority of those liable to behave homosexually when in prison have no distinguishing features, and have never been convicted for this offence, they generally remain unidentified. Furthermore, prisoners know they must avoid too obvious associations with those exhibitionistic types who adopt girls' names, or otherwise draw upon themselves the unfavourable attention of the staff.

The demoralizing effect of the prison culture depends upon how long a man has to spend there, and whether relations with the staff are too formal to counteract the influence of the closely-knit, oppositional inmate group. By no means all prisoners participate in homosexual activity; but it has been amply demonstrated that the prison environment stimulates homosexual feelings and releases homosexual behaviour among many people who have never shown the slightest tendency of this kind before. Fortunately, the available evidence suggests that most of them revert to heterosexual pursuits immediately upon release. Possible exceptions to this general rule are older men who have spent very many years in prison and find the prospect of life outside altogether too frightening. During my own interviews with long-term prisoners, some of them confessed that their interest in women had waned, or that they had come to the conclusion women were not worth bothering about [373]. Douglas Gibson comments on the disillusioning humiliations some of these men experience when they come out of prison and try to go with a woman prostitute [131]. The unfortunate youths who have spent the greater part of their formative years in institutions, with minimal opportunity to acquire either the sexual confidence or the social skills needed for heterosexual courtship, are also liable to be permanently affected.

A flare-up of homosexual behaviour during imprisonment is not peculiar to criminals; the same happens in prisoner-of-war camps, as G. Westwood [377] described in an account of conditions in Japanese and German camps.

In these camps a minority of confirmed homosexuals would take the chance to run riot and provoke large numbers of 'normals' to indulge with them. Many of the men, while professing hostility to all forms of homosexuality, had secret 'affairs' of their own, most of which sooner or later became common knowledge owing to the lack of privacy. According to Westwood, after an initial battle the majority ultimately succumbed to the temptation. He gave several illustrative sexual histories of interned men. One of these, a young R.A.F. officer, was captured when he was twenty-one, He had had no previous feelings of the sort that he could remember. Men had approached him, but he had always kept aloof. In the German prison camps he had plenty of advances, from guards as well as prisoners, but he never gave way. He had a particular friend with whom he spent most of his time. One day he found himself admiring his friend's body, and felt very ashamed and angry, but could do nothing to banish the thoughts. He reached such a pitch that he could not bear his friend out of his sight. Then one day he let the friend kiss him. 'It wasn't just a way of relieving ourselves as it seemed to be with most of the others. I can't really explain it. All I can say is that I have never seen a girl and a boy who love each other more than we do.' On return to civilian life this man, though he wanted a family and children, went to live with his friend because they could not bear to be separated.

A reversal as complete and permanent as this is unusual. In a study of the effect of imprisonment, Greco and Wright

[143] concluded that, in general, only those sensitized to seduction by previous experience or prior emotional bias became permanent deviants as a result of experience in prison. Most men regain an interest in women after their release, although some remain confused and disturbed sexually for a long time. The R.A.F. officer cited by Westwood noticed a crucial point. He and his friend were emotionally involved with each other to a greater degree than most of the other men who similarly indulged. Those who really fall in love in the prison situation are liable to have greater difficulties later on than those who merely play with each other as a change from masturbation.

On the whole women's prisons seem to have an even greater incidence of homosexuality than men's prisons [168], which seems curious in view of the relative unobtrusiveness of lesbianism in the outside community. In discussing the situation in prisons in New York, Bluestone [37] comments that: 'In institutions for female offenders, a homosexual orientation is so common that no attempt can be made to separate these individuals . . .' Some eighty to ninety per cent of the inmates of the Women's House of Detention have a history of homosexuality. A close study of a women's prison in California [371] yielded a smaller incidence than this, but still an excessive incidence in comparison with male prisons.

The Californian study brought to light some interesting qualitative differences between the homosexuality of male and female prisons which probably reflect differences between lesbian and male homosexuality in the wider society. For example, the women were much less aggressive in their sexual approaches, courtship took the form of personal attentions, sympathy, flattery and gifts rather than intimidation or force, and those who maintained that they wanted to stay faithful to someone (male or female) outside of the prison were not molested. Once formed, these attachments became highly charged with romantic feeling, passionate letters were exchanged freely, and scenes of grief or attempted suicides might follow action by the staff to separate the women. Manipulation of sex to gain goods or status, or brief mechanical contacts purely for the purpose of attaining orgasm, were most untypical among the female prisoners. In fact, deprivation of heterosexual intercourse, so prominent a feature of the pains of imprisonment for men, came low on the women's lists of complaints. They felt much more acutely the loss of the affection and support they normally received from friends and family. A yearning for something to fill this emotional vacuum appeared to supply the main driving force behind the conduct of those women (the 'jailhouse turnouts') who took to lesbianism for the first time after coming into prison.

In attitude and sexual behaviour many prison lesbians fell into distinct categories of pseudo-masculine ('butch') or pseudo-femine ('femme') types. The former affected mannish hair styles and starched collars, and ruled their girlfriends' lives on the principle that they were helpless females in need of protection. These 'butch' types were in the minority, most of them had been practising lesbians in the outside world, and a higher proportion were single women. However, the fact that even among this group four-fifths had been married at least for a time suggests that comparatively few women lead permanently and exclusively lesbian sex lives. Unlike their effeminate counterparts in the male prisons, the 'butch' women were not ridiculed or discriminated against by the other prisoners, perhaps rather the reverse, since there was always a surfeit of 'femme' types looking and hoping to find a friend and protector.

In view of the popular psychological theory that female prostitutes have little true feeling for their male clients, being lesbian from the start, or turning to lesbianism from an acquired disgust for men [146], it is interesting to note that the women prisoners who behaved homosexually, both 'butch' and 'femme' varieties, had been involved in heterosexual prostitution significantly more often than the other women prisoners.

Two fairly obvious factors contribute to the prominence of the homosexual problem in women's prisons. First, the feminine need for affection and support, which leads to emotional and then sexual attachments. (The incidence of lesbianism in the Californian prison research would have been much greater had the investigators conformed with the view of many staff and inmates and counted as lesbianism such acts as hand holding and affectionate embraces which, in the wider community, might pass as normal.) Second, whereas men take fairly readily to crime, and many male offenders are quite healthy characters from a psychological standpoint, women criminals, especially those who get themselves into prison, are generally speaking social misfits and unstable creatures, and hence likely to be more confused and uncertain in their sexual orientation than the average female [93].

Whatever one's views about the long-term dangers of seduction, sending homosexual offenders to prison clearly encourages the spread of this behaviour within the institutions, and places the homosexual himself under intolerable temptation and stress [65, 202]. The use of ordinary imprisonment for homosexual importuning, public indecency or indulgence with (or between) young men under twenty-one, may be inevitable, since this is the only severe punishment available to the courts, but it should surely be used only as a last resort. One can understand that homosexuals passing through prisons feel they have been scapegoated as they discover how many men and youths will indulge when it suits them, in spite of their protestations of contempt and disgust for 'queers'.

Child molesters, if put among typical criminal prisoners, often become terrorized outcasts. In view of their serious problems of social and psychological adjustment, and their pressing need for the most effective treatment possible—both for their own sakes and for the benefit of the community—simple imprisonment seems, in their case, particularly inappropriate.

In spite of all that has been said about the evil effects of heterosexual deprivation, nothing has been done about it in England, and very little in America. However, in one State

Penitentiary, in Mississippi, rooms have been set aside where men can receive conjugal visits in private during Sunday afternoons, and this seems to have had the effect of much reducing the incidence of homosexual conduct in the prison, as well as helping to preserve the prisoner's marriages [278].

6. *Male Prostitution*

Heterosexual men patronize female prostitutes more often than women employ gigolos. Similarly among homosexuals, the clients for commercial sex are males rather than lesbians. Incidentally, this example shows yet again the tendency for deviants to retain many of the characteristics of their true gender.

Because of social barriers to homosexual 'marriages', and also perhaps because something in the nature of their perversion militates against lasting love affairs, many male homosexuals appear drifting and unattached, and often irretrievably promiscuous. Their inclination to seek an outlet with prostitutes is greater than that of heterosexual males, who are usually married, and hence have a less pressing need, as well as less time and opportunity.

The female prostitute finds many clients among the minority of frustrated heterosexuals whose physical or temperamental disabilities interfere with success in marriage. The male prostitute might be said to cater for a minority within a minority, but all the same his potential clientele is quite extensive. The appearance of their partners counts for more in the sexuality of men than women, and beyond a certain age a great many male homosexuals find themselves much frustrated because they can no longer obtain desirable new partners by means of their own sexual attractiveness. Hence the temptation to buy the favours of young men by presents, patronage or an actual fee. Moreover, brief, impersonal encounters with prostitutes suit the convenience of many furtive homosexuals, particularly those who, having got married, or having accepted some sensitive public position, dare not allow themselves to become entangled socially with a male lover. Some homosexuals find prostitutes particularly exciting because they are attracted by the rough, working-class type, or because they derive an added thrill from the sordid atmosphere and the need to run the gauntlet of a watchful police.

All over the world, this trade flourishes in the big cosmopolitan cities, where clients with money are plentiful, and personal habits are shielded from critical scrutiny by the anonymity of large, drifting populations. The Danish police officer Jersild [197], who made a special study of male prostitution, remarked that the trade was particularly rife in the countries of the Mediterranean coast. This does not necessarily mean that these populations have more sexual deviants. More likely the situation reflects socio-economic factors, like unemployment, the effects of rapid urbanization, and the stark contrasts between rich and poor. The tourist towns in poorer countries tend to attract, during the season, numbers of unsettled youth without visible means of support who turn to other crimes than prostitution during the rest of the year. To quote just one example, according to police reports, a quarter of the male tourists visiting Southern Portugal are homosexuals seeking adventures and prepared to pay. Since girls in that region are closely guarded from any premarital sex experience, young men turn all the more readily to homo-erotic practices. In Lagos, the police rounded up some of the most popular of the juvenile homosexuals, shaving their heads and painting their scalps, and then parading them in the market place to excite public scorn. Their action proved rather ineffective, because it aroused sympathy for the branded youths [19].

In Jersild's research (which, incidentally, shows how the realistic and practical approach of the policeman can be combined with a humane attitude) he found that young male prostitutes very often came from those emotionally and socially impoverished family backgrounds which are the well-known breeding-grounds of delinquency in boys and immorality in girls. There was a very high incidence of broken homes, police records, reform school committals, excessive drinking, educational backwardness, unemployment and work-shyness. He found that many of the boys had been socially unsettled, badly behaved or delinquent long before they took to professional prostitution, but some of them became considerably more delinquent later, apparently stimulated further in this direction by their experience of the joys of a parasitic existence and of the ease with which money could be got by bullying and robbing perverts. However, as he remarked, 'It is true these boys are cruel, hard-boiled and arrogant, but it is also true—as we have seen—that they have become so as a result of gross abuse'.

Since it is the unstable, demoralized or frankly antisocial type of youth who is most likely to take to prostitution, the risk of this activity leading to more serious crimes is easy to see. Clients who take prostitutes back to their homes—as they often do because alternative accommodation involves other dangers and expenses—expose themselves to blackmail, or, more commonly, to assault and robbery at the time and housebreaking subsequently, either by the prostitute himself or by his criminal accomplices. In turn, the young prostitutes get a brief and unsettling taste of a way of life and a standard of living quite unattainable to them by legitimate means. The impetus this may give to a criminal career will be readily understood by those familiar with the sociological theories of crime propounded by Merton, Cohen and others [375]. The Hegelers, a psychologist couple who have written a Danish marriage manual in a commendably earthy, sensible and humorous style [164], suggest a further reason for the gravitation of boy prostitutes to crime. When they want to give up the game and settle down they find that they have put themselves beyond the pale socially, and in their disappointment it becomes tempting to lash out in retaliation, perhaps by blackmailing their former friends for having seduced a minor. Thus, quite apart from the fact that male soliciting and prostitution contravene the law of many countries, the police have good reason to keep an eye on the male prostitution trade.

The male prostitute's career differs in a number of significant respects from that of his female counterpart. He is less likely to make it a full-time or exclusive occupation, or to persist in it for many years. When not actually 'on the game', he is quite likely to be working on a job, either in the normal or the criminal sense of the word. One reason may be that, being a man, unless he limits his sexual repertoire to passive sodomy or fellatio, his physiology will not permit him to satisfy a series of clients in quick succession after the manner of women of the brothel. Furthermore, since many of them are primarily heterosexual, they are likely to spend their best energies, as well as their immoral earnings, upon girl friends. A few are recruited or organized by older 'pimps', but again, being men, they have less need of protection, they are unlikely to be bullied by their customers (rather the other way round), and they mostly prefer to go their own way and keep their own counsel. The amateur prostitute is very common among these young men, the sort of person who has learned how to make a little money on the side now and then, without hindrance to an otherwise ordinary working-class mode of life. Simon Raven has published a vivid description of this type [309]. In London, they are often members of the services stationed near the metropolis who have learned from their more experienced mates what bars to visit if they want free drinks, liberal hospitality, and a good tip at the end of it.

Michael Craft [69], in his study of English boy prostitutes under treatment in medico-penal institutions, pointed out the very uneven geographical distribution. In some towns epidemics of cinema masturbation seemed quite common, whereas in other areas, where the local culture afforded no opportunity, the prostitution practice had never caught on except among youths in institutional confinement.

In a study of the experiences and attitudes reported by boys at an American penal establishment, Reiss [313] found that the practice of taking payment from an adult 'queer' in return for letting him perform fellatio was fully accepted in the working-class delinquent culture. Most boys knew all about the usual meeting places and fees before they began to take advantage of such opportunities. A boy incurred no threat to his masculinity so long as the contacts were brief and purely for business and there was no question of being persuaded to reciprocate the client's sexual routine. If a queer broke out of the accepted pattern, wanting other forms of sex, using terms of endearment as if to a girl, or displaying familiarity outside the customary meeting places for trade, the only appropriate response was to beat him up on the spot, or as soon as assistance was at hand. For the self-respecting juvenile gangster prostitution was a good and acceptable means of making easy money, but for the older career criminal other forms of crime held out more prestige. In America, the specialist male hustler of mature years (well-portrayed by the novelist John Rechy)[1] has a low status in the hierarchy of criminals, and a tough task in preserving his masculine image. Thus the social system of the criminal classes, while favouring homosexual prostitution up to a point, also acts as a limiting and circumscribing influence, discouraging a too intimate or too prolonged involvement of the boy prostitute with the world of permanent homosexuals.

In his sample of three hundred male prostitutes known to the Danish police, Jersild found that a third were under eighteen years, and about four-fifths under twenty-one, when first they began to take money for sexual activity. He thought that the percentage of real homosexuals and bi-sexuals among them was only fifteen per cent, the majority being distinctly heterosexual in their natural preferences. The dangers to these youths' heterosexual adjustment did not appear very great. Few of them established any permanent liaisons with the homosexuals they encountered, and most of them drifted away from the homosexual *milieu* as they got a little older. The police observed a perpetual

[1] John Rechy (1964) *City of Night*. London, McGibbon and Kee.

change of young faces around the homosexual resorts. Cynics might suggest that this was not due to any increased social and sexual scruples as the youths grew to manhood; but merely reflected their decreased attractiveness to homosexual customers as the bloom of adolescence receded into the past. However, other evidence exists to show that homosexual attractiveness does not really wither so quickly as this. (See page 117.)

As with most research on criminological topics, studies of prostitutes tend to be biassed by the fact that samples known to police or medical authorities are not altogether typical. In this instance they are probably overweighted by the delinquent type who has no particular predilection for prostitution as opposed to other forms of criminal profiteering, and so has every chance of coming into the hands of the police for all sorts of reasons. The more circumspect and successful, who make a speciality of prostitution, and avoid other crimes, are more likely to evade detection. The police have an easier task identifying female prostitutes, since women do not normally approach strange men indiscriminately, but men have a certain liberty to strike up conversations in bars, and the experienced homosexual prostitute takes care to make contact covertly, by unobtrusive gestures or innocuous sounding remarks, leading to a more discreet rendezvous elsewhere. Such successful prostitutes are also likely to be homosexual themselves, otherwise they would neither choose to specialize in this line nor be so indulgent and pleasing to their clients.

In some of these relationships no sharp distinction can be drawn between friendly patronage and definite trade, especially where the junior partner has some legitimate daytime employment. Just as some female prostitutes dream of settling down one day, so some of these young men hope to find a well-established friend with whom they can live in comfort on a permanent footing. Sometimes it happens, and who is to say when it does whether the arrangement is commercial or romantic? The state of matrimony has been described before now as legitimized prostitution, on the grounds that the woman gives herself in return for a contract providing security. Homosexual matrimony has no contract, only a promise or a hope.

Nearly all who have written about male prostitution, including Jersild, Raven [309], Doshay [83], Reiss [313] and Craft [69], have emphasized the youthfulness of the prostitutes, the comparative shortness of their careers, and the fact that most of them retain a sexual preference for women in spite of their experiences with men. Such observations have an interest beyond the immediate topic, for they tend to support the view that experience of seduction is not an important cause of homosexual fixation, and that the forced practice of uncongenial sexual relations may not be the best way to change a person's erotic orientation.

7. *Venereal Diseases*

Venereal infections are just as easily transmitted from one person to another during homosexual as during heterosexual intercourse. Specialists have expressed concern about a phenomenal increase in the numbers of men appearing at V.D. clinics with syphilis contracted homosexually [355, 194]. Indeed, at some London clinics, and in some American cities, over half of the male syphilitics attribute their infection to homosexual contacts [270].

Some of the apparent increase is due to patients having become more willing to confide to the doctor the truth about their sexual habits [325], but this can be no more than a partial explanation. The incidence of anal sores fairly confidently attributed to homosexuality—whatever the client's story—have also increased significantly. Unless, in the past, men with such symptoms kept away from doctors until the incriminating phase of illness was over, it looks as if there has been a real increase in homosexually contracted syphilis in recent years. Incidentally, some authorities have fastened upon this observation as evidence of a widespread increase in homosexual behaviour; but it could equally well be due to the introduction of a new source of infection (from increased travel, for example) followed by rapid dissemination, among a group of men of already well-established promiscuous habits.

Syphilis, the most serious of the common venereal infections, is produced by a germ known as a spirochete, which is present in the blood, saliva, semen, vaginal secretions or sores of an infected person. This germ can only pass to another person by direct contact, entering the body through one of the mucous linings (i.e. mouth, anus, vagina, or glans penis) but not through the ordinary skin, unless there is some cut or abrasion. A variable incubation period of a week to three months passes before any symptoms show, and then a spot, which rapidly develops into a hard, painless ulcer (the primary chancre) develops at the place where the infection gained entry. In the heterosexual male, the primary chancre usually appears on the penis, or occasionally on the lips, sites where it cannot be overlooked, but should it appear around or inside the anus it may not be noticed or may be mistaken, even by the doctor, if he is unsuspecting, for a haemorrhoid or fissure. Left untreated, the chancre heals, but after two to three months the secondary stage of the illness begins, during which a generalized rash appears over the trunk, the lymphatic glands swell, the person may feel slightly unwell and feverish, and inconspicuous, painless ulcers may develop in the mouth or around the ano-genital area. During all this period of incubation and secondary phase the patient is infectious, and a promiscuous woman or passive homosexual whose sores are in a hidden place, may continue sex activity unaware (or unwilling to admit) that anything is the matter until it transpires that scores, or even hundreds, of men have acquired the illness from the same source.

If still untreated, the secondary phase clears up in a month or two, but the spirochetes remain alive in the blood stream, and may in time play havoc with the circulatory and nervous system and, in the case of a female, may cause irretrievable damage to any baby she produces. Fortunately, modern antibiotics, if taken conscientiously during the early stages, will successfully eradicate the disease in nearly all cases. Hence the great importance of the prompt and confidential treatment provided free at special clinics in England, and the advisability of promiscuous passive homosexuals reporting for blood tests every four months as a precaution against concealed infection [3].

Gonorrhoea is a less dangerous infection. It attacks the male urethra, causing pus to dribble from the penis, and a burning pain on passing urine. It is contracted by inter-course, either from the female vagina, or homosexually, from an infected rectum. It clears up very quickly with treatment, but if left it will persist and may lead to arthritis and other serious complications. Again, the passive male homosexual with a gonococcal infection of the rectum may have some slight anal soreness or discharge, but this can easily pass unnoticed or be attributed to the minor abrading or stretching often produced by a too ardent devotion to sodomy. Hence, his first awareness of the disease may come from complaints by his sexual partners, who usually develop their symptoms a few days after contact.

Between homosexuals, gonorrhoea is always propagated by anal intercourse and syphilis usually so (although oral-genital contacts and even kissing may occasionally suffice). Promiscuous heterosexuals often use a contraceptive sheath during intercourse, and this affords considerable protection against infection. The use of germicidal ointments is not effective. Mutual masturbation and embracing rarely trans-mit venereal infection. Lesbians, on account of their dif-ferent techniques of intercourse and their avoidance of promiscuity, rarely transmit venereal infection to each other; but of course the really promiscuous Lesbians, especially those who have contacts with both men and women, may well do so.

CHAPTER VI

TWO TYPICAL CASES

Before discussing in the abstract some of the varied theories of sexual deviation, it would be well to have a picture in mind of some actual instances of individuals who have failed to conform to normal standards. A study of such cases helps to show how aberrant tendencies develop, and provides a background against which to judge the plausibility or otherwise of the commoner explanations. Here, then, are the personal histories of two homosexual men, both very typical of their kind.

CASE I

The first example is a person known to me outside the patient-doctor relationship, an architect by profession, who agreed to answer my questions for interest's sake. He was not seeking psychiatric help; in fact he would be the last person to consider himself ill or in need of treatment. In this respect he provides a good example of the type of homosexual the psycho-analyst rarely sees because they do not come for treatment.

He was of medium build, slightly thickset, with a manly face and body, rather muscular considering his sedentary habits, and with normal genitals. He dressed carelessly and one would never notice him particularly in a crowd. In fact the keynote of his personality was ordinariness. He avoided sports, walking, and exertion generally, more from laziness and lack of interest than special aversion, but liked swimming, which he did well. Though not brilliant in his profession, he was successful by dint of a capacity for persistent application coupled with considerable practical ability. Outside his own technical sphere he had few

intellectual interests. He held naïve views on political affairs
and questions of philosophy or religion failed to interest
him. His approach to life savoured of rather earthy common
sense. He knew how to look after his own interests, was
even a little egocentric, but more from absence of imagination than lack of goodwill. His disposition was placid and
he co-operated with his colleagues easily. They looked
upon him as a steady, dependable chap, calm, efficient and
businesslike. They would have been greatly surprised to
hear about his unorthodox sexual life.

His family background was equally unremarkable. He
came from a typical upper-working-class provincial home.
His father, one of a large family, had known real poverty in
his earlier days. His mother, too, had not had an easy life.
She had been reared by a domineering mother and then left
to fend for herself at an early age. She was an attractive
woman, cheerful, energetic, and sociable. Many men had
taken an interest in her, but ultimately she married a man
much older than herself, a weedy, anxious type of distinctly
retiring disposition. She had inherited something of her
mother's strong will and soon she became the dominant
partner in the marriage. She it was who made the family
decisions, looked after the finances, arranged the holidays
and punished the children when necessary. She it was who
saw to it that her son worked hard, visited his school to
make sure all was going well, and urged him on until he
won a scholarship.

He could not remember having any preference for one or
other parent when he was tiny, although his father used to
make a fuss of him, taking him on his lap to read to him. By
the time he was ten, he felt more drawn to his mother. It
was clear to him that she was the real boss and that his
father was content that it should be so. He grew rather
contemptuous of his father's weak character, and this attitude persisted into adulthood. His father seemed to him
limited in outlook and lacking in understanding and he
confided more easily in his mother.

As far back as he could remember he had always had

some curiosity about sex, but he could not remember ever being interested in girls. The only exception he recalled was an incident at the age of six when he and a small girl showed each other their private parts. He vaguely remembered that even before that he had got some erotic pleasure from a game they played together. The only woman he had ever had a real fondness for was his mother. At school he picked up sex information from obscene drawings and talk and also by reading. He listened to dirty jokes, but was neither specially interested nor specially revolted by them.

It was as early as seven years of age that he first found himself attracted to another boy, one slightly older than himself. He found the boy's company very pleasurable and used to wonder what he would look like undressed. When he was about eleven he remembers there was mild sex play between the boys at school in which they poked at each other's privates. He used to like this being done to him. When he was alone he tried various ways of pleasurable stimulation, but it was not until he was thirteen that he discovered by experiment how to obtain orgasm by regular masturbation. Thereafter he indulged frequently, but he did not feel guilty or worry about its effects because, about this time, his mother lent him a book on sex. On one occasion his father caught him masturbating and warned him that it would make him ill. He could not believe this, and the incident only made him more disillusioned with his father.

At first his masturbation was no more than a bodily manipulation, but around the age of fifteen he suddenly found he could increase his pleasurable excitement by imagining naked men, or looking at photographs of male nudes. Many of his school-fellows indulged in mutual masturbation, and he used to get erections and orgasms by watching them, but he refrained from joining in himself, because his particular friend said it was a nasty practice. As he grew older and his friends talked a lot about girls he remained uninterested. He was not frightened of girls; he just did not bother to seek them out. He had no desire to see girls undressed, but he was very excited by the sight of men with athletic bodies at the swimming baths.

During his later school years, and during his period of national service, he continued to masturbate to the accompaniment of homosexual fantasies, but he made no actual contacts with other men, From reading about homosexuality he gathered that he would never be able to marry, and at first this thought worried him. He also read about sodomy, and was disgusted at the thought of it. It was not until he was twenty-two, when someone in a crowd made advances to him, that he first went with another man. They had mutual masturbation in a secluded spot, and it was brought home to him that there were plenty of other men who wanted the same thing as he did. During the ensuing years, however, while he was pursuing his studies, he had only occasional furtive contact with men he met in public places. In the course of these clandestine adventures he was initiated into the practice of *fellatio* and he learnt to obtain great pleasure from taking the passive role in sodomy.

After some four years of these casual encounters, during which he never went with the same man more than once or twice, he met someone older than himself to whom he was attracted mentally as well as physically. 'Anthony', the man in question, was a fastidious, mannered *poseur*, artistically inclined and over-emotional, full of neurotic symptoms, in fact very close to the ordinary man's picture of a male homosexual. At their second meeting Anthony swore eternal love. Anthony introduced him to homosexual circles and they went about together to shows and 'gay' parties. By the time he had finished his studies, however, he had tired of Anthony. Thereafter he made friends with one homosexual after another, each 'affair' lasting only a few months. He thrived on being chased by some ardent lover, whom he would encourage up to a point, while being at pains to assert his independence. At the same time he spent a large part of his leisure hours in bars and meeting places where he could be sure of finding men like himself, and became exceedingly promiscuous. He maintained that he did not want to belong to anyone, he was out for a good time. It was nice to have homosexual friends, but too exclusive a relationship with one person led to jealousies and scenes, and he would have none of it.

Despite his promiscuity, he longed secretly to find someone with whom he could have a love relationship as complete and stable as a happy marriage between man and woman. Eventually he met someone better suited to him in age and temperament than Anthony had been, and the two of them began to live together and organize their lives as one, just like any married couple. His attitude changed abruptly, his promiscuous wanderings ceased, his life became more ordered, he took a new interest in clothes, meals, domesticity, he saved money to make a home for the two of them, and declared his firm resolve to make the arrangement last.

Throughout these developments X pursued his work as usual. He liked his colleagues well enough, but most of them were engaged in settling down and rearing families, and he made no intimate friends among them because their personal interests were different. At ordinary social events he felt rather shy and out of things and distinctly bored. This was not noticeable to casual acquaintances, but it was sufficient to keep him away from much of the normal community life. He did not feel deprived, for he preferred to spend his time in the company of fellow homosexuals with whom he could be his natural self.

In women's company he was quite at ease in formal and professional situations, but quickly shied away from any amorous approaches. At the mention of having sexual relations with a woman he gave a little humorous shudder. His only real female friend was his mother. For her he preserved a great fondness, taking her out to the theatre and visiting her regularly after he left home. The two of them would joke together as familiarly as companions of the same age. 'We two are so alike,' he said. 'She understands me and knows what I am going to say almost before I have spoken.' He admitted that there was a noticeable lessening in his feelings towards his mother at those times when he was involved in passionate affairs with men. He knew about the psychological theory that male homosexuality arises from mother fixation, but he did not seriously think that this had much relevance to his own case. However, after a discussion of his behaviour towards his mother and its contrast with his attitude to his father, he developed a violent headache.

He agreed that if there were some magic treatment that would change him into a heterosexual overnight he would no longer want to have it. All his friends and interests were homosexual, and the idea of a wife and children left him cold. Of course, he said, if he were heterosexual he might feel differently.

Apart from his sexual habits he was a well-adjusted person and showed no signs of neurotic conflict. From his point of view the only problem arose from the legal and social condemnation that forced him to live secretively in order to avoid the prying suspicions of neighbours. Consciously, at least, he displayed no guilt, and did not consider he was doing wrong to live, as he would put it, according to his nature. It brought harm to nobody and he would not mind explaining to any understanding person how he felt about it. Hence this case history. He was seen again twelve years after this was first written. He had continued all that time to share his home and to spend most of his leisure time and his vacations with the same homosexual friend. The companion was a person who liked keeping house, and who therefore performed many of the tasks ordinarily done by a wife for her husband, although in sexual roles their preferences showed no corresponding division. As often seems to happen in long-standing male liaisons, both partners had reverted to promiscuous sexual dalliance with outsiders.

CASE II

Now, in contrast, a second case. Unlike the first, who

accepted the situation with no trouble at all, this man engaged in a constant struggle with himself. He came before medical scrutiny at the age of thirty years, when he went to his doctor and complained of a tired feeling, aching pains in his muscles, poor appetite, and insomnia. He also suffered from moods of depression when he felt no interest in anything and spent all his time moping indoors. Eight years ago he had had an illness involving muscular pain, and for no obvious reasons he had been suffering from similar pains ever since. The doctor sent him to a psychiatrist. At the first interview he revealed that his indulgence in homosexual practices was worrying him terribly. He thought it very wicked, but he could not stop himself. He was deeply ashamed, and not at all sure he had done the right thing in telling his guilty secret. He confessed to a vague fear that the hospital case histories might be subject to inspection by some high official of the National Health Service, and that he would be prevented from obtaining decent employment in future.

He was a quiet-spoken man, of medium build, with a normal masculine body and genitals. He displayed no effeminate mannerisms. He had fair intelligence, but self-blame and a deep feeling of inferiority had brought him to a pitiable position. For some five years he had held a steady job as a skilled worker. Although there was never any complaint about his work, he lacked confidence in himself and was always wondering whether he was doing as well as the next chap. Then he did a period of national service as a private. He liked physical training and assault courses, but he panicked on being selected for clerical training, because he feared he would not be able to cope with memory work. At his own request he secured a transfer to something else, but still he was unsure of himself. Fear of doing the wrong thing haunted him, especially when there were other men around. He dreaded what others would think of him if he made some stupid mistake. His pains returned worse than ever and he slept badly. Finally an army psychiatrist saw him and he was discharged as psycho-neurotic.

Two Typical Cases

After this he drifted from job to job, taking on simple, menial tasks that would make no demands upon him, and becoming quickly miserable and bored in each one. He had applied for better jobs, but sometimes he failed to turn up for interview, and sometimes, after having got so far as to be accepted, he backed out on account of last-minute fears that he would prove a failure and show himself up. He would have liked to do an interesting job of some social value, but he felt it would be wrong for him to try for anything decent. In any sort of public work he might be found out and bring disgrace all around. Although he held strong religious convictions, and would have liked to take part in the social life of his church, he kept away because, as he said, it would be a mockery of religion for a homosexual to attend a church.

Although very different in his attitudes from the first case, there were points of similarity in his personal history. He too had been mother's favourite, and described her as kind, understanding, and his best friend. He used to stay in with her of an evening and not feel the need of other company. She had been a strongly-built, vigorous woman who could get her own way without domineering. She had brought up her family strictly and competently, but when her son was twenty years of age she died suddenly. It was at this point that he first lapsed into homosexual habits.

Whatever environmental influences may have caused his homosexual development, they did not seem to have affected his brothers. His elder brother, a happy-go-lucky type who always got what he wanted out of life, was already married and raising a family, and his younger brother seemed likely to be married before long.

As with many male homosexuals, his relations with his father were somewhat odd. His father was a healthy, care-free man, who had held the same job for forty years. He admired his father in some things, and wished he himself were half so steady, but he never felt at ease with him. He complained that his father had never taken much interest in him, never found time to attend his school functions as other parents did. He thought that his father preferred his elder brother to himself, and he remembered particularly that when first he began to complain of nervous troubles his father remarked unsympathetically, 'You're weaker than I thought you were.' After his mother's death his father took up with another woman. He disapproved strongly and left home when the father remarried.

About his childhood sexual feelings he could recall very little. (No doubt he had repressed a great deal.) He said that as a boy he had been completely ignorant and innocent, and was greatly troubled by the obscene talk at school. Although he was nervous, afraid of the dark, and a nail-biter, he thought that his early childhood was happy. But at the age of eleven, he failed in a scholarship examination that he had expected to pass, and after that everything went wrong. The teacher told him there was no reason why he should have done so badly. The failure upset him terribly, and, for the first time, he began to feel helpless and to become awkward in everything he tried to do. Bit by bit he dropped out of school activities and lost all his friends. It was to this disappointment at the age of eleven that he traced back all his present troubles.

Owing to an accident in early childhood he had a somewhat crooked nose. On reaching adolescence he became extremely sensitive about this, especially in the presence of girls. His embarrassment about it made him so clumsy and self-conscious that he had to give up an attempt to learn to dance. Even after his nose was put right by an operation the embarrassment persisted. Moreover, he could not outgrow his childhood disgust of sex, and heartily wished that such horrid desires did not exist. The crude conversation of his workmates revolted him. When he was sixteen another youth introduced him to masturbation, and thereafter he indulged himself in solitude while thinking about girls. He feared having anything to do with girls except in imagination in case he made one pregnant. He thought that about the most terrible thing that could happen. He remembered very vividly his mother, who had old-fashioned ideas about sex, saying that she would feel like killing any son of hers who got a girl into trouble.

After his mother's death he took to spending time in bars where he encountered groups of homosexuals. In their company he felt more at ease because he thought they would be less critical of him than normal men. Soon he was indulging in illicit sex, but not without many qualms and inhibitions. He always let the other man make the first advances. He hated another man to kiss or fondle him, he disliked having to masturbate another person, and he would never agree to *fellatio* or to be the passive partner in sodomy. His preference was for the active role in sodomy, but he liked it to take place in the dark as then he felt less ashamed. He made it a rule never to meet his sexual partners a second time. He had only one permanent male friend, of whom he was very fond, but they had ceased having sexual relations after their first encounter. The reason he gave for having relations with men was not that he preferred them but that in so doing he avoided the dread of pregnancy that assailed him when he approached a woman.

In point of fact, he did have a girl friend with whom he went about off and on for over five years, but they never had sexual intercourse and never became engaged. This girl liked to cuddle him in doorways, and on these occasions, when he felt her body pressed against his, he would become sexually aroused, but then his panic fears of pregnancy would overcome him, and he would have to hurry away. Quite apart from this phobia about pregnancy, the idea of intercourse before marriage seemed to him utterly wrong. On the other hand, he feared to marry in case his homosexual tendencies should get the better of him, forcing him to return to his old haunts and be unfaithful to his wife. 'What should I do?' he asked. 'Should I take the plunge, forget everything, and get married?'

CHAPTER VII

GLANDS AND HEREDITY

1. The Physical Basis of Sex

For the benefit of readers unfamiliar with the elements of heredity and glandular physiology, a few preliminary explanations need to be made. Although the bodily contours, temperament and sexual desires of men and women are often contrary or overlapping, the vast majority are unambiguously distinct in their genitals. This clear-cut difference is hereditarily determined through the chromosomes. These microscopic constituents of the reproductive cells carry the genes which are made up from complex protein molecules of DNA, the famous messenger of heredity. The genes provide the template for growth from a single cell to a complete human being, and transmit everything that is physically passed on from one generation to the next.

Each human cell has forty-six chromosomes arranged in twenty-three pairs. In the formation of the reproductive cells, that is the female egg and the male sperm, these pairs split up, leaving only twenty-three single chromosomes. When the reproductive cells from mating couples come together at fertilization, the chromosomes reform into the original twenty-three pairs, one set coming from father and the other from mother, so that some of the qualities of each parent appear in the offspring.

In twenty-two of the pairs the member chromosomes look alike. In the remaining pair, the sex chromosomes, they look alike in the female (the XX combination), but in the male one looks smaller (the XY combination). Normal female eggs always have a single X chromosome, but male sperm cells have either an X or a Y chromosome. The sex of the offspring is set at the moment of fertilization according to whether an X or Y type sperm unites with the egg.

When things go wrong with this mechanism, for instance if the Y chromosome is abnormal or perhaps missing altogether, the baby is likely to suffer from serious genital deformities. In recent years, cellular biology has made rapid strides, and some of the microscopic anomalies of the germ cells which cause various types of physical intersexuality (hermaphroditism) have been conclusively identified. Fortunately these conditions are quite rare. For this reason, and also because the obvious deformities of hermaphrodites set them apart, an explanation of the generality of homosexuality along these lines does not seem likely.

The sex chromosomes transmit directives, but their accomplishment depends upon favourable conditions during growth. In particular, the quality and concentration of hormones in the circulating blood has great influence upon the growth and function of the sexual organs. Hence, even in individuals possessed of normal sex chromosomes, development still depends upon the endocrine glands maturing at the right time and secreting into the circulating blood the right amount of the required chemicals. In experiments on animals, physical sex reversals have been produced by giving artificial concentrations of the wrong hormone to the (previously) normal growing embryo. Hens' eggs treated with oestrogen during the first week of incubation hatch into normal females, intersexual monstrosities, and a very reduced proportion of ordinary male chicks [121].

The endocrine glands do not relate exclusively to sexual development. They include the pituitary, the thyroid, the pancreas, and the adrenals, as well as the ovaries or testes, which produce hormones as well as eggs or sperm. They influence the development of most bodily functions, and throughout life they continue to act as chemical governors for regulating the speed of physiological changes, and for inducing appropriate adjustments of gear when the body has to respond to stress. They tend to act in unison, the hormone of one affecting the activity of other glands, so that a flaw at one point may result in a wide range of disturbance. For instance, lack of some pituitary growth-stimulating hormones not only causes abnormally short stature (dwarfism), but indirectly, because the ovaries or testes are not stimulated, prevents the physical changes of puberty, so that the affected female fails to menstruate and the affected male remains sexually infantile, with a tiny, impotent penis.

The hormones produced by normal female ovaries and male testes (in principle oestrogens and androgens respectively) stimulate the growth and maintain the function of the physical sexual apparatus. Failure of these hormones naturally causes greater havoc when it occurs before the sexual apparatus matures at puberty. Thus a boy who is castrated in infancy not only remains permanently sterile, because the sperm-producing equipment has been removed, he grows up into a eunuch, with smooth, beardless skin, high-pitched voice, sparse body hair, plump figure, and small ineffectual penis. The corresponding female type remains flat-chested, with small genitals and rudimentary womb, incapable of child-bearing. The male eunuch is well known in history from the custom of castrating boys for various purposes, such as initiation to priestly cults, to preserve a high singing voice, or to produce slaves to guard harems. The type is also well exemplified in domestic animals like the large, sleek and lazy 'doctored' tom-cat, or the plump hen-like capon. If destruction of the secreting cells of the testes occurs in a fully grown man, as a result of castration, injury or disease, the physical consequences are less extreme, although, in the course of time, changes in weight, beard, voice and size of penis usually become obvious. The use of castration by some countries as a penal measure for adult male sex offenders has led to a better knowledge of both the physical and psychological effects [42].

2. Sex Performance, Desire and Preference
Physical ability to perform sexually, and the desire for

sexual activities, do not necessarily go together, as some old men discover to their chagrin. Furthermore, the preferred means of obtaining orgasm, or the choice of sexual partner, have little to do with the degree of lust. These three elements, capacity, lust, and preference, though interconnected, develop somewhat independently. It seems that heredity and glandular factors are primarily responsible for the physical growth and function of the sex organs, although psychological factors may play some part, usually in limiting sexual performance. For example, social anxiety may render a young male impotent with women, but if he is normally endowed his physical potential will appear in spontaneous erections and nocturnal emissions.

The strength of sexual desire, on the other hand, is very much a combination of physical and psychological factors. On the whole, one expects persons inadequately endowed physically, such as the eunuch, to experience less pressing sexual desires, and on average this holds true, but the exceptions are remarkable. For instance, Perloff [293] described a young woman with Turner's syndrome (one missing X chromosome, the XO combination), who had no ovaries and no circulating oestrogens, no breasts and only a rudimentary vagina, who nevertheless experienced erotic arousals to an embarrassing extent, and regularly attained orgasm by masturbation. In humans, sexual responsiveness is largely a matter of the individual learning an expected social role. With normal physical equipment, the learning task comes that much easier, but even severe sexual cripples may experience some erotic sensations, and hence develop a powerful need for sexual gratification. The fact that erotic responsiveness is a unique instrument for gaining affection and attention provides further incentive to learning. At the same time, physical conditions do play an important part too, as is obvious from the loss of sexual appetite during illness and following orgasms, or the striking increase in lust that is produced in some people by injecting hormones.

Traditional beliefs, exemplified by the fairy story of the innocent ivory tower princess suddenly awakening to love on the arrival of a handsome prince, suggest that the third facet of sexuality, choice of love object, is determined by some hereditary lock-type mechanism which only the appropriate key will bring into operation. Instances of this kind are familiar enough in the animal world. For example, the mating season releases a whole chain of nest-building and egg-hatching activities by young birds who have never before behaved in such fashion or had the chance to learn by imitation. However, factual observation suggests a different story in the human species. Sexual feelings develop slowly, from the first confused gropings of infancy to the final stage of mature heterosexuality. Sexual behaviour is not a stereotyped pattern of copulatory activity suddenly released fully-fledged by appropriate stimulation; indeed the means of attaining orgasm which a normal adult may resort to, or a youngster is likely to experiment with, includes day-dreams, solitary or mutual masturbation, reading about or watching the sex acts of others, as well as various physical intimacies between members of the same or the opposite sex. All this serves to emphasize the plasticity of sexual behaviour in humans, and the essential role of social conditioning and individual learning in determining sexual preferences. It is one of the chief contentions of this book that although physical and hereditary factors play a large part in governing the strength of sexual urges, psychological factors are more decisive in channelling these urges into either heterosexual or homosexual directions. The remainder of this chapter is taken up with arguing this out in a little more detail.

3. *The Hormonal Contribution to Lust and Deviance*

Experiments with mammals have demonstrated the close dependence of animals' sex behaviour upon the blood concentration of hormones [393]. In females oestrogen levels have a natural periodic variation, and only when the cycle reaches its peak is the animal 'on heat' and willing to mate. Removal of the ovaries, by cutting off the source of oestrogens, renders the female animal permanently unreceptive. Likewise castration of the male, which seriously lowers androgen levels, abolishes copulatory initiatives, reduces aggressiveness, and may result in the animal being mounted in sexual fashion by other males.

In lower animals the pattern of sex behaviour can be actually reversed by giving androgens to a female or oestrogens to a male. In hens the effect is quite dramatic. Hen communities preserve a social hierarchy or pecking order, with the cock bossing all, and the most powerful and aggressive of the hens pecking at all her sisters below, while the most submissive hen in the roost gets pecked by all and sundry. Feeding androgens to a hen of low social status causes her to start pecking aggressively at those above her, so that she quickly rises to the top of the social ladder. Her comb enlarges, giving her a masculine appearance, and she assumes male postures and attempts to mate with other hens. Of course the analogy between this behaviour and human homosexuality must not be pressed too far. One cannot get in to the mind of a hen to know if she notices or likes the distinctive appearance of the cock, and one cannot be sure whether the adoption of a dominating or masculine copulatory stance is an expression of 'desire' or merely the result of the relative strength and vigour of the participating animals.

In animals higher on the evolutionary scale, and especially in human beings, sexual behaviour is largely independent of immediate hormonal control. Female chimpanzees, like women, will mate during any phase of the oestrus (menstrual) cycle, regardless of oestrogen levels, and castrated male chimpanzees, like some castrated men, will persist in attempts to copulate. In human females, oestrogen production falls and menstruation ceases in middle age, but sexual desire generally continues, and may even become stronger, perhaps as a consequence of removal of all fear of further pregnancies. Nevertheless, some women do experience a falling off of sexual interest at the menopause, and in certain cases giving oestrogens will restore their lust; but this effect might be an indirect result of the relief

156

which oestrogens give from hot flushes and other uncomfortable symptoms associated with the menopause. Oestrogens never cure the frigidity of younger women with normal hormone levels; their difficulties are psychological.

In a young man with mal-functioning testes, who suffers from a poorly developed penis, partial impotence and lack of sex drive, the administration of androgens to restore the hormone deficit often produces remarkable improvement in physical appearance, potency and desire for sex. Androgens have also been used to some purpose in the treatment of male sterility, and sometimes have a temporary rejuvenating effect upon elderly men with failing physical and sexual capacities. In the endocrinologically normal male, however, taking an artificial excess of androgens may sometimes increase lust, but usually it has but little effect.

Artificial reduction of androgens by castration has variable consequences. When a fully mature young man has his testes destroyed, as sometimes happens through wounding or tubercular infection, eunuchoid bodily changes may not occur at all or may be quite slight. The effect on sexual desire is inconstant. The Romans knew very well that even eunuchs were not always to be trusted with women. Although castration of an adult often causes his sexual desires to diminish, in some cases it appears to make no appreciable difference. Some castrated adults continue an active sexual life, although they are sterile. The nervous reflexes governing erection and ejaculation, once established, can continue unimpaired in spite of considerable hormone deficiency. Moreover, the testes are not the sole providers of androgen. A variable amount, produced in the adrenal glands, continues to circulate even after castration.

On the analogy of what occurs in hens, one might expect normal women to respond to doses of androgens by becoming lesbian, and homosexual men to become heterosexual, but in practice nothing of the sort happens. When given to male homosexuals, androgens, far from having a curative effect, are likely, if anything to increase their desire

for whatever type of sexual activity they are accustomed
to [16]. Out of eleven homosexual men so treated by Glass
and Johnson [136], the majority experienced no change in
their desires, while five noted an increased drive towards
homosexual activity. Androgens have been found to have
no influence upon the pseudo-feminine mannerisms, attitudes, and interests displayed by certain male homosexuals.

The effect of large doses of androgens on women is well
known as a result of naturally occurring adrenal tumours,
which secrete excessive amounts of androgens, and also
because big doses of androgens have been given as treatment for certain cancers. The woman's appearance under-
goes a striking change in the direction of masculinity. The
voice deepens, a beard grows, breasts regress, clitoris enlarges, features coarsen, and feminine fat disappears. Sexual
desire usually increases, but remains normal feminine
desire, unless of course lesbian inclinations were already
present [104, 144, 252].

Correspondingly large doses of stilboestrol (synthetic
oestrogen) have been given to men in the treatment of
cancer of the prostate gland. Far from inducing homosexual
desires, oestrogen simply brings about a reduction of male
libido. If continued with for long enough and in sufficient
doses oestrogens destroy testicular tissue and thus have the
same effect as castration. This fact has been made use of in
the treatment of sex offenders. Stilboestrol sometimes
effectively quells desire and so helps the homosexual to
control his behaviour [85, 101, 141].

Stilboestrol treatment, like castration, is not invariably
successful in abolishing sexual feeling [151]. It also has unfortunate side effects, such as the stimulation of feminine
breast development, which is both painful and embarrassing [85]. Moreover the ethical justification for interfering
with the little-understood endocrine balance of a physically
healthy man might be called into question. Taking stilboestrol as a 'cure' for homosexuality is rather like 'treating'
a bad leg by amputation. However, if a man earnestly
desires this pseudo-castration as a possible escape from

conflict with the law, then one can hardly withhold it from him.

The situation may be best summarized by quoting the conclusions of the very experienced endocrinologist W. H. Perloff [293]. 'The administration of large doses of androgen to normal women may intensify their libidos—possibly by increasing the sensitivity of the clitoris—but does not cause them to assume male roles. Treatment of the [male] homosexual patient with the hormone of his somatic sex will in no way influence his sexual behaviour unless this substance be androgen, in which case his sexual activity may increase but always in a direction determined psychologically.'

One further line of evidence from endocrinology deserves mention. Normal male blood contains some oestrogen, but relatively little compared with the amount of androgen present. According to one theory, a naturally occurring imbalance of androgen-oestrogen ratios may provoke deviant sexual behaviour. Thus the man who has too little androgen in relation to the oestrogen he carries may be expected to become homosexual. In the past, some investigators have claimed to find just this anomaly in hormone measurements taken from male homosexuals [137, 272, 392].

These old findings are very doubtful. Other investigators have failed to discover significant alterations in the androgen-oestrogen ratios of male homosexuals [11, 334]. In the past, the determination of hormone levels has depended upon taking extracts from the urine of the human subject, and then estimating the potency of the extract by watching the physical changes in sex characteristics which it produces when given to mice or other small animals. This method suffers not only from the variability of animal reactions, but also from the fact that urine concentrations do not necessarily correspond at all closely to the levels of hormone in the blood. Adequate techniques of direct chemical analysis of the blood have not been fully developed. Chemical estimations of the substances known as

17-ketosteroids have been widely used to give an indication of androgen levels, but in point of fact these derive from other hormones as well as androgens, and so may be misleading. Furthermore, in referring simply to androgen and oestrogen the actual hormone situation has been oversimplified, since their action may be masked or altered by the presence of other types of sex hormone such as those from the pituitary. Perloff [293] states categorically that direct measurements of hormone levels present a still unsolved problem. It would be fair to conclude that so far no clear evidence exists of any peculiarities in the sex hormone levels of homosexuals, although no one can be sure what more refined techniques may reveal in the future.

To summarize the implications of all the endocrinological evidence, it seems that the development of lust at adolescence and the strength of lust in later life partly depend upon glandular functions; but that in humans the choice of male or female as love object has nothing to do with the hormones [268]. One small exception is the partially impotent, feminine-looking man who suffers from glandular insufficiency. It is arguable that a man with these disadvantages may be slightly more likely than a healthy male to take to passive homosexuality. Be this as it may, a negligible proportion of homosexuals suffer from any demonstrable glandular disturbance.

4 . A Biological Anomaly?

So far as can be demonstrated at present, homosexuality manifests purely psychologically, with no accompanying physical stigmata. Nevertheless certain theorists maintain that the condition may still be due to some innate biological anomaly as yet unidentified. The abnormal chromosome constitutions responsible for some physical intersexuality have only lately been discovered, so it is not unreasonable to look for something analogous to explain the psychological counterpart of hermaphroditism. The theory that homosexuality is one form of biological intersexuality deserves some consideration [302], although it must be admitted at the outset that the evidence adduced in support is, to say the least, equivocal. Some people, especially homosexuals themselves, find the biological theory appealing less for genuinely scientific reasons than for the implication that sexually deviant individuals bear no personal responsibility for their condition.

Many grades of physical intersexuality have been observed and studied. In some cases the nature of the internal reproductive glands, the ovaries or testes, are at variance with the bodily appearance. In some cases the glands are neither ovaries nor testes but a mixture of the two, containing both androgenic and oestrogenic cells. In some cases there is a testis on one side of the body and an ovary on the other. The external genitals may range through every intermediate stage from male to female. Thus an individual with an apparently normal penis may have in the position of the scrotum a small cleft leading to a rudimentary womb. Body build and other external appearances may be equally confusing.

Sometimes an endocrine disorder beginning during foetal development will produce intersexuality. A rare example of this is over-activity of the adrenals in a female foetus of three to four months, causing masculine growth of the sex organs in what would otherwise have been a normal girl. In most cases of human intersexuality, the foetal endocrine disorder is itself the consequence of a flaw in chromosome constitution.

One type of sex chromosome abnormality that has attracted medical attention recently, called Klinefelter's syndrome, is due to the male receiving an additional, feminizing 'X' chromosome, so that his sex chromosomes have an 'XXY' or even an 'XXXY' combination, instead of the normal male 'XY' complement. The clinical effects of this anomaly are very varied, and may be slight or severe. Usually, however, the individual is recognizably male, although testes and penis are small, breasts may be enlarged, and the figure feminine. In some types of hermaphrodite, the external bodily appearances may closely simulate those of the opposite sex, so that a genetic male will look and act like a female, although surgical exploration may perhaps reveal rudimentary testes buried inside the abdomen. Public attention has been drawn to such cases by the suggestion that genetic maleness may account for the success of some of the professional athletes who compete as women. Other abnormal sex chromosome combinations have recently been identified, notably an XX-YY and an XYY combination. Both these types of males are usually very tall. All these unusual chromosome combinations are particularly common among patients in institutions for the subnormal and in hospitals for the criminal insane, so presumably they exert effects upon behaviour and temperament as well as upon sexual function and physique. In the general population, however, their incidence, in total, cannot be much more than one or two per thousand.

Arguing by analogy from these physical transformations, the suggestion has been made, notably by Lang [226], that male homosexuals are really genetic females whose bodies have undergone a complete sex reversal in the direction of masculinity. On this theory it is difficult to explain the normal bodily appearance of the great majority of homosexuals. If their condition were due to a sex-reversing process one would expect to find many cases of incomplete masculinity. However, Lang adduced one curious piece of evidence in favour of his theory. He investigated the family background of 1,517 male homosexuals whose names he obtained from a German police register. He found that in the aggregate they had 2,534 brothers but only 2,034 sisters, a male-female ratio of 124 to 100. This figure differed significantly from the male-female ratio for the population as a whole. Seemingly male homosexuality was associated with an excess of boys in the family. The observation fitted in well with Lang's theory. The excess of apparent males would be accounted for if some of them were in fact genetic females whose sexual development had undergone a radical reversal towards masculine appearance. Their sexual preferences, instead of being regarded as being perverse, could then be looked upon as the persistence of natural feminine impulses in spite of their bodily masculinization.

More recent research has disproved Lang's theory. An easy microscopic technique has been developed for identifying cells with a normal female 'XX' chromosome complement by observing the presence of chromatin spots which appear in the nuclei of cells from all parts of the body. Pare, at Maudsley Hospital [288] examined microscopically cells scraped from the linings of the mouths of fifty homosexual men, and fifty normal male and female 'controls'. All the men, including the fifty homosexual males, were identified as biologically male, and all the women as biologically female. Since then, several other investigators have repeated Pare's observations with the same result [289]. Additional confirmation was provided by Pritchard [299] who went further and made a detailed microscopic study of the actual chromosomes in cells taken from six exclusively homosexual men. They all had normal male sex-chromosome constitution.

The preponderance of brothers in the families of male homosexuals reported by Lang might have been a fallacy of selection. His findings were confirmed in a later large-scale study by Jensch [196]; but both these investigators based their work on police lists of homosexuals. Since the homosexuality that comes to the notice of the police is often connected with other forms of crime, and since large families of boys are peculiarly susceptible to delinquency, homosexuals from such families are likely to be unfairly over-represented among police dossiers. In a later American survey by Darke [73] no significant excess of brothers was found in the families of 100 male homosexuals. J. E. Morrow and others [269] have challenged the significance of the excess of brothers found in certain samples of homosexuals. They demonstrated a similar excess in an unselected group of male college students. They suggest that the result may be due to a tendency for some families to have children all of the same sex, a phenomenon which has been noted by other observers. If so, although the ratio of

163

males to females in the total population may approximate to 1 to 1, any all male sample might yield more brothers than sisters on account of the frequency of one-sex families.

Studies of physical intersexuals shows that by and large the direction of their sexual inclinations goes according to the sex in which they have been reared rather than the sex of their internal organs or chromosome constitution. Despite their bisexual appearance, intersexuals are not necessarily bisexual in their desires. One might expect that their sexual impulses would follow the pattern of their internal sex glands, that those with ovaries would develop feminine inclinations, those with testes masculine inclinations, and those with mixed glands bisexual characteristics. But it does not work out like that. An intersexual's desires are more likely to fall in line with the sex in which he is reared than to conform to the sex to which his endocrine glands belong. Many of them are brought up as boy or girl on the basis of an arbitrary decision made immediately after birth after an inspection of the genitals. Sometimes the decision runs contrary to the true sex as reflected in the internal organs. When this happens upbringing is apt to triumph over the sex glands. Ellis demonstrated this point by abstracting from medical literature all the cases he could find in which an intersexual's glandular constitution and sexual preferences were both known [89]. He found 84 cases distributed as follows:

INTERNAL SEX GLANDS (GONADS)

Reared as—	*Male*		*Female*		*Mixed*		*All Types*	
	Male	*Female*	*Male*	*Female*	*Male*	*Female*	*Male*	*Female*
Attracted to men	0	19	0	3	0	11	0	33
Attracted to women	11	2	5	0	18	3	34	5
'Bisexual'	0	1	0	2	0	0	0	3
Immature	0	1	0	1	5	2	5	4
Total	11	23	5	6	23	16	39	45

A Biological Anomaly?

The table shows that of 39 intersexuals reared as males 34 showed definite sexual desires. In all 34 cases their desires followed the normal male pattern, although 23 of them had either mixed or female sex glands. The inclinations of intersexuals seem, therefore, to correlate more closely with their upbringing than with their hormonal constitution. In a later study of 100 patients with different types of intersexuality Money and Hampson [266] confirm that, with occasional exceptions, the psychology of these patients follows the sex of rearing, even in cases in which their chromosomes, and the predominant charactertistics of their external genitals and their internal reproductive organs are those of the opposite sex. This is strong evidence in favour of the view that heterosexuality and homosexuality are psychological attitudes acquired by training and not automatic responses preordained by physical constitution. Money and Hampson [265] also comment on the fact that the sex of assignment appears quite firmly established in the child's behaviour and sense of gender identity by the age of two or three, and attempts to change this sex identity become increasingly difficult after that age. The theory that sexual preference arise from social training is not inconsistent with the observation that such preferences are decided, and probably fixed for all time, in the earliest years of life.

Some British workers have drawn attention to the exceptions to the general rule. Children reared contrary to their biological gender sometimes show signs of behaviour more appropriate to their true sex, e.g. tomboyish tendencies and a preference for urinating in a standing position on the part of supposed girls [81]. Berg and others relate the history of a boy with hypospadias (a relatively superficial genital deformity) who was mistakenly reared as a girl up till puberty. He fully accepted his feminine position, played happily with dolls and so forth, and only came to medical attention because his voice broke. Successful surgical repair of the genital deformity was carried out. In this instance, in spite of his relatively advanced age, the boy showed an amazing willingness to discard female things and to take up life as

165

a boy, and a surprising change towards masculine imaginative fantasy in his responses to psychological tests [29]. Considering how often normally constituted children show homosexual interests, or become dissatisfied with their sex roles, it would be surprising if the same did not happen occasionally among these intersexuals.

One may safely conclude that the presently recognized sex chromosome and endocrine anomalies do not play a significant part in the cause of homosexuality. Homosexuals rarely suffer from these conditions, and physical intersexuals do not usually suffer from homosexuality (if by that one means sexual desires contrary to the sex of upbringing). But that does not altogether settle the issue, since relevant genetic abnormalities may exist which are as yet undiscovered. The technique of counting the total number of chromosomes is a very crude method of deciding genetic normality. Pare has likened it to trying to recognize a symphony from the location of the intervals between movements. Many abnormal genes may be carried within a single chromosome, and genes carried on other than the sex chromosomes might be responsible for a predisposition to homosexuality.

One item of evidence in favour of an unidentified chromosome abnormality is the work of Slater [337], who found a statistical tendency for male homosexuals to be the younger sons of elderly mothers, that is to be born in the later years of their mother's reproductive cycle. The same observation holds true of individuals with identifiable chromosome abnormalities, such as Klinefelter's syndrome, or Mongolism. However, the observation is no more than suggestive, since it could easily be explained in other ways. If maternal attitude is an important factor, one can well imagine that the youngest sons of elderly mothers stand a greater risk of being 'smothered' and 'babied' and so pushed into homosexuality.

5. *An Inherited Factor*
The theory that sex deviation is caused by a hidden

constitutional defect would seem a little more plausible if the existence of some hereditary tendency towards homosexuality could be demonstrated. Many difficulties stand in the way of the necessary research. In the case of a rare and clear-cut defect, like a webbed finger, the mere observation of several instances in the same family affords good evidence of a hereditary factor. But homosexuality is so common that the discovery of a number of cases in the same family would have no significance. Even if investigation revealed some families with an unusually high proportion of homosexuals in several successive generations, this still would not amount to proof of hereditary causation. Like infectious disorders, homosexual tendencies might be transmitted by association. A homosexual father's peculiar outlook might so influence his sons that they develop the same way, even though they have no inborn peculiarity and under other circumstances would develop normally. Nor should the possibility of seduction be overlooked. If several brothers are affected, this may be the result, not of hereditary defect, but of one brother having introduced the others into perverse practices. In addition to the difficulties arising from alternative theoretical interpretations, actual data are hard to obtain. The extreme secrecy which surrounds sexual habits, especially within the family circle, makes it almost impossible to secure reliable estimates of the numbers of relatives of homosexuals who have similar tendencies. A voluntary patient would not permit the doctor to ask such questions of his relatives for they, of all people, are the ones from whom he most desires to conceal his sexual deviations. Inquiries among the relatives of convicted persons would scarcely lead to much information for they would naturally be antagonistic and reluctant to make admissions of any kind.

In the teeth of all these difficulties, both practical and theoretical, Kallmann [201, 200], an American authority on human heredity, achieved remarkable success in research with male homosexual twins. The study of twins enables the investigator to sort out the effects of hereditary and environmental influences. There are two types of twins. Dizygotic or ordinary twins, produced by the simultaneous fertilization of two separate eggs by two separate sperm cells, are no more alike than ordinary brothers and sisters. Monozygotic or identical twins, supposedly produced by the splitting of a single egg into two shortly after fertilization, descend both from the same egg cell and sperm cell and so have virtually the same hereditary endowment. Identical twins are always of the same sex and bear an uncanny resemblance to each other in general appearance and in such identifying characteristics as finger-prints and blood groups. Now, if the same anomaly occurs among several brothers the explanation might be that it was a hereditary condition, but it might also be due to the fact that the brothers had a similar upbringing and similar life circumstances. In studies of twins, if it is found that a condition occurs more often in both members of pairs of identical twins than it does in pairs of ordinary twins of the same sex, this affords strong evidence of a hereditary factor. Ordinary twins and identical twins are both brought up in similar environments, but only the identical twins have the additional factor of precisely similar inheritance.

Kallmann naturally experienced some difficulty in securing homosexual men with twin brothers and in following them up once he had found them. He had the co-operation of such organizations as the New York City and the New York State Departments of Correction, but it cannot have been easy. He remarks that this is 'not a promising field of exploration for research workers who are in any way anxious for their conventional peace of mind . . . the problems and attitudes of a sexually aberrant group look less wholesome in the twilight of gloomy hiding places than they do from the perspective of an ornamental desk or from a comfortable therapeutic couch.' In the end, Kallmann secured 85 homosexually-inclined twins. Most of them were more or less exclusively homosexual, that is to say they would be rated 5 or 6 on Kinsey's scale. All of them were at least 3 on the Kinsey scale. Of these 85, 40 were identical twins, and of these 40, Kallmann succeeded in tracing the brothers of 37. He found that all 37 twin brothers were homosexually inclined (with a Kinsey rating at least 3) and 28 were more or less exclusive homosexuals (with a Kinsey rating 5 or 6). In striking contrast the brothers of the ordinary, non-identical twins showed no particular homosexual trend. Twenty-six were traced, and only 3 had a Kinsey rating of 3 or more. This represents an incidence no higher than that of the population at large.

One cannot put too much reliance upon the results of one isolated investigation. Kallmann's findings run directly counter to all the evidence demonstrating the importance of upbringing in producing homosexuality. So far, in spite of the great scientific interest of the issue, no one has been able to stage a repetition of this research. Moreover, Kallmann has been criticized for lack of objectivity in his investigations. In his research on schizophrenia, his findings were doubtful because they were based upon a selected population and upon uncorroborated diagnoses made by himself [291]. In his homosexuality research, he was forced to obtain his cases from among the criminal and the severely abnormal. Out of his 40 identical twins, one was actually schizophrenic, and at least 22 were 'definitely schizoid', 'severely unstable with obsessive compulsive features' or else alcoholic. The use of such seriously pathological personalities not only increases the difficulties and sources of error involved in the social inquiry, it also limits the value of any findings, since they might not hold true for a more normal population. It could be that certain very abnormal types are particularly prone to homosexuality—that point is considered later—and it could be that these abnormalities, and hence the homosexuality associated with them, are to some extent inherited, but even so this would not necessarily apply to homosexuality occurring in otherwise normal individuals.

The close resemblance in behaviour between identical twins need not be due entirely to heredity. They look so alike that they tend to get treated alike, almost as if they were really the same person, and they learn to react in the same way, identifying with each other and imitating each other to an extent quite unusual among dissimilar twins. It is when identical twins are separated at an early age and reared apart that the resemblances in their behaviour provide the best evidence for heredity. Kallmann's twins were reared together, but he did emphasize that they all claimed to have started their homosexual practices on their own initiative, independent of any influence from their brothers.

On the face of it Kallmann's figures imply that if a man inherits the appropriate genes he has 100 per cent certainty of developing homosexuality, but even Kallmann does not go so far as to advance this conclusion. In fact, he suggests that homosexuality is not inherited in any simple or direct fashion, but has a multiplicity of causes, and is not necessarily unalterable. He thinks a number of different genes may influence sexual maturation at various stages, and he likens the inheritance of sexual deviation to that of left-handedness.

In any event, the idea that pairs of identical twins must be either both homosexual or both heterosexual has been disproved by individual case studies. The German investigator Lange [227], himself an ardent proponent of the importance of heredity, described a pair of identical male twins, of whom one, Otto, was a vain, painfully skittish-mannered homosexual, passive in sex habits, who had never got pleasure from women, while his twin brother Erich, who was about to marry, was completely heterosexual and disgusted by the thought of homosexual activity. Better verified examples of identical twins differing in sexual orientation have been published in recent years by Rainer *et al.* [304], Klintworth [214] and Parker [290]. In fairness to the hereditary theory, however, one has to realize that the cases selected for publication may be exceptional. Such differences, when they do occur, presumably come about through some environmental influence encountered by only one of the twin pair. By reviewing their respective life histories, one may obtain clues as to what kind of influences can tip the scales in the direction of homosexuality.

An Inherited Factor

One of the examples described by Parker was a married man with children who had had no homosexual interests since the common masturbatory experiences of early adolescence. In contrast, his identical twin brother had never shown the slightest heterosexual interest, and from the age of sixteen had indulged in promiscuous relations with older men contacted at lavatories and clubs. Eventually he settled down to a pseudo-marital relationship with a man of his own age. Both twins were intelligent, free from neurotic symptoms, and of normal masculine physique. The one striking difference between them lay in the way they had been mothered. Their mother had wanted a girl, and when the boys were born she fastened upon one of the babies, put a bracelet round his wrist, and treated him from the start in a subtly different fashion because, as she put it, he was pretty enough to be a girl. Both the brothers and the mother herself were aware of this special relationship. The affected twin became a sensitive, home-loving boy closely attached to his mother, whereas his heterosexual brother preferred to go out to football and swimming. Thus studies on twins, far from always supporting the hereditary theory, may sometimes point to the importance of other causes.

Even in cases in which identical twins resemble each other very closely in their deviant behaviour, heredity may not be the whole explanation. Dr. H. M. Holden [174] reported the treatment of a pair of male twins both of whom had developed strong and exclusive sexual attraction to elderly men. However, as he pointed out, the example could be used to support either the congenital or the acquired theory, since both men had experienced the same dominating, possessive mother and weak father, a pattern which many psycho-analysts have identified as a prime cause of male homosexuality. In addition, this pair were closely identified with each other, they lived together, worked together, and in many ways acted as one person. Psychotherapy helped them attain some individual independence, but did not change their sexual orientation.

CHAPTER VIII

THE PSYCHO-ANALYTIC APPROACH: AN INTRODUCTION

Of all the brands of psychological theorists the psycho-analysts have most to say about the causes of homosexuality. Their method depends upon making the patient talk about his most intimate fears and fantasies, and in particular encouraging him to recall the emotional reactions of early childhood, since these seem to set the tone for a great deal of what happens later in life. One may well doubt the general validity of some of the interpretations analysts put upon their patients' musings, but most psychiatrists would agree that the method has proved a very fruitful source of ideas about the origins of abnormal behaviour and that it has greatly increased our understanding of human motives and human vagaries.

Outside evidence contradicts the analysts on some points, vindicates them on others, and leaves them unsubstantiated on a great many more. Unfortunately, psycho-analytic tradition demands that one accept the system as a whole, as if in the entire corpus of somewhat inconsistent speculations by Freud and his followers all the ideas were of equal worth. This is not my own approach. In regard to the cause of homosexuality, I prefer to try to sort out the essentials of the Freudian view, to state this in the simplest terms, and to see how far it fits the known facts.

Many of the concepts laboriously formulated by psycho-analysts after prolonged study of the material recounted by their patients are really matters of common observation put into technical language. The first essential is to recognize, as most people do today, that human behaviour is often impulsive, guided less by rational reflection than by a host of emotional attitudes and tendencies, the strength of which the individual does not fully realize. Only by prolonged rumination and agonizing self-questioning can one gain insight into some of the remote influences that determine conduct and feelings. The analysts call this exploring *unconscious motives*.

In ordinary life we do not go in for introspective searchings. If our motives are questioned, we are apt to *rationalize*, to put forward some reasonable-sounding but spurious justification that did not really occur to us until after we had acted. It is easier to see this happening in other people. Listening to a woman giving vent to her feelings by criticizing a friend for extravagance we may be perfectly sure from her tone of voice that her motive is jealousy, but she herself would be the last to see it, and if challenged she would firmly assert and genuinely believe the rationalization that she was giving helpful advice.

Psycho-analysts have drawn attention to the great extent to which our thinking and acting rests upon these unconscious self-deceptions. They give names to the commoner mental tricks—*repression*, for example. When we are repelled by our own feelings, when they clash with our self-respect, we try to deny or to banish the offending thoughts. Often we are successful, and unwanted, inconvenient memories fade much quicker than pleasant, reassuring ones. The process has its uses. But for the development of a few healthy repressions civilization could not work, for, like wild beasts, we should be the victims of each other's untrammelled murderous impulses. We can deal with the nasty side of our natures in two ways, by repression, or by acceptance plus rational control. We can, for instance, accept the unpleasant fact that we sometimes feel like murdering our relatives without necessarily acting on the impulse. But many find repression the easier solution. Trouble arises when repression has not been complete and the repressed tendencies keep peeping through. This happens particularly in neurotic individuals who have the unfortunate habit of trying to repress too much and too often.

The Psycho-Analytic Approach: an Introduction

When the effort to repress is strong, but the repressed tendencies will not stay quelled, the individual feels tense and miserable without knowing why. Torn between his conscious wishes and his unconscious, repressed feelings, he is said to be in a state of *neurotic* conflict. The sufferer does not appreciate the nature of the conflict. He feels neurotic symptoms, anxiety, depression, irrational fears, and so forth, but he does not know their origin. The second of the two cases described in Chapter 5, the man who could not associate with women on account of his pregnancy *phobia*, was a typical instance of neurotic conflict. Phobias are the neurotic's danger signals, and they come on most acutely in situations that stimulate partially repressed tendencies. In the case of this young man, for reasons not yet clear but doubtless related to his puritanical attitude to sex, he had tried to repress his desire for women. Confronted by a situation of temptation, in which his desires threatened to get the upper hand, his symptom would appear—a feeling of unbearable tension. The pregnancy scare was just his way of rationalizing his fear and explaining why he ran away from women. His phobia, like most neurotic symptoms, provided a form of escape, a means of retiring from the conflict situation and at the same time drawing attention away from the unpleasant dilemma that was the real cause of the trouble.

Sometimes the real nature of the conflict appears perfectly obvious, at least to outside observers. In wartime, pilots who had been specially selected for their toughness and mental stability nevertheless fell a prey to neurotic symptoms under the enormous strain of long-continued and desperately dangerous duties. The conflict between the partially repressed desire for self-preservation and the urge to fulfil a duty ultimately became intolerable. Without realizing what was happening or why, a man would succumb to obscure ills and depressions. In such cases the element of conflict counts more than the actual danger. Narrow escapes from drowning or the like rarely cause neuroses, but protracted battles between irreconcilable im-

174

pulses eventually result in breakdown. In experiments with animals the conflict situation can be artificially staged and the process of breakdown watched and studied. The poor beasts are given increasingly complicated choices to make, and for every wrong choice they receive a painful electric shock. The point comes when suddenly the animal breaks down and becomes too trembly and excitable to make even the simplest choice. Again it is the element of conflict and not the severity of the punishment that precipitates the breakdown.

Psycho-analysts contend that problems of love and sex are at the root of most cases of neurotic conflict in humans. Certainly the majority of neurotics seen in civilian life have trouble in their sexual relations. Once food and safety are assured, sexual release and affection become man's most pressing needs, and the two are closely associated. Analysts are at one with poets and romantics in believing that love is the great fount of all human striving. They call it *libido*, a word standing for both the sensual and the spiritual urges of love. Libido is present in infancy. The sensual cuddling and suckling of the infant are the veritable precursors of the passionate embraces of the grown man. Libidinal urges are strong and their manifestations varied, but in the interests of family and social institutions they must be brought under rigorous control. At all costs such inconvenient manifestations as incest and homosexuality must be prevented. The individual must therefore learn to repress if he is not to find himself in a cleft stick. He cannot accept society's standards, including the sense of unutterable disgust for sexual nonconformists, without repressing a great deal of his own instinctive impulses. Unfortunately not everyone succeeds in maintaining a healthy appetite for the legitimate marriage partner, while repressing all socially undesirable tendencies.

Neurotics fail to achieve this adjustment. In an effort to conquer completely all sexual desires of a forbidden nature, they repress too much, and so cannot enjoy uninhibited relations with another person under any circumstances.

Hence impotence, sexual frigidity, guilty feelings, and general *gaucherie* are the prime features of neurosis. The process begins in childhood. The infant possesses libido but lacks adult discrimination. He becomes attached to whoever tends him and, unless restrained, he enjoys himself playing with his own and other persons' bodies. Such behaviour occurs quite openly in societies that make no attempt to suppress their infants' sexual curiosity, but in our community these free and easy ways are usually curbed as soon as they appear, and the child quickly develops a sense of shame that spares his parents' susceptibilities. From then on until puberty he passes through the so-called *latency period*, during which overt sexual behaviour is said to be in abeyance.

The psycho-analytic conception of sexual development agrees with outside evidence in maintaining that the infant's first responses are bisexual. Both boy and girl embrace the mother that suckles them, the question of gender scarcely arises. Heterosexual and homosexual developments come later. A boy of five, however, is old enough to have an acute appreciation of sex differences. He realizes that women have secret, hidden parts to their bodies, and that if he feels fascination or curiosity on the matter he must conceal it from his mother. He knows that he is meant to grow up like father, and he looks forward to the day when he will have the same power and privileges; but meantime he has to play second fiddle, let his father have first place in his mother's affections, and stifle his jealousy as best he can. This stage of development is the notorious *Oedipal Situation*, so named from the legend of Oedipus the foundling who returned as an adult to his native land and unknowingly killed his father and married his own mother. When he found out what he had done remorse made him gouge out his own eyes. Psycho-analysts claim that young children indulge in 'incestuous' fantasies of ousting and replacing the rival parent. When such thoughts appear they arouse intense guilt feelings and fears of punishment, especially punishment by mutilation or castration. Altogether the situation is so unpleasant and frightening that the whole matter is vigorously repressed.

Put so baldly, and in adult vocabulary, this description sounds implausible, but direct observation of children confirms that they do indeed harbour fantasies of the kind. In games like 'fathers and mothers', in scribbled drawings, in dreams, in fact in any situation in which the child's imagination has free play, the theme of Oedipal rivalry with fears of retributive punishment obtains thinly-disguised expression. After a time, however, such is the uncomfortable, guilty flavour of these fantasies, the idea is firmly repressed.

The theory of Oedipal conflict was first propounded by Sigmund Freud from a study of the *free associations* of his neurotic patients. They lay on a couch and let their thoughts flow in a day-dream while the analyst passively recorded what came forth. They were urged to speak aloud and with absolute frankness everything that came to their mind, however personal or unpleasant. In spite of their inhibitions, their thoughts tended to run on to topics that they found most painful. Ideas that ordinarily they would keep repressed would seep through into their reverie, and slowly the conflicts responsible for their symptoms would emerge. Time and time again the Oedipus theme cropped up. Freud did not invent the story; patient after patient related it to him, and such has been the experience of hundreds of analysts ever since.

Confirmation has also come from other sources, from child studies, from researches among primitive tribes, and from observation of psychotics. The ravings of the insane are apt to break the bonds of repression and display in brutal, undisguised form the same incestuous fantasies that the analysts first discovered in neurotics.

The analyst's use of technical terms to describe emotional life gives an exaggerated impression of clarity to the chaotic fantasies with which he deals. Conceptions such as 'incestuous guilt feelings' and 'castration complex' are the analyst's intellectual crystallizations of the general tenor of the patient's half-conscious fears and fancies. In the patient's own mind matters are never so clearly formalized. Incest guilt is not a clear-cut precept derived from formal prohibitions. Normal parents would never talk to their children in such language. Nevertheless, disgust and disapproval in certain contexts are efficiently communicated without verbal instruction. The child senses his parents' unspoken feelings and responds intuitively. In the process, he builds up a fantasy pattern of his own, an unreal, dreamy constellation of emotional ideas. In this private fantasy-world the Oedipus complex takes shape, but it is never verbalized, never conceived in such harsh, unequivocal terms as 'incest' and 'castration' unless an analyst happens to come along and force the patient to consider the meaning of his fantasy.

Normally the Oedipal situation is left behind in childhood, but persons who have experienced a particularly intense parental attachment accompanied by severe guilt feelings may continue for the rest of their lives to try to fight against all sexual responses. In adult life such persons cannot enjoy any sexual relations without conflict because, unconsciously, they continue to associate all sex feeling with the incestuous desires they had to battle against in childhood. They are said to suffer from an Oedipal complex. This complex, or variations of it, accounts for many manifestations of sexual neurosis.

Nothing can so well convey the reality of the Oedipal complex as actual contact with a neurotic sufferer in whom this feature is prominent. A young woman, for example, without in the least realizing what she is doing, may select a man friend resembling her father in a thousand little ways and then, when he makes love to her, she breaks out into a state of acute neurotic tension with all the usual fears and symptoms. The process becomes understandable when the lover is recognized as an unconscious father-substitute with whom sex is impossible.

Frigidity and attachment to a parent-substitute are only two particular examples of the ways in which an unresolved Oedipus complex may manifest. To take another case, a woman may act on the unconscious theme, 'If I can't love father at least I can be like him.' I knew one such person. She suffered from feelings of anxiety and depressed moods that were so severe that she could hardly carry on with her work. Her love life consisted of one long, forlorn attachment to an older man. He had left her years before after a brief flirtation, but she continued to worship him from a distance. She worked at a routine job in a factory. One day she discovered that she had a talent for composing songs. She had no musical training and couldn't even write down the themes that came into her head. What is more, she developed a hoarseness of voice for no discoverable reason which prevented her doing more than hum the tunes. But she flung herself into the business with passionate intensity, and she found a musician who would transcribe and harmonize her inventions. At the same time as all this was going on, she also developed a great fondness for cats, and although she could ill afford to feed them, she took several cats into her home. The inner meaning of her behaviour became clear when it came to light that her father had been a musician who had a great passion for cats. He would have been a singer but for a throat trouble contracted early in his career. He had deserted his family when she was a child and at the height of her emotional attachment to him. Consciously she scorned his memory, but unconsciously she was for ever trying to follow in his footsteps.

Another common manifestation of Oedipal conflict is the man who finds himself impotent with women of his own social set, yet capable of relations with prostitutes. Women at all like his mother are forbidden fruit to him; he shies away from them, or is content to put them on a pedestal of purity. Some mother-fixated men go one stage further and are cold to all women and able to respond only to their own sex. This is the essence of the Freudian interpretation of how homosexuality comes about.

A boy with a too intense and exclusive relationship with his mother develops correspondingly violent guilt feelings and fantasies of punishment by castration. The whole painful constellation of ideas is repressed, and for a time all sexual thoughts are banished, but as the boy grows up and the sexual urges become more insistent the conflict re-awakens. He fights shy of any sexual feeling towards women because they are too like the forbidden feelings towards his mother that he was at such pains to repress. He feels no pleasure at the contemplation of the female form. Their lack of male organs suggests castration and stirs up his re-pressed fears. In his dreams he may visualize the woman's genitals as a dangerous, biting instrument ready to trap and injure him [97].

The best evidence for these interpretations comes from the rich harvest of fantasy produced by free association during many sessions of analysis, but even without this aid one can often discern the Freudian themes running through the life histories given by homosexuals. For example, the point about the undue attachment of the male homosexual to his mother is in many cases easily seen without any special investigation. It is nothing out of the ordinary for an adult homosexual to stick to his mother, to take her about with him and fuss over her like a 'best girl'. Inability to come to terms with women of his own age may be one factor contributing to the symbiosis of bachelor son and lively mother, but the process dates right back to childhood days when the intense mother-son relationship first developed. Both the cases given in Chapter V showed the importance of the mother figure in the lives of these homosexuals. The second of the cases brought out this aspect particularly well. The man wanted to be heterosexual, but when he tried to have relations with women he failed because his inner tensions were too great. Memory of his mother's warnings about 'getting a girl into trouble' filled his mind with guilt, and he had to run away. In addition his feelings of unworthiness and inferiority, and his peculiar sensitiveness about his nasal deformity, lend themselves to interpretation as the outward signs of the unconscious fantasy of having been 'castrated' as a punishment for sexual guilt. Sensitive-ness about imagined or unimportant deformity and neurotic fears of lack of manliness are characteristic of what the analysts call castration complex. It will be remembered how this man emphasized with shame his father's taunt of many years ago, 'You're weaker than I thought you were.'

Many male homosexuals assert that as far back as ever they can remember they have found their own sex attractive, but never have they had the least interest in women sexually. The theory that their trouble arises from repressed or inhibited heterosexuality strikes them as absurd. However, their assertions on this point deserve sceptical treatment; they are on a par with the 'normal' man's assertion that never in his whole life has he had the slightest homoerotic feeling. Analysts maintain that whenever the mental life of a homosexual is thoroughly explored, past heterosexual feelings come to light, and vice versa in the case of heterosexuals. In the first of the cases previously quoted, the man was as exclusive an homosexual as ever one would come across, but he admitted to one slight experience with a girl when he was very young. Actually, this admission cost him more embarrassment than the recital of all his homosexual adventures.

Granting, as I think we must, that fantastic notions born of guilt and fear do operate in neurotic minds, it is still an open question how important they are as determinants of homosexuality. Oedipal fantasies have been laid bare in thousands of psychological investigations. Whether a subject is healthy or neurotic, homosexual or heterosexual, the persistent analyst will eventually unearth some traces of Oedipal conflict. Even when the conflict rages with peculiar severity, the outcome is not always the same. Some men find refuge in impotence, some in prostitutes, and some in homosexuality. Other factors must come into the picture. The Oedipal theory explains certain features of sexual development, but it by no means tells the whole story.

Apart from the abnormalities already mentioned, of which the commonest are frigididy in women and homosexuality in men, a reaction against normal sexual relations may show itself in other peculiarities, such as exhibitionism or fetishism. Exhibitionists derive their sexual pleasure from exposing their private parts in front of a member of the opposite sex. Fetishists use personal articles belonging to the opposite sex, usually pieces of clothing or undergarments, to excite themselves while masturbating. Traces of these tendencies may appear in the love play of normal persons, but they amount to real perversions only when they constitute the sole methods of obtaining sexual release. Both forms of perversion are usually found in men, and they clearly represent a form of inhibited heterosexual approach. The exhibitionist has to keep a safe distance from the woman; the fetishist cannot bear a real woman at all and contents himself with a harmless, inanimate symbol. As with other perversions, once the individual has become accustomed to respond sexually in a particular situation, his pattern becomes strongly conditioned and difficult to alter. In these two perversions the sexual drive is diverted from the normal love object to a highly artificial substitute. The selection of a lady's shoe, for instance, as the only means of sexual gratification, is a psychological quirk that cannot have been inborn. Such extreme examples make it easier to appreciate how choice of love object may be determined psychologically rather than genetically. The homosexual differs from these other types of pervert in that his sexual pattern does involve a close relationship with another person. This encourages emotional maturation, and is partly responsible for the fact that many homosexuals achieve a commendable personality development in spite of their sexual handicap.

Reduced to the simplest and most general terms, Freudian theory states that sexual perversion is due to a neurotic fear of heterosexuality, deeply instilled during early life, and arising out of the child's intense, conflictual feelings towards his parents. Clearly this explanation will not account for all forms of homosexual behaviour, and indeed the psycho-analysts do not claim that it does. The theory does not apply to homosexuality indulged in as a matter of convenience when the opposite sex is not available, for in such instances no heterosexual inhibition exists. It cannot very easily account for persistent bisexuality, or for the experimental homosexuality of adolescents, and it does not explain why some homosexuals identify strongly with the characteristics of the opposite sex while others do not. On all these matters the analysts have other theories.

The primary Freudian theory outlined above refers to the compulsive, obligatory type of homosexuality and accounts quite plausibly for a number of facts. Homosexuals themselves commonly recall the first awakening of their deviant impulses in childhood, or at least early in puberty. When cross-sex identification occurs dissatisfaction with the assigned sex role is usually apparent to relatives by the time the child is ten, and often before then. As will be seen from the discussion in the next chapter, independent investigators have demonstrated that disturbed or anomalous relationships with parents, roughly on the lines expected by Freudian theory, occur particularly frequently in the early histories of homosexuals. As a further point of confirmation analysts also claim that the recall of Oedipal guilt feelings sometimes enables a homosexual patient to conquer his aversion and to form heterosexual attachments for the first time. This does not happen often, however, and when it does all sorts of factors might be responsible. The occasional cure does not really help the theory very much.

If the homosexual condition arises from a neurotic phobia of heterosexuality, one would expect it to occur among the type of persons most prone to such symptoms, namely those of morbidly anxious, unstable personality. Indeed many psycho-analysts, such as Bergler and Cappon [52], have commented on the emotional immaturity and neurotic disposition of the sexual deviants they see. Edmund Bergler [31], in particular, emphasized that they are *sick people*, so much so that 'Even if the outer world were to leave them in peace, homosexuals could lead miserable lives'. Yet systematic inquiries, such as those of Curran and Parr [72], Liddicoat [232] and Loeser [234], have failed to confirm this, and point to the existence of a large proportion of apparently non-neurotic homosexuals. Furthermore, the results of psychological tests given to homosexual volunteers (see page 51) suggest that they are not particularly maladjusted. Some analysts, such as Bieber [35] disagree so violently they can only challenge the validity of the tests, suggesting that the homosexual's neurotic conflicts are so deeply repressed that he can put up a show of equanimity in the face of superficial inquiry. Perhaps so, but this interpretation, like so much else in psycho-analytic literature, savours of the 'heads I win tails you lose' type of argument.

The plain fact is that many people find in homosexuality a workable adaptation to life. Unlike a person suffering from impotence or frigidity, who obtains no release from sexual tension, and finds himself frustrated in all his most intimate relationships, the homosexual does obtain satisfaction, both physical and emotional, and so long as he can bear with social disapproval, he achieves a passable adjustment. Though he has not solved his sexual conflicts in the best possible manner, he has at least arrived at a solution which leaves him free of immediate tension and capable of developing his personality in other directions. The point has been put very clearly by the psychiatrist Dr. K. Soddy.

It is not within everyone's power to develop completely, and a small minority of both sexes remain in a state of homosexuality. Nevertheless their emotional adjustment may be stable and secure at the immature level; their physical means of gratification may remain within society's canon of adolescent conduct, and meanwhile the development of other aspects of their character and intellect may proceed normally. When this happens no social evil will result, other than loss to society of potential parents [343].

Provided he accepts his position philosophically and mixes with others of like mind, the homosexual can leave behind the emotional turmoil that originally drove him away from women. Neurotic conflict only remains evident in those who do not fully accept either homosexual or heterosexual adjustment. The man with the pregnancy phobia was like that: he could not face women, nor could he accept homosexuality. As a result his conflict was never stilled and preoccupation with it ruined his work and prevented the maturation of his personality in other respects. His was a case ripe for psychological treatment, whereas the mature homosexual, one who has arrived at a calm outlook and a tolerable way of life, would scarcely be helped by a revival of long-resolved conflicts. In many cases the mature homosexual suffers from his efficiently repressed heterosexuality no more than the mature married man suffers from the complete repression of homosexuality. Explanation in terms of 'burnt out' or 'completely resolved' conflict accounts for the many homosexuals who, though nervous, shy, and inhibited in their younger days, became later in life mature and gifted personalities without ceasing to practise their perversion.

A more serious objection to psycho-analytic theories is the variability of the interpretations advanced by different exponents of the art. An orthodox Freudian pondering the feelings expressed by a homosexual patient may well convince himself that the key to the man's problem lies in the unconscious guilty association of women and incest. An analyst[1] of another school of thought confronted with a similar patient will find other themes more important. He may perhaps feel that the real cause of the man's fear of women is an early experience of rejection by a mother who was cold and contemptuous towards all the males in her family. Emotional development being such an individual process, this clash of interpretations could be due to genuine differences between one case and the next. If taken too far, however, this line of thought could undermine the whole psycho-analytic approach by making generalizations impossible. A further complication arises

---

[1] Strictly speaking, only the Freudians count as true psycho-analysts, and other words should be used for Jungians, Adlerians, Kleinians, etc., but here the name is used in a wide sense to cover all varieties.

from the natural tendency of the patient to dwell upon whatever themes best evoke the interest of his particular analyst. Preconceived ideas about the causes of homosexuality, or of any other condition, may thus achieve a spurious self-fulfilment.

These dampening considerations do not refute the psycho-analytic theories, but they point to several reasons for caution. First, one has to distinguish interpretations, such as the Oedipal theme, which apparently apply to large numbers of cases, and may thus be susceptible to statistical verification, from interpretations that apply to just a few individuals and have correspondingly slight general validity or interest. Second, one has to realize that psycho-analysis is an intuitive process, often leading to contradictory interpretations. For all these reasons psycho-analytic conclusions must be regarded as tentative ideas that require point by point verification before they can be accepted as scientific theories. A common means of checking and refining scientific theories is to make predictions from them and see if they work out. Most analysts would say that human nature is too complex for it to be possible to identify the children who will later become homosexuals. If this is a genuine uncertainty, and not merely a lack of courage to put their theories to the test, it really means that the causes pin-pointed by analysts are less crucial, or less well understood, than their writings seem to suggest.

CHAPTER IX

SOME PSYCHOLOGICAL FACTORS

1. Searching for Explanations

Homosexual impulses are abnormal only in relation to our own culture's standards of correct conduct. The point requiring explanation is not the existence of homo-eroticism, but the inability of a minority to conform with the social taboo against it. Why is it that the majority either lose interest or repress homosexual feelings, whereas a minority, in spite of society's discouragement, maintain an unshakeable preference for their own sex? According to Freudian theory, this fixed preference becomes established in early childhood through the emotional interaction between the infant and his parents. The life stories of many homosexuals bear witness to the peculiar upbringing to which they have been subjected [235]; but in order to put the matter on a better scientific footing one needs something more than a haphazard collection of individual and possibly unrepresentative case histories.

A more systematic method of tackling the question would be by deliberate sampling of a wide range of homosexual types, and a careful point by point comparison of specific features of their upbringing with those of a corresponding group of heterosexuals of similar social and cultural background. Unfortunately, researches of this kind have rarely been accomplished. As has already been pointed out, grave difficulties stand in the way of assembling and investigating a fair sample of male homosexuals. The co-ordinated efforts of a research team such as Kinsey's might succeed, but so far psychiatrists have shown no inclination to initiate research or foundations to sponsor the project. Distaste for the whole business, and the professional man's fear of compromising his reputation by displaying too great interest, have had a lot to do with this neglect. In consequence, clear scientific evidence as to the important causative factors is simply not available.

Perusal of psychiatric literature yields little more than a collection of opinions based, for the most part, on personal observation of a limited number of cases without any attempt at systematic comparisons with normal groups. The psychiatrist notices that a number of homosexual men in his clinical practice are only sons. He therefore gives out the opinion—and he may be right—that this is a factor in the genesis of the condition. But he does not and cannot check his impression scientifically, for that would involve a prolonged and systematic statistical inquiry. Limited experience and personal bias affect nearly all psychiatric opinions on this topic and give rise to the most varied and contradictory viewpoints. One psychiatrist will assert that in his experience seduction plays a major role in homosexual development [87], while another pours scorn upon the same idea. A meticulous review of the contradictory assertions contained in psychiatric literature, appropriately labelled with the date and author's name, might give an impression of studious learning, but it would be a waste of labour. The best one can do is to give an over-all picture of the more authoritative opinions which have gained wide acceptance, and to attempt a reasonable synthesis taking into account the evidence from non-psychiatric sources that has already been discussed.

No single causal explanation can possibly cover all cases. All kinds of psychological influences may combine to tip the scales towards homosexual development, and the factors important in one case may differ radically from those most concerned in another. Generalizations true for many cases will not apply to all. With these reservations in mind one may now consider some of the psychological explanations, and some of the evidence supporting them.

2. *Parental Behaviour*

Laymen, psychiatrists and psycho-analysts alike commonly believe too intense or possessive mothering risks making a boy homosexual [156]. Neodoma [276] and Nash [273] note that, in addition to having an unhealthily fierce attachment to their mothers, many male homosexuals have either no interest in their father or else positively dislike him. While the dominating mother gets most of the blame, some observers, including Anna Freud [108], have pointed out that the weak, unsatisfactory, or absent father forms an important part of the picture [5], [236], [10], [382]. Psycho-analysts stress these points they fit so well the expectations of the Oedipal theory. In his classic exposition of psycho-analytic theory [97] Fenichel comments: 'The majority of homosexuals not only present an Oedipus love for their mothers, just as do neurotic individuals, but for the most part the intensity of the mother fixation is even more pronounced.' Sometimes the devotion to mother is not unconscious at all but frankly talked about. 'The homosexual man identifies himself with his frustrating mother in one particular respect. Like her he loves men.' The Oedipal situation also involves rivalry and rejection of father. Fenichel goes on to say: 'The probability of a homosexual orientation is increased the more a boy tends to identify with his mother. Children in general tend to identify with the parent from whom they have experienced the most impressive frustrations. This explains Freud's findings that those men are more inclined to become homosexuals who have had a weak father or no father at all, who, in other words, were frustrated in crucial things by their mother.' In a typical case history one finds father a meek, unassertive underdog who lets mother rule the home. Sometimes one finds no father at all; he is dead, divorced, deserted, or gone to gaol. Or else, what amounts to the same thing emotionally, father cuts himself off from his children by an over-stern or aloof attitude. In all these cases mother dominates the children's lives. If, in addition, mother adopts a possessive attitude and keeps her offspring tied to her apron strings, and if it happens she has an only child who has no brother or sister relationships to offset the maternal domination, then the situation becomes that much more acute.

Both the cases described in Chapter 5 conformed to the dominant mother pattern. In the first case father was a weak individual, despised by his son. He kept in the background and let his wife run everything. In the second case father was said to be aloof and unsympathetic, whereas mother was the good friend and stable companion.

In any collection of case histories one finds the same pattern repeated again and again. The first few examples from G. W. Henry's book *Sex Variants*—a valuable source of case histories—serve to illustrate the point. The very first case, Thomas B., happens not to run to type. His father was a violent-tempered, frightening person against whom his mother was passive and defenceless. The second case, Nathan B., is more typical. His father was extremely puritanical, rigid, and a slave to discipline; he used to strap the children frequently. Nathan was a timid child, afraid of his father, afraid of rough boys, and generally a 'sissy'. His mother was highly strung, but energetic. He was the youngest child and he was petted outrageously by his mother and his elder sister. In the third case, Rodney S., father was an alcoholic, who was garrulous and popular with strangers, but hardly opened his mouth at home. He spent periods away having treatment. Mother was a person of 'charm and breeding' who was affectionate with her son and liberal in her attitude to sex. Rodney began by being un-selfconsciously attracted to both sexes, but he had no special ambition for masculinity. He went to work in theatrical circles, and slowly developed a definite preference for relations with other men. The fourth case, Michael D., is classical. He was the only son of a family dominated by women. Mother was a competent business executive who bossed the home. Father was a submissive man often in disgrace in the eyes of his womenfolk. His wife kept him waiting years before it suited her to marry him. His son had scant respect for him. Michael himself was a nervous child, handicapped by bad health, and teased as a 'sissy'. He felt very lonely. He had physical experiences with women prostitutes, but only men could give him emotional as well as physical satisfaction, and so he slowly developed exclusively homosexual inclinations. In the fifth case, Eric D., father was 'inclined to be quiet' and 'slightly effeminate'. Mother, an ex-school-teacher, was 'mildly domineering' and 'somewhat a matriarch', but she was never demonstrative in her affections. As Eric expressed it: 'I never had any affection and I always wanted it.' Malcolm E., the sixth case, said his father was 'an extremely indifferent sort of man'. Mother 'took the initiative' and saw to the disciplining of the children. She had to urge her husband to give her some support. Malcolm used to help her about the house, much more so than his brother did. Well over half conform to the pattern of absent or unsatisfactory father and a mother who dominates the child's life to an unusual degree. But Henry's examples also show how other factors obtrude in even the most clear-cut instances of mother fixation [167].

These impressions need confirmation by comparisons with heterosexual groups, in order to show that the peculiarities recorded really do occur more often among homosexuals. Since the homosexuals in question are usually neurotic patients, they ought to be compared with other neurotic patients who are not homosexual, since it could be argued that mother fixation is a feature of male neurosis in general and not of male homosexuality in particular. Several such comparisons have been reported. P. J. O'Connor [280] compared fifty neurotic men, seen in the course of psychiatric work in the Royal Air Force, with another fifty who consulted him about homosexual problems. The homosexuals mostly came along on account of symptoms of anxiety or depression, and indeed they had as many psychiatric symptoms as the heterosexual neurotics. The homosexuals differed from the other neurotics in having a much higher frequency of attachment to mother more than to father (62 per cent compared with 8 per cent), poor relation ship with father (28 per cent compared with 6 per cent)

and a history of long absences of father during their childhood and adolescence (24 per cent compared with 2 per cent).
They also differed in more often choosing artistic hobbies
and disliking robust sports. O'Connor concluded that un-
aggressive, artistic men devoted to their mothers were the
prototypes of male homosexuality.

In another study of the same topic, C. H. Jonas [198]
obtained similar results by putting a series of set questions
to 60 overt homosexual male patients and to a corresponding number of non-homosexual controls. He found that 43
of the homosexuals stated their unqualified favouring of
mother over father, as compared with only 18 of the controls, whereas only one of the controls expressed hatred of
father compared with 9 of the homosexuals. In a study
based on case histories collected at Maudsley Hospital,
West [372] copied out the descriptions of each parent
from the notes of 50 overt male homosexual patients and
50 non-homosexual neurotic controls. The descriptions
were given to an independent judge for rating, who did not
know the diagnosis. It was found that a combination of
abnormally intense relationship with mother and definitely
unsatisfactory relationship with father occurred commonly
among the homosexuals but not among the controls. A
wide range of defects were found in the fathers of the
homosexuals, including denigrating attitudes, aloofness,
ineptitude, absence from home, and inability to hold their
own against a dominating wife. The mothers of the homosexuals were some of them soft and indulgent, others
strong and domineering, but in either case they tended to
be bound up with their sons to an unusual degree. It was
the combination of unsatisfactory father and dominating
mother which was particularly characteristic of the male
homosexual patients' backgrounds.

Psycho-analysts do not often go in for organized research, but in 1962 Irving Bieber [35] published the results
of a survey among New York members of the Society of
Medical Psycho-analysts concerning the personal characteristics and family backgrounds of male homosexuals

under treatment. The analysts were sent a long list of questions which had to be answered with respect to both homosexual and heterosexual male patients, so as to provide a basis of comparison. Of course the patients concerned were a very selected group, consisting of men of favoured educational and economic status, who were willing to invest a substantial sum in protracted private treatment. The parents of the homosexuals were described as much more peculiar than those of the heterosexual patients. The majority of the homosexuals' mothers had formed a close, binding intimate relationship with their deviant son, favouring him over their other children and even over their husband, spending an enormous amount of time with him, exchanging confidences with him, over-protecting him, discouraging masculine attitudes and interfering with heterosexual interests. Most of these mothers were themselves sexually frigid or puritanical. The sons' feelings towards them were strong but mixed, and often resentful. In contrast, the fathers of the homosexuals were usually emotionally detached or actively hostile, favouring their other children and often expressing open contempt for the deviant son, who reciprocated with fear and hatred of the father. Most of the homosexuals' parents had very poor marital relationships with each other, and often the mothers disparaged and tried to dominate the fathers. The investigators concluded that nearly all the homosexual patients had had highly abnormal upbringings, worse than the heterosexual group, and that as children they had acted as scapegoats who brought out the worst in their unhappy parents.

The investigations so far mentioned have all concerned the parents of neurotic patients, which leaves open the question whether similar disturbances would have been found in the backgrounds of homosexuals at large. P. R. Miller [261], who studied fifty male homosexuals of 'effeminate' type, who were serving sentences in an American Federal Prison, found that the commonest parental pattern was what he called an 'over-protective' mother combined with a negative, hostile or absent father. It is impressive that a group of deviants of utterly different class, circumstance and behaviour from the New York analytic patients should have had similar features of parental background, but still both were abnormal groups.

In Westwood's English survey [378], he collected a sample of 127 male homosexual volunteers from the community, who might be expected to be better representative of homosexuals at large. The most obvious contrast between his results and the surveys of patients or prisoners was that a half of the homosexual volunteers had come from reasonably happy homes and complete homes, in which neither parent was dead or absent for long periods. Even so, 38 per cent reported unsatisfactory relations with their father, 44 per cent were of the opinion that their mother was possessive or over-protective in some way, and 57 per cent named their mother whereas only 29 per cent named their father when asked which was the more dominant parent. It looks as if the community homosexuals showed similar background tendencies, but less often, and less extreme. Unfortunately, Westwood's investigation included no control group of heterosexuals with which to compare these incidence figures, so the findings remain suggestive rather than conclusive.

Eva Bene [23] succeeded in recruiting 83 self-confessed male homosexuals from the community, and also the same number of married men of roughly equivalent age and class. She gave to both groups a test consisting of a series of descriptive items of character or behaviour. The volunteers were asked to think back to their early years and to say which member of their childhood family most closely fitted each description. For example, one item read 'used to nag too much'. Of the homosexuals, 35 per cent applied this unfavourable comment to their mothers, compared with only 13 per cent of the married men. A quarter of the homosexuals, but only 6 per cent of the married men, thought the comment 'did not love me very much' true of their fathers. Bene's results amply confirmed that homosexual men recall bad relations with their fathers; but she did not find the expected evidence of strong attachment to mother or maternal over-solicitude. Indeed, certain negative evaluations of mothers, like 'used to be mean to me' were reported more often by the homosexuals. Maybe male homosexuals who have got away from binding, maternal attachments, and are freely practising their perversion in the community at large, are better able to express their resentment of maternal domination than a group of anxious, neurotic homosexuals. Be that as it may, the evidence from all these systematic investigations agrees that unsatisfactory fathers are at least as prominent as dominating mothers in the backgrounds of male homosexuals.

Kräupl Taylor [358] has pointed out that one cannot deduce with certainty that parental mismanagement causes homosexuality, since the recollections of adult homosexuals may be subject to bias, and even if the parental behaviour described really took place, it might have been provoked by the homosexual child's innate peculiarities. A soft girlish boy might well arouse a mother's compassion and a father's contempt. The answer to both these criticisms lies in long-term research, beginning with an objective scrutiny of parental behaviour from the moment a child is born, before any question of disappointment with the child's personality arises, and ending with a study of sexual adjustment in adult life. Something approaching this was done by W. McCord and others [240], who had the good fortune to have access to a mass of psychological information on the upbringing and reactions of a large sample of Boston schoolboys who had been selected to participate in a delinquency prevention scheme known as the Cambridge Somerville Project. Observation began, not at birth, but around the age of eleven, when psychologists and social workers began to study the boys and take histories from their parents. Observation continued for at least five years, by which time sexual problems of adolescence had become evident.

Some Psychological Factors

Analysing the material sometime later, the McCords identified three kinds of sexually disturbed adolescent. The anxious-inhibited type feared any form of sex. The 'perverted' type indulged in a variety of disapproved activities (e.g. public masturbation, voyeurism, fetishism, exhibitionism) in addition to ordinary heterosexual outlets. The 'feminine' attitude type were clearly unhappy in the male role, preferring girls' company and girls' pursuits, and being liable to overt homosexual activity. Compared with the sexually undisturbed youths of similar class and ethnic background, all three types of sexually maladjusted boys came from parental homes characterized by sexual anxiety and prudishness, maternal authoritarianism, quarrels between parents, and paternal punitiveness. This finding fitted quite neatly the psycho-analytic view that a repressive, anxiety-ridden type of upbringing favours the development of sexual disorders of all kinds. In addition, the investigators noted that the 'feminine' type deviants had been exposed to particularly unsatisfactory fathers. Half of the fathers were absent from home most of the time, most of them openly despised or neglected their sons. A third of the fathers and three-fifths of the mothers were clearly neurotic or mentally ill. These findings suggest that sexually repressive homes are particularly liable to generate homosexual or 'feminized' sons if the father is absent or is a rejecting, aggressive disordered person who forces the child to view masculinity as an unattractive role. Again one sees the importance of the father figure as well as the mother. The authors commented that the personalities of these parents were clearly abnormal in the objective assessment of outside observers, and that some of their peculiarities must have been present long before the birth of the deviant son.

3. Development of Sex Roles

The McCords' research draws attention to some of the factors that may upset a child's acceptance of the social role appropriate to his sex, and thus lead, indirectly, to a homosexual orientation. Observations have been quoted earlier (see page 165) to the effect that by the time they are four children with physical sex deformities have developed a strong and possibly irreversible identification with the gender assigned to them. The typically distinct social attitudes and reactions of normal boys and girls are easily demonstrated at age three or four by observing their reactions to standardized doll-play situations set up by an experimenter. Boys more often make the dolls behave in a physically aggressive manner; girls tend to limit their aggressions to indirect or verbal expressions. Moreover the girls' aggressions tend to take a socially approved form, such as spanking the naughty child, whereas the boys' aggressive play more often takes the form of hurtful, destructive acts. R. R. Sears [332] has led a number of fascinating investigations of parents' behaviour with their infant children, and has tried to pin-point the influences which help or hinder this clear differentiation of the infant's gender role. Four factors were found to be important. First, was sexual anxiety on the part of parents, and especially the father, which discouraged the child's sexual interests or curiosity. Second, was the mother's punitiveness and non-permissiveness towards the child's aggressive behaviour. Third, was frequent use of punishment and ridicule. Fourth, was severe demands on the child to conform to correct social habits at table, toilet, etc. All four influences favoured strong conformity with typical female attitudes on the part of girls, but favoured feminine attitudes on the part of boys. From this work it would seem that the ideal feminine type is produced by a strict upbringing with insistence upon social conformity and suppression of aggression, whereas the same medicine applied to a boy may produce a miserable sissy. The ideally masculine boy, it seemed, was more often disciplined by father, and by physical punishment rather than withdrawal of love, was encouraged to fight back if attacked, and was treated more leniently while learning social habits. Such observations fit in well with what clinicians like C. C. Hewitt [171] have been saying about the character structure of feminine identified male homosexuals. According to Hewitt, a wide variety of early experiences or conflicts may teach a boy that masculine attitudes are dangerous, reprehensible or unrewarding, and thus engender a homosexual character who is passive, compliant and compulsively self-effacing.

These considerations introduce a new set of factors not taken into account in the simplified version of Freudian Oedipal theory given in the last chapter, in which undue attachment to mother was the most important element. The need for a growing boy to have a certain freedom of expression, and an adequately masculine father upon whom to model himself if he is to assume his expected social role, provides a plausible reason for the observed fact that fathers as well as mothers have a decisive influence upon their sons' sexual orientation.

In matters of sex role the boy normally identifies with his father, and takes upon himself his father's manly, assertive approach to life. Though customs are changing, man still retains something of his lord and master role, and is allowed and expected to show more leadership, self-assertiveness, and adventurousness than the submissive, demure, dependent woman. The process of *identification*, whereby the child adopts as his own the ways of thought of his parents, is something more than deliberate imitation. However much they may seem on the surface to battle against parental injunctions, children need the security of parental approval, and they do in fact absorb most of their parents' ideas and attitudes. If it were not so, cultural characteristics could hardly be passed on from one generation to the next. Unfortunately they absorb anxieties and prejudices as well as more wholesome values. A father who is himself unhappy and uncertain in his role as husband may unwittingly inculcate a corresponding fear and distaste in his son. Moreover, a father who is conspicuously lacking in interest and affection, and arouses negative feelings in his son, thereby discourages the emotional attachment upon which the identification process depends.

Development of Sex Roles

Absence of father from the home may contribute to a boy's difficulty in establishing his sexual role. P. O. Tiller [364] compared the families of Danish sailors with a control group of families of similar social level. The mothers whose husbands were persistently absent tended to overprotect their children. As a result, their boys displayed a distinct excess of feminine traits. At the same time, many of these boys also showed a tendency to fight against their own feminine characteristics by a compensatory assertiveness of masculine status and attitude in particular situations. Thus, pressures which drive one boy towards femininity and possible homosexuality may turn another boy into a tough, defensive, hypermasculine personality.

Although successful copulation has nothing directly to do with masculine or feminine interests in other respects, a boy's close psychological identification with femininity may cause him to reject or repress heterosexual behaviour in much the same way as others reject homosexual behaviour. But very often the process of cross-sex identification goes less far, and a youth may feel inadequate and a failure as a man, although he would still like to be one if he could. Even so, he may be unwilling to experiment heterosexually because he fears to fail in this as he has already failed in other masculine pursuits. The boy who has had no adequate father figure to emulate, and has had no help in counteracting maternal domination, will likely prove timid and unassertive at school, and may be ostracized as a sissy because he lacks the toughness and aggressiveness of the average boy. These experiences will drive him still further away from conventional masculine interests, and will further undermine his confidence and his ability to establish relations with members of the opposite sex.

Difficulty in conforming with an uncongenial or too exacting masculine social role may cause some boys to take what seems to them the easier path towards homosexuality. It was pointed out in Chapter I how some primitive communities that make heavy demands upon their menfolk in the way of prowess in hunting and warfare, also have a *berdache* system which provides an officially recognized homosexual alternative for the occasional misfit. Our own culture makes less spectacular demands, but all the same men are supposed to be effective economic providers, to take the lead in sexual matters, to initiate advances, to show a certain competence. In order to win a desirable mate, the man must arrive at a socially acceptable compromise between the moral dicta regarding continence and chastity and the need to prove his worth as a lover. The young man with too many scruples finds himself at a disadvantage. For some temperaments the task is far from easy.

Dissatisfaction with their sex role occurs most often in women, owing to the fact that our society tends to despise some of the qualities which women are expected to possess. The feminine-mannered homosexual man evokes universal contempt, as if feminization were the worst fate possible. If a masculine group has petty squabbles it earns the reproach, 'You're behaving like a bunch of women.' Jobs with the best pay and the most prestige usually go to men, while the task of looking after the home and children has not quite lost its inferior status. Reaction against an imposed inferiority explains why some women assume an excessive heartiness, take to trousers or tailored suits, and find pleasure in masculine pursuits.

Of course, not all shy men are homosexuals nor all aggressive women lesbians, but the possession of temperamental features contrary to the accepted criteria of masculinity and femininity makes sexual adjustment more difficult. The shy man inclines to run away from women, the aggressive woman finds that men run from her. Such persons may regress to an earlier phase of adolescent homosexuality if their first attempts at heterosexual experience prove too humiliating.

Those who believe that the homosexual trend establishes itself once and for all in infancy, as a result of Oedipal conflicts, find it hard to accept that the young adult's social frustrations can have anything to do with the determination of his sexual orientation. But a predominantly homosexual youth may sometimes overcome his inhibitions (provided they are not too deeply ingrained) though experience with a sympathetic and not too demanding woman, and it seems reasonable that the reverse process may sometimes occur and a precariously heterosexual youth become inhibited as a result of a painful rebuff or an initial failure. Psychologists are coming round more and more to the view that, though emotional trends may become established in childhood, they are susceptible to reinforcement or counteraction by later influences. Admittedly the man who has led an exclusively homosexual life for many years cannot change his ways, but that may be due to the strong conditioning of physical experiences and emotional attachments rather than to the fossilization of reaction patterns in infancy. In fact, when a homosexual succeeds in changing his outlook as a result of psycho-analytic treatment, the change depends as much on the strength of his current motivations as upon his ability to resuscitate and deal with Oepidal guilt.

4. More Psychological Interpretations

Quite apart from the embellishments and variations introduced by later analysts [134] Freud himself worked out many more explanatory themes than the simple version of Oedipal theory given in the last chapter. He recognized that not all male homosexuals were mother-bound boys. For instance, boys who have lost their mothers may become homosexually orientated through trying to win the affections of the remaining parent by playing the role of substitute wife. Freud suggested that one reason for the prevalence of male homosexuality in ancient Greece was that boys were tended by male slaves. An all-male atmosphere, as in a family of brothers, may have the effect of instilling a sense of hyper-masculinity and a contempt for women's ways that seriously interfere with the development of relations with girls. The sporty 'man's man', who has no time for the petty limitations of domesticity, exemplifies this type.

The one common factor in all these situations is some

hindrance to relations with the opposite sex. It may be through Oedipal guilt, it may be through maladroitness or 'sissiness', but whatever the most appropriate interpretation in a particular case it amounts to this: homosexual adaptation occurs when heterosexual adaptation proves too difficult. That is why a too puritanical upbringing can be dangerous. A child instilled with disgust for normal sex is all the more likely to try furtive, substitute outlets. The history of sexual perverts, homosexuals and otherwise, suggests very strongly that an over-moralistic upbringing can have a most evil influence. The remorseless progression from sex taboos, through fear and guilt, to repression and homosexuality, was clearly shown in the case in the previous chapter of the man with a pregnancy phobia.

But what of the Oedipal theory? First the case of the pregnancy phobia was treated as an excellent example of Oedipal guilt, now it is used as a stick to beat the puritans! The contradiction is more apparent than real, for the two interpretations are complementary. A dominant mother fosters Oedipal conflict, and at the same time her puritanical attitude ensures that the conflict will be accompanied by the maximum of guilt feeling. Thus in homosexual cases the Oedipal conflict provides the central theme, but any number of subsidiary themes may appear and contribute to the total effect. It is essential to read actual analytic case reports in order to understand the wide variety of emotional dynamics that can enter into the genesis of homosexuality. In some cases such factors as inability to cope with the rivalry of more successful brothers, or intense jealousy of father, may play a decisive role [221, 230, 310, 330].

Freud's more detailed theories of sexual development are particularly controversial, but deserve some mention on account of their relevance to homosexuality [58]. He postulated several stages of infantile sexual development, which take place so closely in unison with character development that the two might be considered different aspects of the same process [109]. He believed that parental mishandling could cause delayed or incomplete passage from one stage to the next, and that this would lead to permanent distortions of both sexuality and character in adult life. One important transition was the transfer of the infant's erotic interest from his own body to that of other persons. If the earlier auto-erotic phase partially persisted, the individual might in later life become homosexual through seeking love objects resembling himself as closely as possible. Freud called this distortion narcissism, from the name of the young man in Greek legend who fell in love with his own reflection [112]. According to Freud, both narcissism and Oedipal guilt feature in the production of homosexual orientation. The male homosexual resolves his Oedipal conflict by identifying with his mother and assuming her sexual orientation. It follows that his choice of love object must be a boy like himself, someone he can love as his mother used to love him when he was young, or at any rate as he would have liked her to love him. An unconscious desire to find another 'mother's little boy' explains why some male homosexuals chase after children.

Arrest of sexual development at a narcissistic level is supposed to lead to a narcissistic personality—a vain, self-glorifying individual who delights in devoted admiration but gives little warmth in return. The narcissistic type of homosexual might be expected to take great interest in his own appearance, cultivating body-building exercises if he has a masculine self-image, or adoring perfume, make-up and dressing up if he has a feminine identification. Having captured the affections of a young man, he would be apt to make self-centred and unrealistic demands upon his partner's exclusive attention, only to turn away without a second thought as soon as some more promising admirer appeared on the scene. Some observers maintain that these very qualities of vanity, self-display and shallowness in personal relationships typify the behaviour of homosexuals, but this impression has never really been confirmed. The fickle and exhibitionistic conduct of some affected city coteries conforms superficially to this pattern, but these comprise only a small and untypical minority, and even in their case their outlook is probably influenced as much by social pressures as by individual temperament. Moreover, narcissistic traits also appear all too often among heterosexuals! According to theory, lovers of little boys ought to be particularly narcissistic in personality, but so far as I know clinicians have not noticed this to be the case. Nor does it appear, when one considers the most obviously narcissistic characters, that they have any special predilection for child molesting.

Possibly narcissism plays a part in some cases of homosexuality, but not generally. In fact Freud himself was more cautious about making generalizations than some of his followers. He was well aware that 'In men the most complete mental masculinity can be combined with inversion', and he emphasized that 'Psycho-analytic research is most decidedly opposed to any attempt at separating off homosexuals from the rest of mankind'.

Freud identified other stages in erotic development. He believed that bodily sexual feelings are at first diffuse. Later they centre primarily upon the mouth, at which time sucking gives the most satisfaction. Later again they centre upon the anal area, at which stage the infant delights in bowel movements and anal stimuli, spends an unnecessarily long time on the chamber pot, and has to be persuaded to let go his stool [113]. Only in the final stage does the genital zone become the prime source of erotic pleasure. In normal adults, though genital pleasure predominates, remnants of earlier stages remain, and some degree of arousal occurs from stimulation of other zones. Since kissing does not qualify as a perversion in our culture, oral contacts remain under less of a taboo than anal practices. Brought up as we are to think of latrines, excrement and all their associations with disgust, the thought of buggery seems to many persons exquisitely horrible, and the way dogs sniff uninhibitedly at each other's anus and excrement they find most revolting. Admittedly faeces carry germs, but the disgust is acquired, and scarcely proceeds from rational considerations. The mental process is not dissimilar from that of the hysterical girl who finds intercourse impossible because the penis passes urine. Before the anal disgust reaction becomes established, infants have to be weaned from the habit of playing with faeces. Lunatics, who lose their repressions as they lose their sanity, sometimes revert to an infantile interest in their own excrement.

Apart from perverts who never relinquish the pleasures of the anal zone, Freud recognized a class of adults in whom anal sexuality is still active, although repressed and manifest only in disguised form. The psycho-analysis of certain abnormal personality types, namely those characterized by a combination of obsessive orderliness, parsimony, and obstinacy, led him to conclude that such persons are influenced by strong, repressed anal interests. The obstinacy and pleasure in hoarding he interpreted as adult relics of the infantile habit of obstinately hoarding faeces. Their neatness, orderliness, and excessive cleanliness he interpreted as reactions against repressed desires to do the exact opposite—to play with dirt. This connection between miserly characteristics and unconscious love of dirt had long been apparent in such everyday expressions as 'filthy lucre', 'making his pile', the 'goose that lays the golden egg', and (in German) 'Dukatenscheisser'. Psycho-analysis of these so-called anal characters confirms that their inner fantasy life tends to be preoccupied with bowel functions and associated matters [110].

In view of the homosexual's predilection for anal intercourse one might expect him to show other signs of an anal character pattern. In fact, the fussiness and tidiness of some passive male homosexuals has been cited as evidence of anal traits, but one cannot set too much store by this, since the same traits can be accounted for as part of a feminine identification. Obviously, not all men who indulge in buggery are anally fixated in the Freudian sense. Since they cannot have normal intercourse, homosexuals must find some other mechanically convenient form of gratification.

Some Psychological Factors

The man who takes part in buggery need be no more anally fixated than the man who kisses his girl friend need be arrested at the oral stage. The connection between homosexuality and anal and narcissistic fixations is, to say the least, tenuous.

Other psycho-analysts believe they have traced the causes of homosexuality to developmental disturbance at the oral stage [32]. Melanie Klein [212] thought that fantasies of sucking and devouring, belonging to the oral stage of sexual development, led to unconscious fears of being eaten up in turn by the love object, and hence to a fear of the dangerous devouring vagina. Bieber [35] has reviewed the contrasting interpretations of later analysts, such as Kolb and Johnson [216] who believed covert encouragement and permissiveness on the part of parents to be an important factor in fostering overt homosexuality in children. Several authorities have suggested that homosexuality arises because it fulfils the needs of an emotionally distorted character. Karen Horney [185] believed it to be a means of playing out, in the sexual sphere, abnormal urges to subdue and conquer others, or alternatively to submit to and to please others. Ovesey [285] identified a type of pseudo-homosexual male who was primarily motivated by a wish for dependency and a fear of asserting himself. Clara Thompson [361] also regarded many cases of homosexuality as the result of abnormal dependency needs. This confusing proliferation of psycho-analytic interpretations casts doubt upon all theories based upon unsupported clinical intuitions.

Traditional psycho-analytic views seemed all agreed on one point, namely that the conditions which determine an obligatory homosexual orientation are laid down in early childhood, and that the events of adolescence merely unfold a preordained disposition. This view gains support from the evidence that seductive homosexual experiences in youth have little importance in fixing permanent sexual orientation and that the peculiarities of some effeminate male homosexuals appear long before adolescence [175].

On the other hand, many authorities, including some of the modern psycho-analysts, have suggested that where some tendency towards homosexual deviation exists, difficulties and discouragements encountered by the adolescent at his first attempts to establish heterosexual contacts may tip the scales unfavourably. For this reason, the wounding rebuffs experienced by persons of unattractive appearance or inadequate social skills (e.g. the over-sensitive male of feminine appearance, or the clumsy mannish-looking woman) may act as a last straw in diverting them from normality. So, perhaps, may continued warnings, threats or punitive responses on the part of repressive parents. One completely inverted male seen by the present writer recalled a single attempt during adolescence to make contact with a girl. The unexpected arrival of his harsh stepmother, who boxed the girl's ears and sent her packing, brought this experiment to an end, and may have ensured that it was never repeated. Personally, I believe that the turbulent emotional experiences of adolescence and early adult life have been far too much neglected in the search for psychological causes. In the fascination of tracking back sexual deviation to the first infantile beginnings, it tends to be forgotten that false starts predispose to further mishaps, each of which may contribute a quota to the final disaster.

5. *Explanations of Lesbianism*

Hereditary and glandular factors probably play no greater part in lesbianism than in male homosexuality; but since virtually no research has been done into the physical characteristics of lesbians this presumption remains unverified, except for the trite observation that most lesbians look like normal women and are capable of having babies. Psychological theories generally assume that both male and female homosexuality arise from an inhibition against contact with the opposite sex. Indeed, many lesbians express their fear or aversion more openly than do most male homosexuals, who try to maintain that they are simply uninterested in the opposite sex.

Some Psychological Factors

Compared with the average man, women in our culture tend to be more socially submissive, less inclined to rebel or to break the law, and more prone to anxiety and panic. In so far as sexual inversion represents a panic flight from heterosexual contacts, one might expect women to have a greater liability to this development than men. The fact that they do not calls for some explanation. One plausible suggestion is that given the same pressures and conflicts women are more liable than men to be frightened off sex altogether, becoming sexually frigid rather than sexually perverted. Of course frigidity, like male impotence, is not always due to a dampening of sexual desire; a combination of eagerness and fear can have the same result. Moreover, frigidity sometimes masks a strong homoerotic preference which the woman strives to suppress. Curiously, homosexuality and sado-masochism are the only sexual deviations to which women become addicted in any great numbers. Fetishism, peeping Tom activities, the urge to indecent exposure, and child molestation are almost exclusively masculine phenomena.

Psychological interpretations of male and female sexual deviation are mostly based on psycho-analytic ideas and follow roughly similar lines in both sexes. It seems generally agreed that the early emotional interplay between infants and parents is of crucial importance. In the experience of most clinicians, peculiarities in parent-child relations and in early upbringing are even more noticeable in the case of lesbians than among male homosexuals, but authorities differ about the details of the process. Eva Bene [22] made a systematic comparison of a group of volunteers from a lesbians' organization with a group of married women. She used the same psychological questionnaire concerning family background that she had previously applied to male homosexuals (see page 194). She found that, to a significant extent, the lesbians were more often hostile towards and afraid of their fathers, and also less affectionate towards their mothers, than were the heterosexual women. Each woman was asked if her parents had

208

ever mentioned wanting a boy or a girl when she was born; to which 38 per cent of the lesbians, against only 13 per cent of the married women, replied that their parents had wanted a boy.

As was remarked in Chapter III (see page 70), dissatisfaction with their assigned sex role, and emulation of the interests and attitudes of the opposite sex, seems to be rather common among lesbians. This dissatisfaction may sometimes have been instilled at an early age by the behaviour of parents who, for reasons of their own, treated a little girl as if she were a boy. Caprio [53] suggests that a girl who senses her father would like to have a son may try to fulfil that role in order to win his attention. I am indebted to Mrs. June Hopkins for the following history, which represents a well-recognized pattern:

This woman volunteered to give her history for research purposes. She was the first and only child born to middle-aged parents both of whom wanted a son more than anything in the world. A girl's name was given her on her birth certificate, but all her life she has been known by a masculine-sounding diminutive. Her toys were all animals (she could not recall ever having seen a doll until she saw one belonging to a girl friend) and she dressed in jeans. Her dark black, naturally curly hair was boyishly bobbed, as that way she could do it herself as soon as she was big enough to hold the comb.

Her father taught her how to hunt and fish and how to clean the game and not to cry if the blood got on her. She actually forgot how to cry and claims she has not done so since she was a baby; although there have been times when she wanted to. She has one dress and several skirts and sweaters which she wears to work now, but she cannot recall ever having had dresses when she was a child, other than one white one for party wear. At a later age she shared her father's hobbies and she remembers having built model cars and airplanes which had powered engines in them, which she and her father played with at weekends. She became quite good at sports and excelled at swimming.

During the war she joined one of the services and enjoyed the experience immensely. She was made sergeant in record time as a result of her competence. It was in the service that she first heard of homosexuality, because someone asked her if she was 'gay'. After experiencing a rather pleasurable lesbian relationship, she decided to leave the service, because she felt it was wrong to hide these tendencies, which were abhorred by the authorities.

She has since become a moderately successful government employee and lives with a competent, self-employed woman. She feels that her life is complete, even though it has never included boy-friends or male lovers. She gets along famously with men as friends socially, but finds female companionship more satisfying. She does not consider herself a man as once she considered herself a boy, but she does feel that she has chosen the proper niche for herself in life.

M. M. R. Khan [205] has reviewed with some thoroughness the psycho-analytic interpretations of lesbian development. Modern psycho-analytic views are quite varied and confusing. Freud's original ideas on the subject ran along similar lines to his Oedipal theory of male homosexuality. The child feels drawn to the parent of the opposite sex, but recoils if the attachment becomes too intense on account of guilt and fear due to incest taboo. The girl child may thus take to female love as being somewhat less dangerous and frightening than an attraction to father or to other men. Girls have a worse hurdle than boys to overcome since they must normally renounce their prime source of love and nurture, namely the mother, in order to develop Oedipal feelings for their father. Hence, in girls, the Oedipal stage may occur rather later than in boys, so that the pre-Oedipal phases, during which she still has an exclusive and dependent attachment to mother, assume great importance in determining subsequent sexual attitudes. Conflicts about her dependent role, or resentment about feminine inadequacy, so-called 'penis envy', which arise during early experiences with the mother, may carry over into the later stage of Oedipal attachment to father, resulting in a sensitive, turbulent paternal relationship, and a tendency to regress back to maternal and feminine attachments.

Such views (here greatly condensed and over-simplified) emphasize the importance of the maternal relationship in lesbian development. In practice, it seems that lesbians are not usually father-bound in the way that male homosexuals are so often mother-bound. As Eva Bene showed, the more typical lesbian pattern consists of hostility to father and an ambivalent attachment to mother. The father's personality may greatly contribute to this development. Helena Deutsch [78] suggested that a brutal or sadistic father can provoke a revulsion against all men. Likewise, it has been said that an unsympathetic, nagging mother may cause her daughter to look for love and security from other women, and hence to develop lesbianism. Of course, psycho-analysts are the first to point out that superficial antagonism may conceal deep attachment. Some lesbians, in spite of protests to the contrary, appear to be very bound up with their harsh, frightening fathers. The analyst Catherine Bacon [13] suggests that some women seek refuge in lesbianism because they fear retaliation from father if they should desert him for another man. A woman partner seems a degree less dangerous. One of Dr. Bacon's patients, having recounted how her father used to admonish her not to let boys touch her, commented: 'He never told me not to be homosexual.' Joyce McDougall [241], reporting on a series of lesbians who came for psychoanalytic treatment, found that whereas they generally regarded their fathers as brutal or disgusting, they had a close, idealistic relationship to their mothers. She thought that some of these lesbians had turned to other women as a reaction against total identification with their mother. Anthony Storr [350] suggested that lesbian affaires often prove unsatisfying just because so many of the women involved are really seeking a substitute mother upon whom they can lean with child-like dependence. The partner may obtain some satisfaction for her maternal yearnings by looking after another woman, usually younger than herself, but since the arrangement involves more give than take on her part resentments tend to creep in.

Psycho-analysts have maintained that a transfer of erotic feeling from the clitoris to the vagina constitutes the final step in female sexual development. Capacity for what has been called vaginal orgasm has been held to indicate satisfactory heterosexual maturity, whereas lesbian sexual practices, involving stimulation of the clitoris rather than vaginal penetration, have been looked upon as infantile methods of sexual stimulation. Freud and many of his followers believed further that sexual inversion was in part caused by physical factors. A woman strongly endowed with clitoral sensitivity, and disinclined to surrender herself passively in the approved feminine manner, might be considered constitutionally different from the norm, and particularly pre-disposed to lesbianism. These ideas receive no support from recent research, which shows that even in the most successfully heterosexual women the clitoris plays an important part in the neurological mechanisms of orgasm. Physiologically, female orgasm is a unified phenomenon which does not vary whether the stimulus is vaginal or directly clitoral. Moreover, physiologically, the vagina is a vigorous organ with an active role in the satisfactory accomplishment of both copulatory and reproductive functions [251]. Even from the strictly physical standpoint, therefore, the concept of the passive female and the active male will not bear too close scrutiny.

Many of the contributing factors discussed in relation to male homosexuality have been said to play some part in the development of lesbianism. Unpleasant or frightening early sexual experience, adolescent disappointments, shyness and inferiority in heterosexual contacts, insensitive or neglectful husbands, and fear of marital responsibilities have all been cited as influencing sexual orientation. The seductive effect of the cultural emphasis upon the beauty and attractiveness of feminine appearance might be expected to influence some women to accept lesbian attraction as a natural feeling. Physical acts of seduction by older women were much discussed by Krafft-Ebing and other early writers; and even Caprio appears to give some credence to this as at least a contributory cause. He quotes several stories of married women being enticed away from

their husbands by scheming lesbians, but the wives involved were probably specially susceptible, either on
account of poor heterosexual adjustment, or previous
homosexual inclinations. As with males, handicaps which
interfere with adolescent heterosexual contacts probably
exacerbate female homosexual tendencies. Physical attractiveness being particularly important to girls, a coarse or
unfeminine appearance may lead to great anxiety. Thus, it
could be psychological reasons rather than glandular
causes that impel some large-boned masculine looking
women to reject the feminine role in favour of 'butch'
lesbianism.

The theory that physically or temperamentally masculine women take naturally to lesbianism has never really
been put to the test. Nevertheless, many authorities confidently assume a high incidence of masculine characteristics among lesbians. Caprio [53], in his concluding
summary, asserts that many crimes committed by women
are the work of jealous lesbians with a strong aggressive
masculine drive. Whether the aggressively 'butch' lesbians,
with strong masculine identifications, are more prevalent
than their male counterparts, the passive, effeminate, girlish
homosexuals, is open to doubt. In both cases these easily
recognized types are in the minority, and their psychology
will not account for the mechanism of sexual deviation in
general.

As was explained in a previous chapter (see page 48), the
basic psycho-analytic assumption that sexual deviants are
immature persons of markedly neurotic personality has not
been confirmed by psychological surveys of either male or
female homosexual volunteers. However, since lesbians
constitute a smaller minority than male homosexuals, it
would not be surprising if they were found to be psychologically as well as statistically more deviant. In clinical
experience, lesbian patients often seem to be more disturbed and unhappy than male homosexuals, but of course
lesbians who decide, or are persuaded, to present themselves for treatment may represent a select and untypical

group. Possibly women tolerate less well than men the guilt feelings associated with socially disapproved behaviour.

6. *Bisexuality*

The causes of bisexuality have attracted even less attention or systematic study than the causes of lesbianism. An ability to respond homosexually as well as heterosexually, such as is found very frequently among criminal types and among adolescents, may merely indicate that the strong inhibitions assumed by the majority in our culture have either not yet been acquired, or are never going to be acquired in the case of social outcasts and rebels. In itself, bisexual responsiveness can hardly be called pathological, although it may betray an underlying defect of character. The individual who acts upon the boast that he can make use of man, woman or beast is likely to be the sort of person who must satisfy his impulses regardless of the consequences to others. Many pathological liars, addicts, criminals and other anti-social types share this same character defect.

The model of the slap-happy, completely uninhibited bisexual does not fit all cases by any means. Many individuals are bisexual in behaviour without being truly bisexual in preference. For example, one finds people struggling to maintain a normal sexual life in marriage in spite of a strong homosexual preference. The psycho-analysts are probably right in regarding such cases as little different in origin from the exclusive homosexuals who stay single. On the other hand, a brief regression to homosexual behaviour on the part of a married man or woman, perhaps in circumstances of emotional upheaval or as a result of special situation of temptation, should not be treated as if it were a chronic homosexual problem. In clinical practice, an evenly balanced attraction to both sexes is relatively rarely encountered, but when it does occur the individual may feel very far from slap-happy, being driven by sexual compulsions to lead a complicated and guilty mode of life, in spite of considerable social scruples. The fact that such patterns can develop shows clearly that flight from the physical aspects of heterosexuality cannot be the explanation of all obligatory homosexual behaviour. In some cases, at least, the sexual problem appears secondary to other difficulties in forming and maintaining intimate personal relationships. The compulsively roaming bisexual may not be scared of sexual activities, but he may be running away from something else, perhaps from the prospect of giving himself up wholeheartedly to a permanent and fully committed one-to-one relationship with a marital partner.

Some bisexuals, like some heterosexual adulterers, succeed in maintaining apparently satisfying marital relationships, in spite of periodic unfaithfulness, perhaps even because of it. Whether these people are more sick than they know, or whether they can pride themselves on a form of sexual adjustment that transcends the petty limitations of the common herd, is a matter of opinion.

CHAPTER X

THE ODD, THE MAD, AND THE VIOLENT

1. Covert, Latent and Repressed Homosexuals

Covert homosexuals are persons who are well aware of an erotic interest in members of their own sex, but keep their thoughts to themselves, and don't put their ideas into practice. In a survey among male students at Cornell University, Braaten and Darling [40] found that covert homosexuals were almost as numerous as the overt types, but they tended to be more seclusive, socially introverted, prone to day-dreaming and to complaints of shyness—in a word more generally inhibited. One can imagine the inhibiting process going a stage further and ending in conscious denial of homosexual feelings, in spite of continued indications of active homosexual drives in the individual's choice of companions and friendships. An unstable state of incompletely repressed homosexuality has been held responsible for much neurotic illness. The affected person experiences considerable anxiety and tension in situations that threaten to evoke his unacceptable homosexual feelings. Psycho-analysts have suggested that men who evince extremely emotional attitudes towards homosexual offenders, advocating castration or the gas chamber, are really compensating for their own insecurity by rooting out the evil in others. Some repressed homosexuals, if placed in a situation in which they can no longer deny homosexual thoughts, break out into a feverish panic amounting almost to temporary manic insanity. This condition, called homosexual panic or Kempf's Disease, is well recognized in American text-books of psychiatry [192]. It explains some of those curious episodes in which a young man who has been solicited, or perhaps allowed himself to be seduced, by an older homosexual, will suddenly turn upon the older man in a fit of murderous rage. He will say afterwards that he was overcome by disgust or revulsion, but the irrational fury of such attacks, in utter disregard of the consequences, reveals how deeply disturbed the assailant must have been at the time. The American psychiatrist A. J. Rosanoff [317], who was particularly interested in the various reactions a person might have on becoming aware of his own homosexual tendencies, believed that panic flight from homosexuality could lead to suicide, alcoholism, drug addiction and even madness. [48]

Psychiatrists have long recognized flight into alcoholism as one way in which some homosexuals seek escape from their conflicts [340]. The sense of well-being and the loss of tension and self-consciousness produced by alcohol comes as a great boon to the conflict-ridden. Moreover, drinking enables men to enjoy intimate male companionship without provoking comment, and so affords a particularly attractive outlet for the covert homosexual. Indeed, as the psycho-analyst Karl Abraham [2] long ago pointed out, alcoholic habits being looked upon as manly vice, the covert homosexual can use them as a disguise to protect his masculine image. Alcohol damps down inhibitions, and some of those who would scorn the thought when sober will indulge in deviant sexual practices when drunk. It also aids forgetfulness. Some men, when their tensions reach an unbearable pitch, rush away on a mad 'binge', during which they have homosexual adventures, afterwards returning to their ordinary life untroubled by any conscious recollection of their lapse. The American novel, *The Lost Weekend*, by Charles Jackson, deals with such a case.[1] In addition it has been noted that alcoholics make unreasonably suspicious and jealous husbands, although they may be virtually impotent, and this has been advanced as an argument in favour of a homosexual component, the jealousy being interpreted as a projection on to the wife of the husband's own desire to be unfaithful with men. Perhaps

[1] The bowdlerized film version of this story contains no reference to the essential theme.

this explanation applies to some cases, but the fact must be taken into account that alcoholic poisoning itself may decrease potency, and this in turn may give rise to jealous fears, quite apart from any homosexual problem.

Psycho-analysts use the term latent homosexuality for conditions in which the homosexual tendency appears more deeply repressed, but remains sufficiently active to manifest in heavily disguised forms. Of course, if one accepts the theory of man's natural bisexual responsiveness, all normal people are in a sense latent homosexuals, and under certain conditions of cultural permissiveness or heterosexual deprivation they may lose their inhibitions and proceed to demonstrate their homosexual potentialities. But in using the term latent homosexual, the psycho-analysts seek to identify a group of persons who seem particularly vulnerable to homosexual conflicts because they are ill at ease with the pattern of behaviour and interests expected of their sex. Freud and the earlier analysts believed that some males were constitutionally lacking in energy and aggressiveness, and hence more femininely inclined in personality, and hence more liable to homosexual conflicts than the average man. In practice, psycho-analysts often label as latent homosexuals persons whose character structure has features considered by society more apppropriate to members of the opposite sex, and also persons who find any kind of difficulty in establishing smooth and successful relationships with the opposite sex.

Leon Saltzman [322] has strongly criticized this tendency to attribute all social and psychological difficulty in the sexual sphere, especially among males, to an underlying or latent homosexual orientation. Shyness with the opposite sex, or enjoyment of the company of cronies of the same sex, does not always indicate a homosexual problem. Indeed, owing to the highly derogatory connotations of the adjective 'homosexual' in our society, the indiscriminate use of this concept may exacerbate a patient's sexual anxieties, and give the less discerning therapist too easy a means of shrugging off his failures.

2. *Homosexuality and Paranoid Schizophrenia*

Freud was the first to put forward the theory that the familiar mental derangement 'persecution mania', technically called paranoia, arises from conflict over homosexual tendencies. In this form of insanity the sufferer imagines himself the victim of wicked plots and scheming enemies. His delusional system of ideas frequently centres upon one particular person who becomes in the paranoic's mind an arch-fiend with diabolical powers. In typical cases he complains of sexual tortures in the form of horrible sensations or disgusting thoughts, which, he says, his enemy inflicts upon him from a distance by means of 'rays', 'hypnotism', or 'telepathy'. Superficially such delusions appear nonsensical, but Freud found that they often have a thinly disguised homosexual flavour. The supposed enemy is really someone for whom the insane person experiences sexual feeling, but a violent reaction against the guilty attraction causes him to fly to the opposite extreme and assert that the offending individual is an object of hate and not of love. Hence the delusion takes the form of a denial, a protest that 'he interferes with me, but I don't like it, I hate him'. In other words this type of delusional insanity consists of an extreme instance of over-compensation for repressed homosexual feelings.

Freud explored this mechanism in detail in the case of Dr. Schreber, a Dresden judge, who fell a prey to a mixture of grandiose and persecutory delusions, and published a mad account of his ideas in a book entitled *Memoirs of my Nervous Illness* [327]. In a lengthy paper Freud examined this book and showed the unmistakable homosexual significance of much of the contents [111]. Dr. Schreber fell ill in October 1893, suffering from hypochondriacal fears and ideas of persecution. He believed that horrible things were happening to his body, that it was diseased and decomposing, and that in addition his sexual parts were being handled and misused in revolting ways. Tormenting voices told him he was being turned into a woman. He would sit motionless for hours, completely preoccupied with these hallucinatory impressions. He hated what was happening to him so much that he tried to kill himself. Gradually the disturbance became less acute. After nine years Dr. Schreber was able to pay attention to the outside world and deal with practical affairs. He secured his release from hospital, but he still adhered to an elaborate system of delusory ideas and felt impelled to write his *Memoirs*.

In the earlier stages of his illness Dr. Schreber believed he was being emasculated for the purpose of sexual abuse, and that the perpetrator of the outrage was his physician, Professor Fleisig. Later his delusion changed in character and he came to accept, even to welcome the idea of conversion into a woman, believing this miracle to be a preliminary to one still greater, namely his assumption of the role of religious Redeemer of the world. He came to believe that God himself, and not Professor Fleisig, was the prime instigator of his persecutions, and that he was being prepared for a voluptuous union with God. He felt he must abandon his former principles of restraint and sexual continence, and acknowledge his duty to assume the role of God's Wife and the world's Redeemer. The bulk of his book consisted of accounts of numerous secondary delusions and elaborations all stemming from this central theme.

Freud noted that Dr. Schreber's illness commenced with a 'nervous collapse' while his wife was away on holiday. One night during her absence he experienced several emissions of semen. When she returned he no longer felt he wanted her. At about the same period, he reported that, while in a state between sleeping and waking, the idea came to him that it would be nice to be a woman and submit to copulation. All this fits in with Freud's interpretation that the Schreber fantasy was a reaction against homosexual desires. At first even the delusions about the abominable Fleisig proved inadequate to salve Schreber's conscience, and he tried to kill himself. Only after he had developed the ingenious delusion about submitting to God, and could indulge in feminine sexual fantasies with a clear conscience, was the conflict sufficiently solved to enable him to make a partial recovery. Once he had achieved a state of 'peaceful co-existence' with his delusions, he ceased to be a suicidal risk.

Freud certainly put paranoia in a new light, and no one today denies that paranoid delusions frequently reveal blatant homosexual conflicts. Sometimes the homosexual trends are apparent in the patient's behaviour, and the conflict is fully conscious [162, 318]. But it is not generally accepted that homosexual conflict is the chief feature in all cases of paranoia [211, 363]. D. Henderson and R. D. Gillespie in their *Textbook of Psychiatry* point out that flight from forbidden heterosexual desires may also form the background of paranoid delusions. Koegler and Kline [215], in measuring the physiological signs of emotion produced in patients by exposing sexually stimulating films, found that anxiety reaction among paranoid psychotics occured as often in response to heterosexual as to homosexual situations.

Some years ago Planansky and Johnston [294] carried out a systematic survey of 150 male paranoid schizophrenic patients in an American mental hospital to try to establish the actual incidence of homosexual conflicts in such cases. Over a half of the patients expressed concern about homosexuality, in the form of hallucinatory voices accusing them of being 'queer', or delusions that other men were trying to tempt or coerce them into homosexual acts. Many of them expressed confused ideas about supposed changes in their genitals, or about belonging to the female sex. On the other hand, a history of habitual homosexual behaviour was quite infrequent, occurring in only 2 per cent of cases. It appeared to the investigators that these patients' troubles arose from their distorted perceptions, and their inability to function in any social role. Their sexual worries were secondary to a much more generalized disturbance, and although they might express fear or confusion concerning homosexual tendencies, in fact this was not a realistic problem in most cases. Furthermore heterosexual concerns were even more frequent, and there was no evidence that those whose delusions were most acutely paranoid had any greater frequency of homosexual concerns. From these findings the investigators concluded that homosexual tendencies and paranoid mental illness were not generally related to each other in the manner suggested by Freud. One also has to remember that even if the psychological meaning of the delusions in certain cases has been correctly interpreted by Freud, this does not fully explain the cause of the illness and does not help to cure it. Paranoics will not respond to reason or to psychological explanations; they have their own fixed ideas and no one can change them. Only a small minority of those with homosexual conflicts react by developing paranoia, so the mere existence of such a conflict cannot fully account for a delusional reaction.

Many psychiatrists do not consider paranoia a disease in its own right, but look upon it as just one form of schizophrenia. Originally paranoia was distinguished from schizophrenia because paranoic patients have delusions but do not display the hallucinations, disturbances of thought processes, and general deterioration of personality so common in schizophrenia. In practice, if paranoics are followed up long enough, other symptoms besides delusions usually appear, and gradually the picture assumes a more typical schizophrenic form. The importance of this lies in its implications regarding the causation of the disorder. There is known to be a big inherited, constitutional element in the tendency to schizophrenic reactions. Recent research also suggests that schizophrenic symptoms may be a sign of an underlying physical disorder, perhaps a poisoning of the brain due to a failure in biochemical processes. The only method of treatment that has had substantial success in these cases is the use of chlorpromazine and related drugs. Clearly, the whole question of the causation of schizophrenia, which is the commonest form of insanity, involves a great deal more than just homosexual conflict. Nevertheless, the prevalence of homosexual behaviour and homosexual preoccupations among schizophrenics and paranoics has been noted by too many different observers to be written off as completely inconsequential [33, 38, 56, 321, 394, 279, 210, 135].

The views of A. J. Rosanoff [317] seem to me rather more realistic than the orthodox psycho-analytic line. He suggested that schizophrenic sexuality is chaotic rather than specifically homosexual, a confused mixture of unsuitably directed sexual impulses which gain symbolic expression in delusions and hallucinations. He agreed with Freud in interpreting many of the characteristic symptoms of schizophrenia, such as aggressive paranoid outbursts, persecutory delusions, and feelings of malevolent influence, as crude defence mechanisms against perverse sexual impulses. He did not consider the perverse inclinations a cause of the mental disorder in themselves, but he thought that the patient's violent efforts to repress their sexuality led to acute tension and a predisposition to psychotic breakdowns.

3. Sexual Violence

Sexual acts accompanied by serious or homicidal violence are almost invariably committed by men. The offenders fall into three categories. In the massive report on sex offenders by the Indiana University Institute of Sex Research [124] it is stated (p. 205): 'The majority of aggressors *vs.* adults may be succinctly described as criminally inclined men who take what they want, whether money, material or women, and their sex offenses are by-products of their general criminality . . . Actually many are suffering from personality defects and stresses which ultimately erupt in a sex offense.' The incidence of this kind of aggression is small in England, but higher in communities in which violence of all kinds is less inhibited. The second category consists of psychotic or insane persons who commit atrocious sexual crimes under the spell of delusions or mad preoccupations, oblivious of the ghastly inappropriateness and terrible consequences of their actions. Happily, this happens only rarely. Most mad people are not at all dangerous. Sadists make up the third category. Whereas any aggressive offender may use force, or the threat of force, to overcome an unwilling victim's reluctance to co-operate in a sexual act, sadists use violence for its own sake, because this gives them sexual pleasure, and because they cannot otherwise fully satisfy their lust. Of course sadistic fantasies of subduing or being subdued are extremely common, as is mildly sadistic sexual fore-play, smacking, biting, struggling etc. Elaborate rituals, in which a sexual partner is tied up, caned, insulted and coerced into humiliating submissions are also quite common, but only rarely do these go beyond the limits of a sort of game, in which both parties participate willingly enough, and no real injury occurs. Murderous sadistic assaults, involving stabbing and mutilations, are very rare, and are nearly always the work of individuals who, in addition to having perverse sexual urges, are of highly abnormal or violent personality, perhaps on the verge of psychosis.

There is no reason to suppose that homosexuals are more prone than heterosexuals to take to any of the three categories of dangerous violence described. The great majority of victims of violent sex crimes are female. From the results of the survey by the Institute of Sex Research, it would appear that in the United States assaults by heterosexuals upon little girls are more commonly accompanied by violence than are homosexual assaults on pre-pubertal boys. The survey included only twelve cases of small boys who were coerced by force, and none of these received physical injury. The worst example was that of a sadistic paedophile who picked up a boy of eleven in a cinema, kept him in his room for a week, and whipped him for going too close to a window. Forceful and injurious attempts at copulation with small girls, especially by drunken heterosexuals of criminal propensities, were a much more frequent offence.

Nevertheless, murderous sexual violence against men and boys is not unknown, although I should guess that of the hundred and fifty or so murders recorded annually by the English police, less than one a year would come into this category. The public gets a misleading impression of the incidence of these crimes because the newspapers always give great prominence to any murder in which sexual perversion may have played a part. Dr. Paul de River [314] has published some horrifying descriptions of such cases, complete with photographs of victims; but he is careful to distinguish between these unusual and highly abnormal offenders and the general run of non-criminal deviants for whom (p. 327) 'psycho-therapy offers a better hope for rehabilitation than care in a penal institution'. J. M. Reinhardt [312], in a chapter on lust murders, describes how one youth, having lured a small boy into a barn, proceeded to kill the victim by throttling him and ripping open his rectum and testicles with a can opener. The youth derived great sexual excitement from these actions, and showed no pity or remorse. He was, in fact, a grossly psychopathic character, whose brain had been damaged in infancy by an attack of encephalitis. He had long been beyond the control of school teachers and parents, and was known as an incorrigible vandal, truant and thief who could not fit into any normal social group. It was his lack of normal feeling for others which made his deviant sexual interests so dangerous.

The mistaken belief that homosexual deviation in itself leads to criminal, insane or sadistic violence arises from several causes. First, sexual perversions of all kinds, including homosexuality, appear with special frequency among criminal types of primitive or anti-social mentality. These psychopaths, as they are often called, have no particular defect of intelligence; they are not anxious or inhibited, like the neurotics, or withdrawn into a fantasy world, like the insane, but nevertheless they are great social misfits. All their lives they remain sullen, aggressive problem children, impulsive and shiftless, unable to knuckle down to a steady job, or to conform to social rules, or to establish prolonged or deep personal attachments. They are the last people to put up any great battle against their instincts. Consequently, in sex, as in other spheres, they seek immediate gratification, and often find easier outlets for their lust in casual homosexual contacts or other deviant habits than in normal courtship. They obey their first impulses regardless of social codes, and show none of the remorse or guilty self-recriminations so typical of the neurotic who tries to repress his inclinations. They are usually the product of disorderly or broken homes, and of numerous childhood deprivations, including periods spent in institutions. No doubt some of them suffer from subtle physical defects (revealed by abnormal brain rhythms on the electroencephalograph, or, more rarely, abnormal chromosome counts), but the most obvious factors in the majority of cases appears to be deprivation of love in their early formative years, and the absence of stable parental figures. They have lacked satisfactory adult models with whom they could identify and have thus missed out on one of the most powerful means of absorbing normal cultural values and restraints [68, 239]. Having failed to experience the consistent training that guides most children into approved social and sexual patterns, many psychopaths remain unstable or confused in their sexual responses, and become disgruntled bisexuals rather than exclusive heterosexuals. Since these difficult characters find themselves perpetually at odds with society, spurned by respectable women on account of their social and economic unreliability, and all too often cast into all-male communities in labourers' hostels and penal establishments, their tendency to indulge in homosexuality on a 'facultative' basis, as the most readily available outlet, hardly seems very surprising. But even among these types, actual homosexual violence is most uncommon, except in special circumstances of confinement in prison or Borstal. Since they mostly take the easiest outlet, it may be that under ordinary circumstances sexual violence towards other men would meet with too much resistance to be profitable!

The supposed connection between homosexuality and schizophrenic madness has already been sufficiently discussed. In so far as their delusions include homosexual preoccupations, the very few schizophrenics who become violent or commit sexual attacks may choose victims of either sex. It has been pointed out repeatedly by criminological authorities, such as Professor Radzinowicz [303] and Nigel Walker [370], that among the mentally sick the subnormals, as a group, have a high incidence of convictions for troublesome sex behaviour, such as exhibiting themselves to women and girls, making sexual approaches to children, or committing homosexual offences. Considering how many of these unfortunates have been reared in institutions under artificial conditions of sexual segregation and deprivation, and how difficult it must be for some mentally handicapped individuals to carry through heterosexual courtships according to socially approved rules, one hardly needs to search for any very deep psychological explanations for the majority of these lapses. In any case, undesirable as they may be, most of these sexual misdemeanours by the mentally subnormal do not in fact involve any serious violence.

Finally, some people believe that the incidence of other kinds of perversion, notably sado-masochistic interests, is particularly high among homosexuals. Quite apart from those socially immature or depraved types who indulge in all forms of sex without discrimination, one would expect to find some individuals with a mixture of perverse inclinations, since the psychological causes of the various perversions seem to be very similar. I know of no factual evidence as to the comparative incidence of sadistic urges among homosexuals and heterosexuals, although some clinicians believe lesbians have a special predilection for flagellation. Dr. River [314] reproduces photographs of women being tied up and beaten by other women, which had doubtless been taken in order to provide pornographic material for the contemplation of sadistic lesbians. In the picture magazines patronized by male homosexuals, illustrations of tied up prisoners, dormitory beatings, and similar situations involving tortures inflicted upon naked men, bear witness to the commercial value of homosexually sadistic titillation.

Since corresponding female pictures also occur with monotonous regularity in pornography intended for heterosexuals, their appearance in deviants' magazines shows
only that homosexuals are not immune from sadistic fancies.
What distinguishes the really dangerous sadist is not a preference for a love object of the same sex, but the blood-
thirsty quality of his fantasies, the inability to curb his
behaviour, and the lack of consideration for the welfare of
his sexual partner. In brief, it is the combination of aggressive psychopathic personality with sadistic inclinations,
whether heterosexual or homosexual, which leads to serious
crime. Incidentally, male homosexuals do appear to be
relatively immune from exhibitionism, which is the urge to
expose the genitals to passing strangers, not as an invitation,
or a preliminary to sexual assault, but as a pleasurable
activity in itself. I suspect that the homosexual version of
this behaviour gives no gratification because a male victim
would hardly be particularly shocked or frightened at the
spectacle.

Jealousy causes more acts of violence than the sexual
urge itself. An analysis of murder records by the Home
Office workers Gibson and Klein [130] showed that lust
was the motive in only ten per cent, whereas quarrels and
jealousy accounted for much more. Even so, murders of
rivals by jealous husbands or lovers are comparatively rare
in England, perhaps because of the stern disapproval of
murderous violence even under these extenuating circumstances. Possibly for this reason, a surprisingly high proportion of murders of wives by husbands are committed by
mentally abnormal men suffering from morbid suspicions
or insane delusions. Such men will misinterpret the most
casual remarks or gestures on the part of their wives as
evidence of infidelity. Because their delusions take this
special form, with sanity retained for a long time on most
other topics, the seriousness of their mental abnormality
may not be appreciated until after the tragedy has taken
place and other symptoms begin to show [271].

In homosexual relationships, cases of insane jealousy,

accompanied by paranoid delusions or hallucinations, do not seem to occur. Possibly this is because, lacking the restriction of the marriage bond, a homosexual partner would be likely to leave long before the symptoms reached a fatal crisis. On the other hand, ordinary forms of jealousy, with endless quarrels and recriminations, seem to be all too common in homosexual and lesbian affairs, but only very exceptionally do they lead to murder. Having looked through the records of a number of cases of murders from jealousy, I found no great over-representation of homosexual as opposed to heterosexual offenders. However, in view of a common belief that homosexuals are particularly prone to jealous violence, the point deserves some systematic inquiry.

Certain circumstances in which male homosexuals are apt to be involved in violence have already been noted. The habit of wandering about late at night searching for sexual contacts, or going home with strangers, incites robbery with violence. Injudicious approaches or seductions risk precipitating a serious outburst of violence if the man in question gets into a state of panic in which he feels his masculinity is in jeopardy. In cases in which a homosexual has been found murdered, and a trivial sum stolen, it may not be clear whether the motive was really robbery, or a sudden panic revulsion, or both. Among offenders compulsively attracted to small children, few are deliberately violent, but sometimes, when the victim makes a noise or threatens to expose the assailant, the man may try to silence the child, and in his state of panic use a lethal amount of force. All of these three situations of violence, of which the last one is fortunately much the most rare, are consequent upon social attitudes to deviants rather than upon any intrinsic aggressiveness in the homosexual urge.

CHAPTER XI

TREATMENT FOR THE INDIVIDUAL

1. Prospects of Cure

Given a simple choice no one in his right mind would opt for the life of a sexual deviant, to be an object of ridicule and contempt, denied the fulfilments of ordinary family life, and cut off from the mainstream of human interests. Many confirmed homosexuals deplore their fate; but self interest and self determination seem powerless to effect a change. As for the prospects of conversion by special treatment, authorities differ wildly, and dogmatic and contradictory statements abound. Some therapists don't care to admit how often their professional efforts prove futile. On the other hand, practising homosexuals, and their sympathizers, prefer the comforting belief that nothing they might do would make any difference. Undoubtedly much depends upon the circumstances of the individual case. At one extreme one has young people in a panic over some quite ordinary homo-erotic experience they fear may have permanently unfitted them for heterosexual life. A little authoritative reassurance is all they need to put them right again. At the other extreme, one has people who have lived as exclusive homosexuals for many years, with no interest in the opposite sex and no wish to change their ways, sent along unwillingly to see psychiatrists because their condition has come to the notice of the courts, or because some officious relative thinks something must be done. In such cases the hope of a successful conversion to heterosexuality by any method at present known is very slight.

On the whole, psychiatrists with the widest experience propound the most cautious views. Dr. Peter Scott writes [331] 'From the very extensive literature and from 10 years' experience of treating and watching the results of others I have to agree . . . that there is no evidence "that the direction of intensely homosexual drives can be successfully altered".' Professor Desmond Curran, a psychiatrist who served on the Wolfenden Committee, has expressed the view that the chances of cure in confirmed cases are negligible and that the psychiatrist should concentrate on making the patient a better-adjusted homosexual and not aspire to convert him to heterosexuality [70]. Referring to the case of an intelligent man of thirty-nine who had practised homosexuality since adolescence without obvious guilt, and then sought advice as to whether he was curable, Dr. Curran stated: 'The only answer that could be given to such a patient was that the prospect of this would be small, and that whether he indulged in homosexual acts or not was something that he must decide for himself' [71].

Some authorities, especially those who believe homosexuality to be a condition fixed by heredity, contend that attempts to attack it are both futile and unjustified. Thus Dr. Stanley-Jones has written [346]:' There can be no question of asking the invert to accept the ordinary standards of heterosexual morality, and any course of therapy which seeks to reverse the fundamental pattern is not only fore-doomed to failure, as all the reported cases testify, but is also quite indefensible when regarded in the light of absolute morality: attempted "treatment" or alteration of the basic personality of an inborn homosexual can only be described as a moral outrage'.

Although some of his later followers have been more optimistic, Freud himself held out little hope of converting the majority of homosexuals by means of psycho-analysis, and believed that treatment should have the limited aim of helping the homosexual towards self-acceptance and better social adjustment. In a famous letter addressed to the troubled mother of a homosexual he wrote [115]: 'In a certain number of cases we succeed in developing the blighted germs of heterosexual tendencies which are present in every homosexual, in the majority it is no more possible . . . What analysis can do for your son runs on a different line. If he is unhappy, neurotic, torn by conflicts, inhibited in his social life, analysis may bring him harmony, peace of mind, full efficiency . . .' Freud believed that homosexuals don't change because they lack sufficient motivation. 'If he comes to be treated at all, it is mostly through the pressure of external motives, such as the social disadvantages and dangers attaching to his choice of object . . . ' Sometimes he secretly hopes for treatment to fail so as 'to obtain from the striking failure of his attempt the feeling of satisfaction that he has done everything possible against his abnormality, to which he can now resign himself with an easy conscience' [114]. The contention that homosexuals desperately resist change until driven by loneliness or fear has been echoed again and again by therapists [276, 267]. By placing the blame for failures upon their patients, therapists manage to preserve the theory that homosexuality is a potentially treatable condition.

Treatment rarely produces a complete conversion of an adult from exclusive homosexuality to satisfactory heterosexuality. The authors of the Wolfenden Report [177], in paragraph 193, remarked that: 'We were struck by the fact that none of our medical witnesses were able, when we saw them, to provide any reference in medical literature to a change of this kind.' Clifford Allen [5] subsequently published a series of case studies from his own experience. He quoted the examples of eight men of mature age, and several women, all of whom had experienced complete reorientation, apparently as a result of psychotherapy. He also cited similar instances in reports published by other psychoanalysts. J. A. Hadfield [152, 153] has also published several such examples of his own, some of which were followed up for many years to establish the permanence of their cure. J. F. Poe [297] published a particularly striking example. A man of forty, who liked the passive role in buggery, and had practised homosexuality for twenty-two years, was completely converted in the course of 85 sessions over a period of nine months.

Prospects of Cure

There seems little reason to doubt that dramatic and lasting conversions do occasionally take place, sometimes after very short periods of psychotherapy, but follow-up studies of groups of patients show that these examples are exceptional. Curran and Parr [72], in a survey of homosexuals seen in private practice, reported that twenty-five patients treated psychotherapeutically received no apparent benefit in terms of changed sexual preference as compared with twenty-five corresponding patients not so treated. Of twenty-four exclusive homosexuals regarded as having very poor prospects, only one in fact reported any change in the direction of heterosexuality. Of fourteen bisexual patients, however, six did change towards heterosexual preference, although three became more homosexual.

In evaluating the efficiency of treatment, one needs to know the probability of spontaneous recovery. Young people often pass through a predominantly homosexual phase of life without permanent ill effect. Kinsey's survey of males [207] showed a substantial shift towards heterosexuality with increasing age. Whereas, according to his estimates, 8 per cent of males were exclusively homosexual (rating 6) for at least three years after reaching sixteen, only 4 per cent were exclusively homosexual throughout their adult lives. Whereas only 81 per cent of males aged twenty were predominantly heterosexual in their current behaviour (rating 0, 1 or 2), at the age of forty-five 93 per cent of males were predominantly heterosexual. Kinsey warned that the magnitude of this shift with age might have been exaggerated by the greater reluctance of older men to admit continued homosexual behaviour, but clearly a quite substantial number of men who are actively and exclusively homosexual in their late 'teens or early twenties become heterosexual later in life.

Kinsey concerned himself more with behaviour than feelings; and one suspects that most of those who change spontaneously towards heterosexuality have some bisexual feelings to begin with. However, some men with very little heterosexual feeling accomplish a form of coitus by dint of conjuring up homosexual fantasies while using the vagina to masturbate. Curran and Parr [72] quoted the case of a married man who used this technique to conceal his true feelings and to produce six children. When he became impotent at the age of sixty, his wife insisted he attend for treatment.

Some psychotherapists put forward quite unrealistic claims for treatment successes. Dr. Daniel Cappon [52] maintained that in his experience of treating 150 private psychiatric patients for sexual problems, 90 per cent of the bisexuals who completed treatment were cured, and had no reversion to either homosexual desire or behaviour. Of male homosexuals, 80 per cent markedly improved and 50 per cent were cured. Since elsewhere in his book this author makes the most surprising and dogmatic statements about the homosexual's shortened life span and susceptibility to illness, and about the historical association of national decay and homosexual permissiveness, one cannot but wonder about the soundness of his therapeutic generalizations.

Another optimistic therapist, Albert Ellis [90], reporting on the results of psychotherapy (anything from 5 to 220 sessions per patient) on 28 men with severe homosexual problems, claimed that 18 improved in terms of hetero-sexual adjustment. He gave no exact information about shifts from extreme positions on the Kinsey scale, so per-haps not many of his cases were of the confirmed, exclusive type that other therapists find unchangeable.

It seems a general rule that the more precise and careful and the longer the period of follow-up, the more modest the therapeutic claims. Mayerson and Lief [255] at Tulane University attempted to follow up forty patients who had had psychiatric treatment for homosexuality. For various reasons information could be got on nineteen only, four-teen men and five women, whose ages ranged from eighteen to forty at the time they had started treatment. The extent of psychotherapy varied from 13 to 420 sessions per patient, and the average lapse of time since completion of treatment was four and a half years. Of 9 patients who were exclusively homosexual to begin with, only 2 were heterosexual at follow up, but of the 10 patients who were bisexual or had had definite heterosexual experience before starting treatment, 7 were heterosexual at follow-up. This shows how much smaller are the chances for the exclusive homosexual. Elizabeth Mintz [263] described the treatment of ten homosexual men by a combination of individual and group psychotherapy, continuing in each case for not less than two years. Three men reported satisfactory heterosexual attainment.

Similarly qualified success was reported by Mary Woodward [389] in a review of the progress of male homosexual patients under treatment at the Portman Clinic, London, which is a centre specializing in the treatment of maladjusted delinquents along psycho-analytic lines. Out of a total of 113 referrals (mostly from courts or probation officers), 92 were selected as suitable for treatment, but only 48 actually went through with their treatment. Of these, only 6 were exclusively homosexual at the outset, and none of them had lost their homosexual impulses or developed heterosexual interests on completion of treatment. On the other hand a majority of the bisexuals (28 out of 42) were said to have lost their homosexual impulses in the course of treatment. One may conclude from this that exclusive homosexuals are less likely to be selected for treatment, probably less likely to complete their treatment, and certainly less likely to achieve heterosexuality than the bisexual cases.

Substantially similar conclusions emerged from the investigation carried out by the Society of Medical Psychoanalysts in New York [35]. Of 106 male homosexuals who undertook private treatment, 27 per cent were exclusively heterosexual when last they reported to their analysts. The duration of treatment varied considerably. At the time the check on sexual orientation was made, a third were still attending, after more than 350 hours of analytic sessions. Very few of those who dropped out of treatment in less than 150 hours became heterosexual. On the other hand, those with an unfavourable prognosis were the more likely to terminate their treatment prematurely. The group who became heterosexual after treatment were distinguished (to a statistically significant degree) by several features which clinicians have long regarded as favourable signs. A half of the 30 bisexual patients became exclusively heterosexual, compared with only 19 per cent of the 76 patients who were either sexually inactive or more or less exclusively homosexual when treatment began. Those who began analysis under the age of 35, those who undertook treatment primarily because they wanted to change into heterosexuals rather than to alleviate anxiety or other symptoms, those who had at sometime attempted heterosexual genital contact, those who had a satisfactory relationship with their fathers, those who did not have an abnormally close, binding tie with their mothers, and those who had not developed effeminate voice or gestures during childhood, all had better chances of becoming heterosexual.

In other words, the less exclusive, long-lasting, and deeply rooted in disturbances of upbringing was the homosexual orientation, the more likely was a conversion to heterosexuality. Although plausible enough, this finding was, in a sense, disappointing, since it showed that signs of well established homosexuality went with poor prospects of cure, even after years of psycho-analysis. Considering that the analysts started out with a particularly favourable group, consisting of men of good education and financial means, who were sufficiently motivated to expend large sums on lengthy treatment voluntarily undertaken, a success rate of one in five is not all that great. Even so, it is larger than most people would have predicted. Dr. F. Kräupl Taylor [357] in a pertinent criticism of this work, has pointed out that no systematic follow-up was undertaken, so no one can say how genuine and lasting were these changes which the analysts said their patients had reported to them during or at the end of treatment. A sufficiently strongly motivated patient, supported by regular sessions with an analyst, may convince himself for a time that he has conquered his unwanted tendencies, but he is not necessarily proof against future lapses.

This criticism may seem a quibble, but in fact heterosexual adaptation established during the treatment is often precarious. Dr. K. Freund [116] found that 45 per cent of the heterosexual adaptations following behaviour therapy were not lasting. I have myself had the experience of giving supportive treatment to a man who had got married on the strength of an analytic cure, only to find himself plagued for years after with homosexual preoccupations, doubts about his performance as a husband, and regrets for his lost freedom.

2. Deciding the Aims of Treatment

If an individual approaches middle-age without having any experience of heterosexual love-making, and if contrary reactions have been firmly conditioned by years of homosexual practice, the prospects of change are obviously very remote. Notwithstanding much unhappiness and self-blame, and even despite considerable insight into the psychological reasons why they first turned away from the opposite sex, many homosexuals remain both unable and fundamentally unwilling to change their outlook. Neurotic symptoms with a purely protective function readily disappear once they have outworn their usefulness, but homosexuality can become an end in itself. Consequently, the homosexual may resist conversion long after the original basis of his flight from the opposite sex has been laid bare. He may prefer his way of life because he has grown up with it and become thoroughly adjusted to it. The fact that a man resists change does not always mean he is weak-willed or obstinate. Shallow, unprincipled characters are content to find sex wherever the opportunity presents, but the mature homosexual has adjusted his loves and his loyalties to a particular style of life. As has often been remarked, it is as difficult to eradicate the emotional and sensual inclinations of a developed homosexual as it would be to quell the natural desires of a normal adult.

Treatment for the Individual

In the ordinary way, the psychiatrist does not have to decide what to do about persons firmly settled into a homosexual way of life, since they do not seek his opinion. Occasionally, however, they get sent along because they have run foul of the police and their legal advisers think that the promise of psychiatric treatment may stop the magistrates sending them to prison. Sometimes the courts themselves refer homosexuals to a psychiatrist, obviously looking for a more constructive method of dealing with the case than by the customary penal sanctions. Sometimes a confirmed homosexual may arrive of his own accord in a fit of despondency or disillusionment, usually after the break-up of a love affair, to see if medical magic will whisk him away from his present difficulties by transforming him into a heterosexual. No matter what outside pressures may be brought to bear, in my opinion the only fair and rational psychiatric response in such cases is to avoid raising hopes of sexual conversion, and to promise nothing more than help with social adjustment and self-acceptance. In view of the limited amount of treatment facilities available, it seems to me a wasteful and misplaced effort to try to convert a settled homosexual of mature years to belated and probably unsatisfactory heterosexual strivings.

Without going so far as Dr. Stanley-Jones, who regarded any attempt to change sexual orientation in established cases as a moral outrage, one must admit the questionable ethics of using psychiatric skills to tear to pieces a person's adjustment to life unless a new and better re-adjustment is expected. Dr. Peter Scott [331] has pointed out some dangers of over-enthusiastic treatment. After the patient's adjustment has been thoroughly disturbed, he may discover the difficulties on the road to heterosexual relationships insurmountable, and react by serious depression, suicide or even a psychosis. If the psychiatrist has made over-optimistic pronouncements in reporting to the courts, and then the patient gets into trouble again, the magistrate may conclude mistakenly that the man has been wilfully unco-operative, and punish him severely. Moreover, the removal of a sexual symptom does not solve all the problems. Dr. Scott instanced the case of a homosexual husband who was induced by hypnotic suggestion to enjoy normal marital intercourse. When an unwanted pregnancy occurred, the husband's homosexual symptoms returned in full force.

To my mind, the worst danger of trying to convert unsuitable cases is the involvement of other people in the patient's unsuccessful attempts to arrive at a satisfactory heterosexual adjustment. A too hasty marriage can turn out a life-long disaster. Some homosexuals misguidedly enter upon matrimony in the hope of curing themselves. Dr. Clifford Allen [5], whom no one could accuse of being pessimistic about treatment prospects, insists that to advise a homosexual to marry in the hope of cure is not only wrong but wicked. Whatever may be the correct sexual morality for normal persons, I have myself not the slightest doubt that persons with homosexual tendencies should obtain experience of normal intercourse, and be fully confident of their heterosexual capacity, before embarking upon marital responsibilities. Unsuccessful marriages, where a mother loses interest in her family on account of lesbian urges, or a father is arrested and disgraced on account of injudicious attempts at furtive homosexual contacts, have most cruel repercussions upon the children. Medical advisers should keep these risks in mind. Dr. Freund [119], a Czech psychiatrist who followed up a sample of treated male homosexuals, found that permanent conversion to heterosexuality was rare, and occurred only if a man married soon after treatment. Unfortunately the great majority of marriages failed, and for this reason Freund concluded that psychotherapy aimed at conversion to heterosexuality should be attempted only in specially selected cases.

In addition to requests for remedial treatment, psychiatrists are often called upon to give practical advice to homosexuals and their families, and the question of impending marriage presents a particularly thorny problem. One can understand the temptation to embark on marriage in spite of a sexual handicap, for the deviant gains the benefits of a stable home and some protection from social discrimination. The doctor finds himself in a most unenviable position if he believes the proposed marriage likely to lead to disaster, but still the homosexual wants to go ahead and does not want the spouse to know about the problem. A man whose inclinations are predominantly homosexual may succeed for a time in the performance of his marital duties (perhaps by conjuring up homosexual thoughts during intercourse) but he is unlikely to make a permanently satisfactory husband either emotionally or physically. Try as he may to remain faithful, the confirmed homosexual tends sooner or later to relapse into his old habits. If he has never confessed his tendency, and his wife discovers it by accident, the emotional shock may lead to the bitterest recriminations, the break-up of the home, and perhaps divorce and public exposure. The psychiatrist has a plain duty to warn an established homosexual against contracting a marriage with a woman who does not know about his problem. Even if she does know, and expresses sympathy, he should make sure she really understands the situation and does not deceive herself that the conversion of a confirmed homosexual is simply a matter of practice. If she thinks her personal charms and her affection will easily wean a man from his perversion, she should be told that there are many homosexuals who can never be won over by feminine influence. Otherwise, finding that her efforts to attract her husband seem merely to irritate and worry him, she might become disillusioned and resentful. Moreover, neither the homosexual himself nor his prospective spouse may comprehend the depth of the aversion to the opposite sex, or the fact that, when it comes to the point of living together, the repulsion may be found to encompass a great many aspects of life besides the matter of genital contacts.

On this, as on other questions concerning homosexuality, the advice must not be too rule-of-thumb. Human nature is so various that the most surprising combinations sometimes succeed. The motive for marriage is important. A great feeling of comradeship, or mutual ambition to rear a family, perhaps forms a better basis than pure social convenience. Some completely homosexual men contract successful partnerships with older women who need an outlet for their motherliness, and are prepared to accept a platonic relationship. Others marry lesbians, and come to a sort of comradely understanding about their sexual adventures. There is also a type of *ménage a trois*, such as was hinted at in the play *The Third Person*, in which there is both a spouse and a homosexual lover. Considering how easy it is for a normal marriage to come to grief through temperamental difficulties, it is understandable that these unorthodox adjustments are particularly precarious.

In my opinion, therapists should concentrate their efforts upon five categories of patient. (1) Those who have fair prospects of cure, especially if they are still young and pliant in outlook. (2) Married homosexuals whose circumstances call for drastic action. (3) Those who are suffering acutely from anxiety or depression about their homosexual feelings, and cannot settle to a homosexual adjustment. (4) Those whose homosexual impulses are anti-social, that is directed towards children, or of aggressive-sadistic quality. (5) Those who cannot be turned down because they insist upon trying whatever treatment may be possible. In the fourth category, a modification rather than a complete re-orientation may suffice, and in the third category relief of tension may be all that can be hoped for.

Sorting out those likely to achieve a complete cure can only be done in a rough and ready intuitive manner. The signs already mentioned as promising include youthfulness, genuine motivation for change, absence of strong cross-sex identification, and, above all, a history of some heterosexual interest or experience. In addition, Albert Ellis [91] has suggested from his own experience that lesbians have better prospects than male homosexuals, perhaps because they can attempt heterosexual relations without fear of impotence. Severe neurotic reactions, although providing a strong motive for treatment, give cause for doubting the ultimate outcome, since they may interfere with heterosexual as much as with homosexual adjustment. In all cases of acute guilt or panic consequent upon conscious or unconscious homosexuality the first goal of treatment consists of bringing the patient to a full recognition and acceptance of his own feelings. In a case such as that of the man with the pregnancy phobia, described in Chapter VI, the patient must come to terms with himself, and get over the worst of his guilt feelings, before he can face up to the second stage, which is the overcoming of heterosexual inhibitions.

Some people might object to this, especially in the case of patients not fully aware of the nature of their own feelings. The effect of bringing out repressed tendencies might be to convert an anxiety neurotic into a practising homosexual. A nice question arises as to which is preferable: neurotic symptoms due to ill-repressed homosexual desires, or homosexual desires undisguised. Fortunately, an individual with a sufficiently sensitive conscience to have repressed his sexual feelings is unlikely to break out into irresponsible anti-social behaviour if his homosexual inclinations become overt. Dr. L. H. Rubinstein [320], an analyst with great experience of sexual deviants, has pointed out that even if the therapist cannot control the direction of a patient's sexual desire, a diminution of his repressions and a more rational understanding and acceptance of himself may release creative powers and improve personal relationships and thus produce a real social gain. At the same time, all psycho-analysts emphasize that a homosexual adjustment is very much a second best way of life, and many of them agree with Gershman [127] that even the best adjusted homosexuals are by the nature of their condition anxious and despondent personalities who can never attain full self-realization.

Psychiatrists can often give more relief by attending to secondary symptoms than by tackling sexual orientation. Many sexual deviants suffer from neurotic guilt feelings, and to alleviate this source of distress is a desirable end in itself, and a task much easier to accomplish than a conversion to heterosexuality. The mere fact that the psychiatrist accepts him and enters into sympathetic relation with him has a beneficial effect on the guilt-ridden patient. In this way miserable, isolated sufferers, who hitherto have felt that their shameful peculiarity cuts them off from all decent human contacts, gain a new faith in the possibility of helpful relations with other people. Release from neurotic guilt not only relieves their suffering but makes them more effective members of society. The man with the pregnancy phobia, once relieved of his abnormal preoccupation with his shame, would be able to concentrate on his work and enjoy normal friendships. From a solitary, drifting, useless character he could be transformed into a self-respecting individual with normal ambitions and interests, even though his homosexual inclinations might remain. But once again the question arises as to the justifiability of giving free rein to homosexual tendencies by removing the protection of neurotic guilt feelings. The answer lies in the qualification 'neurotic'. The psychiatrist does not remove the patient's sense of right and wrong: he can still decide that himself on moral grounds whether or no to give practical expression to his inclinations.

Among those who acquire sufficient equilibrium no longer to experience panic feelings or acute shame on account of their deviant inclinations, many fall a long way short of real contentment. Homosexuals in our society, and especially male homosexuals, cannot be completely reassured because, whether rightly or wrongly, they are in fact the butt of much ill-feeling. They tend to display the reactions typical of any rejected minority. A paranoid attitude, manifest in an uneasy, distrustful approach to people and a hypersensitivity to personal criticism, is all too common among homosexuals. Unfortunately, paranoid attitudes call forth from other people the disapproving, aggressive reactions the sufferer most wants to avoid. Some homosexuals experience great difficulty in their personal relationships on account of their insecurity and touchiness. Even in their love affairs with fellow homosexuals, their sulky, distrustful attitude can mar their relationships and cause much unhappiness and disillusionment. In these problems of personal relations the psychiatrist can give valuable help by means of discussion and superficial analysis.

In addition to the familiar paranoid tendencies, some react in other ways to their feeling of insecurity. A longing for acceptance may cause a person to adopt a rigidly conventional way of life. He does not want to draw attention to himself, and he does want to be one of the herd, so he strives to avoid all taint of unorthodoxy in opinions or behaviour. Few famous homosexuals have been radical reformers. This does not seem a very serious limitation, but it can sometimes produce feelings of severe frustration, as for instance when someone nurses ambitions to branch out into politics, art, social welfare, or other fields but dare not deviate from his formal routine. This type of inhibition occurred in extreme form in the man with the pregnancy phobia. He longed to apply for some worthwhile job but could not do so because he felt he was in too vulnerable a situation to accept a responsible post. The psychiatrist can help with all these difficulties and peculiarities which, fundamentally, arise from feelings of rejection and insecurity. Admittedly homosexuals may have some reason for feeling this way, but often their fears seem exaggerated. Given encouragement they gain confidence in themselves and in their dealings with others, and lose much of their fear-inspired attitudes.

All that has just been said on the side of pessimism and limited goals in treatment applies only to fully developed cases. Curran emphasized that it is unsafe to diagnose a state of established homosexuality before the age of twenty-five. Perhaps he carries the principle too far, but undoubtedly many young men who practise homosexuality in their late teens or early twenties grow out of the habit after meeting a suitable woman and settling down to heterosexual life. These are not true homosexuals harbouring deep-rooted and intractable inhibitions with regard to the opposite sex; they are simply late starters in heterosexuality.

Deciding the Aims of Treatment

In Western culture a youth arrives at physiological maturity long before mature expression of his sexual impulses becomes permissible or practicable. At the time when their impulses first assume adult intensity, most adolescent males are still engrossed in school activities, sports, work-training, and similar masculine pursuits. As a consequence their first sexual essays are so often with their own sex that a homosexual phase, characterized by undiscriminating pruriency and emotional fixations of the hero-worshipping type, is widely regarded as a normal feature of adolescence. Some young persons take a long time to work through this phase, not because they have a fixed homosexual orientation, but because their way of life leaves no room for the opposite sex, so that the full impact of heterosexual influences is delayed. Occasionally relatives seek psychiatric advice on behalf of some young person with an adolescent 'crush' on a friend. In most cases they can safely be reassured. Provided the young person shows no tendency to adopt manners and habits more appropriate to a member of the opposite sex, and provided he has no special aversion to mixed company, then permanent sexual deviation need not be anticipated. Given the right encouragement and opportunity for easy social contacts with the opposite sex, the healthy adolescent soon develops heterosexual interests in spite of early homosexual enthusiasms [21, 305].

Even if a man reaches the early twenties without ever seeking out a woman, it should not be assumed that his sexual inclinations are completely inverted without first carefully investigating his attitude and circumstances. Age is not the only consideration. A man or woman with no practical experience of sex save an occasional homosexual adventure, followed by guilt and remorse, has more chance of developing heterosexuality than a younger person who has regularly indulged in deviant practices for several years. A man who only practises homosexuality *faute de mieux*, because social backwardness or fear of responsibility prevents him making advances to the woman he wants, has a better prospect of cure than another with youth on his side but with no interest in women. When homosexual behaviour represents a precarious solution of current conflicts, or reflects the pressure of external circumstances, a change may well come about. When it arises from deep emotional prejudices against normal sexual contacts, reinforced by long experience and acceptance of a homosexual mode of life, then prospects of cure are slight. But there are no clearly marked dividing lines and no certainty in prognosis. A case considered hopeless may surprise everyone by achieving full heterosexual adjustment. The subtle interplay of external and internal influences can never be completely defined and predicted. Taking into account age, sexual experience, current outlook, and personality factors, the most the psychiatrist can do is to make a rough guess at the probable outcome. But he won't often be proved wrong if he makes a pessimistic prediction in all cases in which a man has practised homosexuality for years without guilt, and has reached the late twenties without evincing any sexual interest in women.

When the situation reduces to a matter of encouraging the homosexual to live with his condition and to make the best of his life in spite of it, he may ask bluntly whether to strive for complete sexual abstinence. The psychiatrist can evade the issue, by saying that the question raises moral and legal issues outside his domain; but a more generous response would be to explain that abstinence forced by fear and guilt often leads to emotional disturbance, but when strong-minded persons make a deliberate choice to live celibately they sometimes succeed without visible harm. The task becomes less difficult if the individual is fortified by a strong sense of purpose behind his sacrifice, as in the case of a priest, or if he can immerse himself in some cause or activity that will use up the energy he would otherwise expend on the pursuit of love. But for many men, especially those who lack conviction of the value of continence, and those who have been used to sexual experience, the attempt frequently fails, and in any case produces intolerable irritability, restlessness, or depression. Most confirmed homosexuals learn that provided they keep their behaviour discreet and private they remain for the most part unmolested; and they learn to bear with the slight risk of accidental exposure or blackmail. Homosexuals rarely find it expedient to emigrate from their native land in search of greater legal or social tolerance.

3. *Techniques of Treatment*

Physical methods of treatment are of little use for homosexuality. As explained earlier, androgenic hormones stimulate sex desire without altering the direction of the sexual interest. However, these hormones may help young males who suffer some retardation in physical sex development. By improving potency and masculine physique the hormone may serve to encourage some men whose fear of heterosexuality stems from an awareness of their own physical inadequancy. Oestrogens also have practical value in some cases, since they reduce the male's sexual desire. This in no sense effects a cure, but it can give temporary relief from dangerously compulsive urges, and this is an obvious advantage in dealing with offenders against children. During the phases of emotional unrest that often occur in the course of psychotherapy, oestrogens may afford some protection from impulsive and foolhardy sexual exploits. Unfortunately the medication is rather slow-acting and not very reliable. In some men it produces impotence without much loss of desire, and it often has to be discontinued on account of disagreeable side effects, in particular painful and embarrassing swelling of the breasts. For this reason, some therapists prefer to use tranquillizing drugs, which sometimes have an indirect effect upon sexual compulsions. Surgical castration is not practiced in England owing to legal complications; but in some countries it has been used to some effect for controlling men who commit violent sexual assaults, whether homosexual or heterosexual. In Sweden and Finland the courts have power to order compulsory castration of certain offenders. According to Slovenko [339], judges in isolated areas of the United

States sometimes grant probation or suspended sentences on condition that a sex offender agrees to this operation, which obviously he will be inclined to do if he thinks the alternative will be a stiff prison sentence. C. T. Duffy [84], former warden of San Quentin prison, believes that in the few cases in which superior court judges in California have put sex offenders on probation after consenting to castration, the outcome has been successful. In his view, most of the Californian convicts who submitted to castration showed dramatic improvement; they became happier, more co-operative, better able to face the future, and were generally successful when put on parole. In Denmark, convicted sex criminals who have been pronounced psychopathic, and committed to prison hospital for an indefinite period, may obtain their release quicker by 'volunteering' to undergo castration, when this has been recommended by the doctors in charge. In Denmark, psychopathic offenders receive a great deal of social supervision and support following their release, and the apparent effectiveness of the system may be due to this factor as well as to the castration [351]. In England, unfortunately, men who have committed serious sexual assaults are all too often released back into the community with minimal help or supervision once the term of imprisonment fixed by the judge has expired. On the other hand, in states such as Maryland that have a legal system for committing dangerous sex offenders for indefinite periods of treatment, the difficulty of deciding when to release tends to result in offenders being detained, perhaps unnecessarily, for very long periods.

As for other physical treatments, one gets the impression that at various times one thing after another has been tried, more for the sake of doing something than on any reasoned plan. The application of electro-convulsant therapy, a method that helps to clear melancholia, has rightly fallen into disrepute [362], although one authority, Dr. Paul de River [314], still advises its use 'in order to bring about a complete change in the pattern of thought of extreme homosexuals'. Another authority claimed to cure both male and female homosexuality by inducing convulsions with the drug metrazol, but the idea seems to have died a natural death [286].

As a means of curing neurotic inhibitions, forceful suggestion, or direct commands under hypnosis, went out of fashion when the psycho-analytic technique gained ascendancy. It was argued that removal of the symptom by suggestion merely led to the appearance of other and possibly worse symptoms, since the conflicts responsible remained unrelieved. Imperative commands to engage in heterosexual intercourse might simply increase the homosexual patient's conflicts, or even precipitate a mental breakdown. Nevertheless, the older German literature describes many experiments of this kind. The Baron von Schrenck-Notzing [328] regarded the establishment of heterosexual intercourse as the principal requirement for cure, and published details of cases in which he and other doctors had succeeded in this purpose by means of hypnotic suggestion. The assumption that actual practice in copulation will necessarily overcome deep-seated inhibitions strikes the modern reader as crude, and some of the pathetic letters from patients telling of their unhappy attempts to comply bear witness to the limitations of this approach. However, Milne Bramwell [41] reported one case (No. 49) in which he treated very successfully by prolonged suggestion a life-long male homosexual. This man had married in the hope of curing himself, only to find intercourse with his wife quite impossible and repugnant. After treatment his married life became normal and he lost his illicit compulsions. In the comparatively few instances in which this technique works and no relapse follows, one suspects that the physician's commands have served to bolster the patient's own strong wish to attempt intercourse. The use of hypnotism to force copulation by persons not ready for it risks producing serious disappointments and complications for both the patient and his sexual partner. The method has fallen into disrepute, although some success was claimed for it recently by Mayer Stone [349] in the case of a young male patient who was both homosexual and mentally subnormal. In modern practice, hypnotism is still used, but as an aid to securing the patient's confidence and to help him bring out his conflicts, and not for the purpose of inducing premature copulation [324].

Many physicians have felt that induction into hetero-sexual experience by a non-threatening, tolerant, and experienced partner might serve to overcome the inhibitions of some homosexuals. The use of a sympathetic woman or a specially trained prostitute has been suggested as treatment for some sex offenders [333] One case of successful seduction therapy in real life, without benefit of medical guidance, is cited later (see page 256). Another case came to my personal attention following a previous edition of this book, when an attractive young lady came to see me to volunteer to help male homosexuals overcome their inhibitions. She had been the girl-friend of a confirmed homosexual, and by dint of persistence in laughing away his inhibitions she had got him to the point of being able to enjoy normal intercourse. Unfortunately for her, once freed in this way, he rather understandably forsook his original mentor and married someone else. Foreseeing a long sequence of further disappointments in store for her, I had to advise her to look for a normal man!

Frankly punitive deterrents seem to make some homosexuals more circumspect in their behaviour. Indeed, the threat of severe reprisals may be absolutely essential to deter some individuals (whether heterosexual or homosexual) from sexual assaults or other totally unacceptable behaviour. But attempts to stamp out all forms of homosexual expression by ferocious methods of ostracism, torture and execution have been no more effective than when similar methods were applied to fornicators. They may intimidate some people into enforced continence, but they do not change homosexual potentialities. The shame and frustration provoked by too harsh an approach may lead to still worse disturbances. Much the same criticism applies to the various forms of financial coercion, threats, exhortations and 'brain washing' by which families sometimes try to force their homosexual off-spring to change their ways. All too often, abuse or lamentation merely adds to the homosexual's miseries without furnishing any solution. Religious exhortation, which places emphasis on the wickedness of yielding to impulse, encourages continence by building up inhibitions based on guilt feeling. If the result were a calm, deliberate decision to behave chastely it would not be unhealthy, but injudiciously expressed religious precepts tend to exaggerate the sufferer's sense of guilt and shame. Instead of inducing strong-minded self-control, this leads to great misery and to desperate attempts to deny the very existence of the offending impulses. The repressions and mental conflicts so provoked may turn the individual into a worse social nuisance and misfit than he would have been if he had simply stayed homosexual. One cannot blame the priest for this regrettable outcome. It is all very well for a psychiatrist like Dr. Desmond Curran to detach himself from moral questions and tell the patient, 'Decide for yourself', but the priest has to teach a set code which includes the rule that homosexual acts are wicked and inexcusable.

Treatment through imprisonment is a contradiction in terms. Those who try to justify prison sentences for homosexuality on the grounds that loss of liberty provides impetus for conversion to heterosexuality are ignorant of the elementary facts of the matter. The argument that punishment acts as a deterrent to potential offenders provides the only rational basis for imprisonment. But for the individual who is incarcerated, segregation in an over-crowded gaol serves only to encourage his homosexual practices (see pages 124-132). This is not to decry the good work of some of the prison therapists, who do much to help the homosexuals in their charge, but prospects of radical cure are greatly reduced by a prison atmosphere [246]. The only hope of changing sexual orientation lies in the removing of inhibitions by means of psychological treatment accompanied by a step-by-step adjustment to heterosexual life. A man submerged in the living death of prison routine, and cut off from all feminine company, is under the worst possible conditions for receiving treatment. As Dr. Stanley-Jones has said, imprisonment 'is as futile from the point of view of treatment as to hope to rehabilitate a chronic alcoholic by giving him occupational therapy in a brewery' [347]. In effect, the circumstances of prison life, and the limited amount of time prison psychiatrists can give to the matter, virtually preclude all hope of radical cures. The most that can be done in prisons under existing circumstances is on the lines described by Dr. J. C. Mackwood, [247], one-time psychotherapist at Wormwood Scrubs. This institution provided a separate ward for prisoners undergoing treatment. There they met together as a group and talked out their problems under the doctor's guidance. This group treatment had a remedial and educational effect on neurotic prisoners. Dr. Mackwood remarked that sometimes the group contained over 50 per cent of homosexuals. He aimed to help them by discussion of their disturbed relations with other people, but he admitted the task could have been done under more suitable conditions. In fact, he advocated legal reform that would make socially harmless behaviour no longer a crime.

In considering the question of therapy in prisons, one must take account of the fact that many of the men who find their way into gaol are not the sort to benefit from psychological treatment under any circumstances. Dr. F. J. Taylor, in a survey of 96 cases sent to Brixton Prison for homosexual offences in 1946, found only one that was suitable for psychotherapy and had good prospects. The 96 men comprised 66 who were classified as pseudo-homosexuals because they were thought to have indulged only as a substitute for normal sexual relations, 5 who were prostitutes, 12 who were bisexuals and capable of full satisfaction with either sex, and only 13 who were complete homosexuals. Of these 13, 7 were in prison in spite of previous psychotherapy and 3 emphatically refused to have treatment [356].

Some sex offenders must be forcibly restrained and dealt with under detention, because their behaviour is much too dangerous to be tolerated, and because they will not co-operate except under duress. This applies especially to men prone to violent assaults, regardless of whether their impulses are heterosexual or homosexual. These are best handled in special security hospitals, if only because every every possible medical effort needs to be made to reduce their dangerousness before they are released. Difficulty arises in knowing how to cope with nuisance offenders, who importune around lavatories, solicit for prostitution, or seek the company of young persons for sexual purposes. In their case, although the penalty of imprisonment carries all the disadvantages mentioned, the courts have no other realistic alternative for dealing with persistent offenders of this kind, especially as psychiatric clinics so often find such persons untreatable and unco-operative.

For individuals with sufficient capacity to introspect and put their feelings into words, the best hope of radical change probably lies in psycho-analysis, either in its full traditional form, or in the various attenuated or modified versions known as analytically orientated psychotherapy. Most people nowadays are familiar with the broad outline of the technique, which consists of long and repeated sessions of talking out inner thoughts and fantasies. The neurotic sufferer has a sort of compulsion to dwell upon topics related to his conflicts, but he tends always to skirt round the edge without ever coming to grips with the real issues. The analyst directs his attention to the focal points of his disturbance, forces him to verbalize ever more fully and frankly his conflicting emotions and fantasies, and by this means guides him along the difficult path of self-revelation. In the process, old conflicts flare up, and the patient relives with dramatic intensity the turbulent emotions of his formative years. For him analysis is a painful struggle. His neurotic symptoms or sexual aberrations represent a com-fortable, half-way adjustment to life. He wants to grow out of this half-way stage, but at the same time he clings grimly to his neurotic refuge. Treatment, therefore, consists of a protracted battle between fears and resistance to change on the one hand and desire for normality on the other. But the process of changing the deeply ingrained emotional habits of a lifetime cannot be hurried. Full psycho-analysis may mean many five hour-long sessions every week for a period of years. Even so, for many patients the task proves too difficult, and they slip back into their neurotic ways. Psycho-analysis is successful only in carefully selected cases. It is a lengthy, costly, and exacting business which demands of the patient a certain intelligence, a capacity for self-scrutiny, and a sincere desire to go through anything for the sake of a cure.

The analyst's technique is essentially the same whether the patient presents obvious neurotic symptoms or whether the only complaint concerns abnormal sex inclinations. Persons in a tense state, with prominent anxiety symptoms and guilt feelings (as in the case of the man with the pregnancy phobia), are easy to help because their conflicts are close to the surface and their miserable condition provides a strong motive for change. The difficult cases are those who have long since adopted homosexual practices as a part of the natural order of things and have no pressing motive for trying to unearth their past conflicts. In all cases the analyst directs attention to the inhibitions that prevent heterosexual development. He is under no compulsion to explain how it is that the patient can love a person of his own sex. To the analyst such love is neither unnatural nor incomprehensible, but simply immature. When the barriers of unconscious fear and guilt are removed the patient is free to choose himself a more appropriate love object. Unfortunately, in many cases the discovery of infantile fears of incestuous relationships and suchlike fantasies, which the analysts believe to have been the original cause of the turning away from normal sex, does not in itself bring about a disappearance of homosexual desires.

Therapists differ in their views about the necessity for full-scale, long-term psycho-analysis, as opposed to psychotherapy of less prolonged duration and more circumscribed character. A lot depends upon the therapist's ideas of the main forces at work in a given case. If the therapist believes that the patient is being held back by present fears of asserting himself, a relatively superficial exploration of this topic may suffice. Even if the therapist believes that the patient's fear of the opposite sex arises from traumatic experiences of childhood, it may be possible to expose and deal with these frightening memories in a relatively short time, perhaps with the aid of hypnosis, or with intravenous injections of anxiety-relieving, tongue-loosening 'truth' drugs. In his reports of quick cures by psychotherapy, Hadfield [152, 153] gives several examples. In one case, a male homosexual's aversion to women disappeared after he had recalled a frightening childhood episode in which a servant girl had made him masturbate her. In another case an illegitimate child recalled how his mother, depressed by the struggle to support him on her own, had actually tried to smother him. After bringing this out, he too lost his fear for women. Many therapists doubt the validity of such recollections, suggesting that they represent fantasy dramatizations of infantile fears rather than actual events. Others have suggested that they are screen memories, that is symbolic fantasy constructs which protect the patient from too exact a recollection of a painful past. One might guess that the dramatic smothering episode was easier for the man to think about than a realization that he had felt murderously resentful towards his rejecting mother, and had carried over something of this feeling in his attitude to other women. If the recollection of an infantile trauma really produces a cure, it hardly matters in practice whether the recollection is exact; but in the experience of most psychotherapists, such dramatic recollections rarely lead to correspondingly dramatic cures. More typically, an aversion towards the opposite sex stems from chronic fear or suspicion, slowly built up over years on the basis of repeated painful experiences until it becomes a fixed and self-perpetuating attitude of mind that can only be overcome by an emotional revolution and much reassuring new experience.

4. Behaviour Therapy

Psycho-analysts conceive of neurotic symptoms as the outward signs of inner conflict. They maintain that delving into the patient's emotional life and exposing his unconscious feelings provides the only really satisfactory method of understanding and cure. Behaviourists, on the other hand, look upon such symptoms as being more like faulty habits that have no deep symbolic significance and may have been picked up almost by accident. The behaviourist would see no more reason to interpret inappropriate sexual conduct in the light of infantile conflicts than to seek an explanation of pencil sucking in terms of oral fixations. Both the pencil sucking and the undesirable sexual habit have become automatic conditioned responses to certain situations. To stop such habits, all one needs is a technique for breaking the link between stimulus and response.

Two main forms of treatment have evolved in practice, the merits of which can be judged independently of the behaviouristic theories that inspired them. The desensitization technique, developed particularly by J. Wolpe, is mostly used to treat specific phobias [388]. The patient is introduced gradually to whatever situations he is most afraid of, while at the same time being given soothing, anxiety-relieving stimuli which inhibit the inappropriate panic response. In principle, the method could be applied equally well to persons with sexual fears, by exposing them to heterosexual seduction in easy stages, to the accompaniment of stiff drinks and moral support from the therapist, but the limitations of conventional decorum and morality prevent the professional man arranging this. Occasionally, in real life, a situation arises spontaneously very like what the behaviour therapist might have designed. Dr. Gebhard [125] described one case of a confirmed lesbian who went to a party at the home of a predominantly homosexual male friend. She drank rather a lot, and then accepted an invitation to stay the night, knowing her host would not be importunate. In fact, he had some homosexual activity in a room adjoining the one where she was sleeping. She overheard and was somewhat aroused. After his friend had gone, her host heard her moving about and called her to him. She sat on his bed without fear, and confessed she was feeling lonely. He laughingly drew her down on top of him—which was her favourite sexual position—and intercourse took place. Taken by surprise in this soothing, anxiety-free situation, she found coitus surprisingly pleasurable, and tried it again the following night, again with satisfactory results. In consequence, her whole sexual orientation changed, and she came to accept and enjoy a full heterosexual life.

Stevenson and Wolpe [348] have reported the successful conversion of two male homosexuals by a less direct approach, but still making use of a desensitization method. In both cases, fear of having to assert themselves was judged to be the main difficulty. The patients were encouraged to experience the satisfaction of taking successful assertive action in small everyday matters so that they would gradually lose their fears. One of them was a twenty-two year old student who had been exclusively homosexual since puberty. The other was a thirty-two year old hairdresser who was a life-long homosexual. The former was under the domination of an unsympathetic stepfather. The latter came from a family background of domineering, critical mother and weak passive father. He had developed habitually fearful, submissive responses in social situations, feeling helpless and tearful in the face of unjustified complaints by customers. Both developed heterosexual interests as they got more used to asserting themselves, and both made satisfactory marriages. These successes might be explained psycho-dynamically, in terms of identification with the therapists rather than as a sort of mechanical desensitization process; but however one looks at it the striking point emerges that the loss of non-sexual fears may lead to loss of associated sexual fears.

The behaviouristic technique more commonly used on sexual deviants, aversion therapy, was well known as a method for treating alcoholics long before it became part of the system of modern behaviour therapy. The alcoholic is given a taste of his favourite tipple, or the homosexual is shown a picture of an attractive nude, but his pleasure is interrupted by some unpleasant, punishing sensation, such as an injection which induces nausea. After frequent repetitions of this sequence the patient finds his former attraction replaced by an automatic reaction of distaste or aversion.

Basil James [190] reported the successful application of this technique to a bachelor of forty who had had ineffective psychotherapy for his exclusive, life-long homosexuality, and was now depressed and even suicidal on account of his perversion. He was given nauseating injections while he looked at homosexually stimulating pictures. Simultaneously, tape recordings were played and re-played, which graphically retailed the misfortunes that homosexuality had brought upon him, emphasized the disgusting and nauseating qualities of his urges, and ended with sounds of vomiting. The treatment had to be interrupted after 30 hours, owing to its physical effects, but after 24 hours it was resumed for a further 32 hours. The patient lost his homosexual urges almost completely. Followed up after 18 months [191], his social adjustment had improved, and he had succeeded in having intercourse with a steady girl friend, although he admitted he did not get quite the same emotional satisfaction from it as he had had previously from his male lovers.

Traditionally, the punishing stimulus is an injection of emetic, such as apomorphine or emetine, but this carries some risk. The severity of the vomiting is not so easily controlled, and it is generally considered necessary to go through the process repeatedly until the patient is thoroughly exhausted. On 7 February 1964, an inquest at Westminster[1] established that the death from heart failure of a male homosexual who had been given aversion therapy was due to poisoning by the emetic. Use of electric shocks in place of emetics avoids this risk, and may be more effec-

[1] *Medico Legal Journal*, 1964, *32*, 95.

tive, since the speed and certainty with which pain follows every pleasurable stimulus is more important than severity of punishment. Solyom and Miller [344] used a combination of reward and punishment, interrupting a continuous electric shock while men looked at a female picture, and introducing a fresh electric shock when a male picture was in view. The technique failed to eliminate the mens' sexual responses to the male pictures.

Psychotherapists naturally look upon aversion therapy with distrust. As an aggressive, punitive approach to an obnoxious symptom, it can have a dangerous appeal to penal and military authorities. In view of the frequent relapses of alcoholics, following temporarily successful aversion, one would expect to find similar relapses among homosexuals. Indeed this has been reported by Dr. Freund [116], who is the one psychiatrist to have followed up a fair number of cases. He used nauseating stimuli (while his male homosexuals were looking at pictures of men) and a sexual stimulant, testosterone propionate (when they were looking at pictures of women). Of 67 patients, 22 established some heterosexual behaviour, but only 12 of them maintained it after the passage of several years, and only 3 broke off all homosexual activity following the treatment.

Feldman [96] and later Mather [253] reported rather more optimistically on the results of a form of aversion treatment with electric shocks carried out in Manchester. In this technique, the patient looks at a homosexually stimulating picture projected on a screen. After eight seconds an unpleasant shock begins and continues until such time as he presses a button which causes the removal of the picture. If he presses the button before the eight seconds have passed, he is rewarded, in a proportion of occasions, by not receiving the expected shock. According to theory, anticipatory avoidance responses, once firmly established, are particularly long lasting. In this study there was no follow up, but at the end of some fifteen or twenty treatment sessions 25 out of the 36 patients who went through with the course reported to their therapists (by interview and questionnaire) some change in the direction of more heterosexual interest or activity. The therapists found, as have so many others, that younger patients and strongly motivated patients responded best, and that a complete absence of heterosexual interest at any time during the patient's history was a distinctly unfavourable sign. Those attracted to children also responded poorly, apparently on account of their greater personality disturbance and greater difficulty in adjusting to adults social life generally.

The aversion approach need not be restricted to homosexuals. On 3 December 1966, the *Daily Mail*, under the headline *How electric shocks took Mr. X's mind off his mistress*, described how two psychiatrists had used the technique to quell an errant husband's illicit and troublesome desires by giving him an electric shock each time they showed him the lady's picture. 'Immediately after the first session, he developed a deep sense of guilt . . .' In a recent paper, Adolf Meyer [260] has produced evidence that in fact behaviour therapy appears to be no more often successful than the traditional psycho-analytic approach. Perhaps the most cogent of the objections to aversion treatment has been voiced by Dr. Peter Scott who wrote [331]: 'One would hesitate to apply this method to a patient who had not already an acceptable means of sexual expression'. The destruction of a homosexual adjustment does not automatically establish a heterosexual substitute. It may cause some patients to undertake heterosexual experiments who otherwise might not have done so, but it will leave others impotent and frustrated and in a worse state than they were before. In my own opinion, use of the aversion method should be limited to those whose perversion takes a dangerously anti-social form, and those who are so tortured by neurotic reactions of guilt, depression and anxiety that they clamour for relief from sexual temptation by any means available.

CHAPTER XII

CONCLUSIONS

1. Causes

Research into the causes of homosexuality has left a lot of mysteries unsolved, but it has cleared up some points, and on certain important issues it has unearthed enough information to make reasonable guesses. Before going on to consider practical measures of prevention, control or toleration, it may be worthwhile to recapitulate some of the main conclusions and inferences.

In the absence of heterosexual outlets, or in circumstances of cultural permissiveness (as in ancient Greece or in some of the primitive societies mentioned in Chapter I) a large proportion, at least of the male sex, behave homosexually. This shows that homosexual behaviour is not always incompatible with normality in other respects. In present day Western society, in spite of the contempt, ridicule and moral condemnation of the majority, the number of practising homosexuals is enormous. If all of them were seriously abnormal, apart from their sex lives, civilization would lapse into chaos. In view of the responsiveness of the sexual apparatus to all kinds of stimuli, the biologist finds no special reason to marvel at the prevalence of deviant habits. The real puzzles are why sexual reactions normally come to be directed exclusively towards other people, and why the great majority of mankind develop a strong heterosexual or homosexual preference.

In regard to physique, genital development, glandular and reproductive functions, and chromosomal constitution, nearly all homosexuals, however fixed or exclusive their homo-erotic addiction, are quite normal men and women physically. Even from the psychological standpoint, many homosexuals and lesbians do not differ very radically from the normal outlook of their sex. Male homosexuals tend to like adventure, and to be promiscuous; lesbians tend to like domesticity and fidelity. Cory and LeRoy, [67] writing from the point of view of male homosexuals, complain that deviants suffer from being looked down upon as something less than 'real' men, and some of them react by trying to assert their masculinity in exaggerated ways.

The balance of evidence favours the view that obligatory homosexual orientation comes about as a result of experiences during the individual's lifetime, rather than as a consequence of any inborn physical peculiarity. Although Kallmann's research on twins suggested the existence of a strong inherited factor, his results have never been confirmed, and they do not accord with the implications of other types of research. In particular, evidence from studies of physical inter-sexuals and psychological transsexuals shows that social training in infancy plays a crucial part in fixing a person's sense of identity with one sex or the other. It seems that this factor sometimes outweighs the influence of inherited bodily characteristics, even when these are quite normal male or female.

Although the causes of an exclusively homosexual orientation are likely to be psychological more than physical, pinning them down has proved difficult. Different authorities assign prime importance to different influences. It seems highly probable that the true causes vary from one case to the next. For example, in attitude, temperament, and in the nature of their conflicts, trans-sexuals and persons with a yearning to belong to the opposite sex, differ sharply from those homosexuals who like most things about their sex roles apart from heterosexual intercourse. Psychoanalysts consider that in most types of homosexuality the crucial causative factors operate during infancy. Certainly, when homosexuality develops in the context of a strong feeling of identification with the opposite sex signs of this development often become noticeable quite early in childhood. But in many instances the future homosexual performs more or less normally in the social role appropriate to his sex, and only appears different from others when he reaches adolescence and fails to evince the erotic interests expected at that age. In such cases, however, it seems a fairly safe presumption that strong forces of repression or denial are at work, and that something must have begun to go wrong some time before the disorder became apparent.

Most typically, the obligatory, exclusive homosexual recalls little or no interest in the opposite sex at adolescence, but an awakening of erotic and romantic feelings towards friends of his own sex, which sooner or later he comes to put into practice. Throughout this book a distinction has been made between this compulsive, obligatory homosexuality (almost certainly based upon inhibitions about the opposite sex, and most noticeably prevalent in the more sexually puritan countries) and the sporadic homosexual behaviour which occurs in situations or places where such activity is tolerated as a convenient extra outlet for the predatory male. In our relatively rigid Western culture, which surrounds youthful heterosexual contacts with a certain aura of anxiety, and at the same time seeks to block the homosexual outlet altogether, two main deviant types appear. First, the rebel class, those who fail to absorb the common standards and indulge their bisexual impulses in defiance of accepted morality. Their sexual peculiarities are often over-shadowed by other rebellious or anti-social trends. Second, the true or obligatory homosexual, whose deviant habits seem to arise from some hinderance or fear that has prevented the development of heterosexual interests. This is the bigger group and the one that represents the worst problem in terms of human suffering and social disruption. Some hidden incapacity prevents them from fitting in with social requirements as far as sex is concerned, although on most other matters they conform quite easily.

Freud attributed the inhibition of heterosexuality, and the flight from heterosexual temptation, to persistence of over-inclusive incest taboos acquired in infancy. Later authorities, psycho-analytic and otherwise, have since put forward a variety of additional interpretations. Whatever the exact truth of the matter, a large amount of evidence exists to show that the circumstances of child-rearing have particular relevance. Males who have had a combination of dominating, possessive, sexually prudish mother, and a weak, absent or aloof father, risk developing sexual difficulties in general and homosexual orientation in particular. The process involved could be just as well interpreted as a crushing of the boy's confidence in his adequacy as a male, rather than a specifically Oedipal situation, in which all erotic feelings towards girls become linked with feelings towards mother. In fact, too close attention to the specific sexual phobia may detract attention from other equally important sources of anxiety, such as fear of the domination or contempt of persons of the opposite sex. In some cases, at least, it seems probable that temperamental difficulties in forming intimate relationships is the root problem, and anxiety about copulation only a secondary difficulty. The repressions that lead to obligatory homosexuality presumably begin early in life, before the heterosexual response is fully established, and while the individual is still sufficiently pliant. One reason why adult homosexuals of mature age rarely change their ways may be that long experience of obtaining sexual and emotional satisfaction in a particular fashion strongly conditions an individual to continue with his habitual pattern of behaviour for its own sake.

Many people, especially the homosexuals themselves, dispute the existence of the hypothetical phobia against heterosexuality, and maintain that it is mere lack of interest, not fear, that prevents contact with the opposite sex. In support of this, they point out that persons subject to other kinds of phobias tend to be demonstrably anxious or neurotic in temperament, whereas tests applied to homosexual volunteers have failed to reveal any general neurotic trend. On the other hand, anyone who has had experience of dealing with homosexuals knows that many of them display a variety of peculiar distrustful, or hostile attitudes to persons of the opposite sex. Very often, the homosexual's aversion to heterosexual situations exceeds the normal heterosexual's aversion to homosexuality. Moreover, following the ventilation of their fears in the course of psychotherapy, some homosexuals have had dramatic cures. These may be exceptional, but the fact that they happen at all suggests that many more homosexuals might change if only their fears could be exposed and overcome.

The puzzling normality of the well-adjusted adult homosexual, and the ineluctable quality of his erotic orientation, can perhaps be understood by analogy with heterosexual development. Some people remain unrepentantly bisexual all their lives, but many more develop a firm and exclusively heterosexual orientation, with no erotic interest whatever in their own sex. We don't think of these healthy heterosexuals as in any way abnormal. Although they have presumably repressed their homosexual responsiveness, they do not suffer from having done so, and they would not show signs of neurotic tendency on tests. They have no conflict, because their behaviour pattern fits in well with the expectations of the culture in which they live, and the functions they perform as husbands and wives. They have lost nothing by complete repression. The well-adjusted homosexual is in a not altogether dissimilar position. He has presumably repressed his heterosexual potential, but so long as he finds both emotional and erotic satisfaction with partners of the same sex, and so long as he has sufficient support from the sub-culture of deviants not to feel isolated or overwhelmed by the disapproval of the heterosexual majority, he has no immediate source of conflict. He has achieved a tolerable, and therefore healthy solution. Repression leads to neurotic disturbance only when pressing needs are denied. With other kinds of sexual perversion, such as paedophilia, exhibitionism or fetishism, the solution is intolerable, because these sexual outlets afford no scope for building up rewarding personal relationships, and because the affected persons find no acceptance among any social group.

If it is true that one's ultimate sexual orientation is firmly laid down in infancy (as is suggested by studies of physical inter-sexuals as well as by psycho-analytic theory), it follows that events of adolescence can have but slight influence. Indeed, such evidence as exists concerning the effects on youths of homosexual experience, either as prostitutes or as victims of seduction, suggests that this has little importance in the causation of obligatory homosexuality, although it may sometimes bring into the open a previous disposition. On the other hand, it seems likely that difficulties and embarrassments when trying to make heterosexual contacts during adolescence have a more deleterious effect, since, by confirming pre-existing fears, they may cause a young person to fall back upon the society of his own sex. But often this retreat is only temporary. The fact that many young people grow out of homosexual habits as they get older casts doubt on the assumption that sexual orientation is always firmly fixed either in childhood or in youth. No doubt some individuals are doomed from infancy, due to indelible aversions or cross-sex identifications, but others remain potentially capable of heterosexual development even in their twenties. The comparatively hopeless cases, for whom no known treatment holds out much hope of change, are older persons who have practised homosexuality for many years and have never tried, or wanted to try, to function heterosexually.

2. Prevention by Tolerance?

No known method of treatment or punishment offers hope of making any substantial reduction in the vast army of adults practising homosexuality. Rather than pretending they don't exist, or hoping to eradicate them by sheer weight of disapproval, it would be more realistic to find room for them in society, so that they can live unmolested and make their contribution to the common good. In previous chapters of this book, and in the public debates on law reform, the point has been made repeatedly that attempts to combat homosexuality by legal and social discrimination tend to exaggerate the very troubles they set out to combat. Even in the United States, where public opinion towards male homosexuals seems particularly unfavourable, experts have come to doubt the practicability or the justice of using the criminal law to condemn all homosexual acts. Edwin Schur [329], discussing the pros and cons of current public policy in America, points out the demoralizing and humiliating effects of the present system upon homosexuals. The disgruntlement and social alienation of a substantial minority of citizens is a high price to pay to preserve laws which quite obviously fail to control the conduct against which they are directed. The low visibility of individual transgressions makes it impossible to enforce continence, and the obvious unfairness of scapegoating the tiny minority of detected offenders brings the legal process into disrepute. The law would receive more wholehearted support from the intellectual sector of the public if the standards were similar for heterosexuals and homosexuals alike, and sexual crimes involving force, or abuse of the young, did not take into account the sex of the participants. Some opponents of the policy of tolerance argue that to permit deviant practices would be to open the flood-gates to a great upsurge of immorality, which would endanger family life and lower the birth rate. Such fears are grossly exaggerated. No such outcome has arrived in Holland or in other countries that have long exercised legal tolerance. No jubilant processions of deviants celebrated the recent relaxation of English law. Pressure of public opinion ensures that homosexuals behave with some discretion. The only unanswerable argument against tolerance is the religious one, that such acts should not be allowed because they are against God's will. But most people would deprecate the use of the criminal law to enforce a religious dogma.

The desirability of greater tolerance appears so obvious that one must look beyond rational considerations to understand why the question remains a focus of controversy. Dr. J. C. Flugel [100] has pointed out that on questions of this sort clashes occur between two opposite points of view, both of which are more closely associated with the emotional development of their protagonists than with the merits of the situation. Persons who in early life have identified strongly with strict parental figures tend to lean towards conservatism and authoritarianism. They are patriotic and loyal to the leader, they uphold traditions and class distinctions, they stress the need for discipline in education and penology, they support religious institutions and the sanctity of family life, and they abhor sexual deviants. The opposite type, those who have undergone an emotional rejection of parental standards, adopt radical opinions, believe in comradeship rather than loyalty to a father figure, dislike the social hierarchy, oppose discipline in education, support penal reform, and are more 'open-minded' about homosexuals. A similar breakdown of social attitudes, with the added refinement of statistical measures, has been carried out by Eysenck, who places individuals on a scale stretching from Toughness and Authoritarianism at one end to Softness and Humanitarianism at the other. At the 'tough' end of the scale are those in favour of such things as flogging for crimes of violence, compulsory sterilization, and corporal punishment for children [95]. It seems that the suggestion of tolerance towards sexual deviants runs counter to a very common constellation of emotionally determined attitudes.

In order to come to a balanced judgement on the matter of the correct attitude to homosexuals, one has to try to cast personal feeling on one side, and to discount the particular prejudices of our society, which has so long unthinkingly stigmatized all such persons as 'perverse', 'heretical', or 'criminal'. The task calls for a high degree of intellectual honesty. Hatred of deviants is so deeply ingrained that, however much an individual may try to preserve a rational approach, he cannot prevent a shudder of disgust at the thought of sexual habits outside his personal experience. Intellectual realization that our own code is arbitrary, and that some people might consider our own kissing habits disgustingly perverse, cannot entirely overcome this revulsion. Nevertheless everyone, and especially every doctor, should strive to approach the problem without bias. Though the doctor may not approve the habits of sexual deviants, he can at least try to understand and to give comfort when it is needed.

Important as it may be, both from a practical and a humanitarian point of view, to help an unfortunate minority by introducing legislative changes, the need for tolerance and understanding goes much deeper than this. Paradoxically, too much intolerance, a too repressive attitude, and a too narrow view of what is natural and unnatural in the sexual sphere, aggravates the situation by instilling at an early age the fears and anxieties that lead to the very deviations that society is trying to suppress. Even if a libertarian attitude were to lead to more people trying homosexual acts, this would be less serious than the present situation, in which so many unhappy individuals find themselves shut off from normal life by a compulsive addiction to their special perversion. The frankness of modern writings about sex gives a false impression of care-free acceptance. The gap between private life and public attitudes remains, as does the communication barrier between generations, while changing and contradictory pronouncements on morality add to the confusion. Indeed, all the public debate about deviations and their dangers can increase anxiety, making adolescents scared and self-conscious about their emotions, and giving parents a wider range of alarming prospects to fret about.

An idea of how a changed social outlook might alter the situation can be deduced from observations on communities with a different scale of values. Take, for instance, the Samoan culture as described by Margaret Mead. The Samoans lived serenely and contentedly in a society in which the accepted standards of good behaviour and social success were within easy reach of the average person. Families were large, stable, and happy, and child training was easy-going. When a child behaved badly he was simply carried outside. Babies were nursed, carried about, and fed generously by many women besides the mother, and later on the child was looked after by his elder sisters, so that exclusive attachments to parents were hardly possible. Father-son and mother-daughter rivalries, which provide the raw material for the Oedipal situation, had no place in their culture. Children were as familiar with nude bodies, pregnancy, and copulation as with the landscape, so no obscene vocabulary was needed to describe these things. The Samoans found nothing disgusting in sex, and there was no association in thought or language between sex and excretion. Adolescents were initiated into the arts of love-making by slightly older members of the opposite sex. Thereafter sexual intercourse was permissible and was undertaken in a light-hearted, unhurried spirit, with both parties expecting and achieving full satisfaction. The adolescent stage presented no special emotional stress, and the onset of menstruation was unaccompanied by fear or pain. The very idea of such pain struck Samoan women as funny when it was explained to them.

Homosexual practices, especially among the young, were very prevalent, but they were neither frowned upon nor given special consideration, being regarded as simply playfulness. They had no important or lasting consequences. Marriage was taken seriously, a partner being chosen by the parents according to social suitability, although the children's wishes were consulted. Thereafter a prolonged liaison followed, and usually resulted in stable marriage, but extra-marital sexual adventures could still continue. Great loves, tremendous emotional fixations on one particular person, were foreign to Samoan psychology. The important place of marriage and children in the social structure prevented their light-hearted adventures from affecting the even tenor of their lives. Most interestingly, not only was compulsive homosexuality almost unknown (Mead found only one man who shunned sexual intercourse with girls) but frigidity and impotence occurred only as a result of severe physical illness, and sexual neurosis was unheard of. The capacity for intercourse only once a night was counted a sign of senility [256].

Prevention by Tolerance?

In contrast, our own culture, which consists of small, isolated family units, tends to stimulate intense emotional relationships between children and their parents. This charged atmosphere makes for insecurity, and, when coupled with an uneasy, guilt-coloured attitude to awakening sexuality, it provokes the nightmarish 'Freudian' conflicts that lead to neurosis and perversion. An obvious way to tackle the problem is to promote a healthier, less tense approach to sex, and thereby to forestall the development of perversion. A direct attack on individual deviants is not so profitable because there are too many to receive psychiatric attention and many of them are not susceptible to conversion.

To advocate elementary principles of mental hygiene as a cure for the burning problem of homosexuality seems almost impertinent. Every modern manual on child-rearing, every book on popular psychology, explains what to do. But although parents know the answers in theory, they often harbour such inhibitions themselves that they cannot fail to communicate their uneasiness to their offspring. Ideally, training in sex should call for no more emotional upheaval than training in any other field. The infant who plays with his genitals should be treated as calmly as one who sucks his thumb. The child who exhibits his own body or explores other children's is no more an unnatural horror than one whose table manners give offence. There is no more reason to fear he will grow up a sexual maniac than there is to imagine that the boy who helps himself to sweets will become an armed robber. At every stage of development the child benefits from a calm approach to sex. Concealment, evasion, or lies arouse anxiety and bewilderment. Strained, ceremonial revelation is almost as bad as uneasy suppression. There is no substitute for the day-to-day, matter-of-fact communication of information by parents who are themselves at ease. What is said is often of less importance than the emotional overtones that go with it. The modern system of imparting theoretical sex instruction in schools scarcely meets the need. The physiology of fertilization is of less concern to the adolescent than the question of how far to go in kissing, petting, and masturbating with the opposite sex. It is some indication of the inhibitions that still plague us that so many adolescents would never dream of mentioning such intimate matters to their parents, and work out their own solutions as best they can.

One argument against a liberal attitude to sex is the theory that freedom leads to social decadence. Psychoanalysts have taught that provided the individual does not succumb to neurosis, enforced sexual continence can have the effects of re-directing into socially useful channels the energies that would otherwise be dissipated in the satisfaction of sex urges. The thesis has been put most learnedly by Unwin, who made a study of the material regulations of eighty uncivilized societies. He concluded that development of social organization, beginnings of discovery, expansion into neighbouring territory, in fact all the signs of energetic society, made their appearance only when sexual freedom was curtailed. Societies in which pre-nuptial and extra-marital intercourse were allowed remained on a dead level of animal sloth [369]. This point of view can be taken too far. Unwin himself pointed out that strictly monogamous societies, in which there was no sexual outlet except through the legitimate spouse, did not usually survive for long. Between racial suicide by complete denial of sex and social anarchy through selfish unrestraint there must be some reasonable compromise. The important point is that whatever compromise we choose for ourselves or teach to our children should be based on informed opinion, free from the taboos of the savage and tolerant towards other standards. Unfortunately, however enlightened we become as individuals, we remain prisoners of our culture. We cannot train our children to behave like some happy, uninhibited primitives, for that would unfit them for the society in which they must live. Changes in cultural attitudes to sex come about very slowly, and meantime one can do no more than help people thread their way through the maze of 'dos' and 'don'ts' without developing too much anxiety.

Prevention by Tolerance?

It must be admitted that no amount of mental hygiene is likely to eradicate homosexuality entirely. However one tries to smooth the path of normal development, so that more and more can attain full stature, a few will always run into difficulties and find solace in this half-way adjustment. Neurosis and perversions have always been with us, and, as Dr. Glover points out, 'We cannot say whether even a satisfactory spread of psychological knowledge, upbringing, and treatment would bring about a decisive modification of ancient patterns of sexual habit and regulation' [138]. The existence of a side track, in the shape of homosexuality, may save some people from getting still more seriously lost. Under existing circumstances, the most civilized attitude to take towards homosexuals and lesbians would be similar to that commonly adopted towards the unmarried. Recognizing that they are missing out on a rewarding experience, we realize that they may be temperamentally unsuited to marriage, that it would be unwise to force them to change their way of life, and that they may serve the community better in other ways than bringing up a family of their own. But tolerance towards homosexuals is not the same as encouragement. No doctor should advise a young person to rest content with a homosexual orientation without first giving a grave warning about the frustration and tragedy that so often attend this mode of life.

REFERENCES

| | Page(s) where | |
Number	cited	Reference

· 1   50 Aaronson, B. S. and Grumpelt, H. R. (1961) 'Homosexuality and some M.M.P.I. measures of masculinity-feminity.' *Journal of Clinical Psychiatry*, *17*, 245–247.

2   217 Abraham, K. (1927) 'The psychological relationship between sexuality and alcoholism.' In *Selected Papers on Psycho-Analysis*. London, Hogarth Press.

3   140 Albany Trust (1966) *The Homosexual and Venereal Disease*. London, 32 Shaftesbury Avenue, W.1.

4   33 Allen, C. (1949) *Sexual Perversions and Abnormalities*. London, Oxford University Press.

5 189, 232, 239 Allen, C. (1958) *Homosexuality: Its Nature, Causation and Treatment*. London, Staples Press.

6   99 American Law Institute (1956) *Model Penal Code* (Draft No. 4). Section 207.5; comments, pp. 276–281.

7   76 Ancel, M. (1962) *La Réforme Pénale Soviétique*. Paris, Centre français de droit comparé.

8   34 'Anomaly' (1948) *The Invert*. 2nd edn., London, Baillière, Tindall & Cox.

9   26 Anon (*circa* 1730) *Plain Reasons for the Growth of Sodomy in England*. London,

10   189 Apfelberg, B., *et al.* (1944) 'A psychiatric study of 250 sex offenders.' *American Journal of Psychiatry*, *100*, 762–769.

11   159 Appel, K. E. (1937). 'Endocrine studies in cases of homosexuality.' *Archives of Neurology and Psychiatry*, *37*, 1206–1207.

12   71 Armon, Virginia (1960) 'Some personality variables in overt female homosexuality.' *Journal of Projective Techniques*, *24*, 292–309.

13   211 Bacon, Catherine L. (1956) 'A developmental

References

theory of female homosexuality.' In Lorand, S. [Ed.] *Perversions.* New York, Random House.

14 73, 97 Bailey, D. Sherwin (1955) *Homosexuality and the Western Christian Tradition.* London, Longmans.

15 47 Barahal, H. S. (1939) 'Constitutional factors in male homosexuals.' *Psychiatric Quarterly, 13,* 391–400.

16 158 Barahal, H. S. (1940) 'Testosterone in psychotic male homosexuals.' *Psychiatric Quarterly, 14,* 319–329.

17 29 Beach, F. A. (1950) 'Sexual behaviour in animals and men.' *The Harvey Lectures,* 1947–48. Springfield, Illinois.

18 70 Beauvoir, Simone de (1953) *The Second Sex.* (Translated by H. M. Parshley.) Ch. IV. London, Jonathan Cape.

19 133 Becker, T. P. (1965) 'Versuche zur Eindämmung der Homosexualität in Süd-portugal.' *Die Neue Polizei* (Munich) *19,* 250–251.

20 120 Bender, Lauretta, and Grugett, A. (1952) 'A follow-up report on children who had atypical sexual experience.' *American Journal of Orthopsychiatry, 22,* 825–837.

21 245 Bender, L. and Paster, S. (1941). 'Homosexual trends in children.' *American Journal of Orthopsychiatry, 11,* 730–744.

22 208 Bene, Eva (1965) 'On the genesis of female homosexuality.' *British Journal of Psychiatry, 111,* 815–821.

23 194 Bene, Eva (1965) 'On the genesis of male homosexuality. An attempt at clarifying the role of the parents.' *British Journal of Psychiatry, 111,* 803–813.

24 20 Benedict, Ruth (1935) *Patterns of Culture.* London, Routledge.

25 17 Benedict, Ruth (1939) 'Sex in primitive society.' *American Journal of Orthopsychiatry, 9,* 570–574.

26 63 Benjamin, H. (1964) 'Clinical aspects of transsexualism in the male and female.' *American Journal of Psychotherapy, 18,* 458–469

275

References

27   76   Bensing, R. C. (1951) 'A comparative study of American sex statutes.' *Journal of Criminal Law, Criminology and Police Science, 42,* 57–72.

28   113   Benson, R. O. D. (1965) *In Defense of Homosexuality Male and Female.*' New York, Julian Press.

29   166   Berg, I., et al. (1963) 'Change of assigned sex at puberty.' *Lancet, 2,* 1216–1217.

30   39   Bergler, E. (1948) 'The myth of a new national disease; homosexuality and the Kinsey Report.' *Psychiatry Quarterly, 22,* 66–88.

31   183   Bergler, E. (1951) *Neurotic Counterfeit-Sex.* New York, Grune & Stratton.

32   206   Bergler, E. (1957) *Homosexuality: Disease or Way of Life.* New York, Hill and Wang.

33   52, 223   Bergmann, M. S. (1945) 'Homosexuality in the Rorschach test.' *Bulletin of the Menninger Clinic, 9,* 78–83.

34   23   Berthe, E. (1907) 'Die dorische Knabenliebe.' *Rheinisches Museum für Philologie* (Frankfurt), *62,* 438–475.

35   184, 192, 206, 235   Bieber, I., et al. (1962) *Homosexuality: A psychoanalytic Study.* New York, Basic Books.

36   126   Bloch, H. A. (1955) 'Social pressures of confinement towards sexual deviation.' *Journal of Social Therapy, 1,* 112–125.

37   70, 129   Bluestone, H., et al. (1966) 'Homosexuals in prison.' *Corrective Psychiatry and Journal of Social Therapy, 12,* 13–24.

38   223   Bosselman, B. and Skorodin, B. (1941) 'Masculinity and femininity in psychotic patients.' *American Journal of Psychiatry, 97,* 699–702.

39   79   Bowman, K. M. and Engle, Bernice (1965) 'Sexual psychopath laws.' In Slovenko, R. *Sexual Behaviour and the Law.* Springfield, Ill., Thomas.

40   216   Braaten, L. J. and Darling, C. D. (1965) 'Overt and covert homosexual problems among male college students. *Genetic Psychological Monographs, 71,* 269–310.

References

41   249   Bramwell, M. (1909) *Hypnotism.* London, 'Cassell.

42   153   Bremner, J. (1959) *Asexualisation.* London, Macmillan.

43   98   British Council of Churches (1966) *Sex and Morality.* London, S.C.M. Press, pp. 30–31.

44   79   Brongersma, E. (1964) 'Revision of criminal law in Morocco.' *Excerpta Criminologica, 4,* 267–272.

45   62   Brown, D. G. (1958) 'Inversion and homosexuality. *American Journal of Orthopsychiatry, 28,* 424–429.

46   98   Buckley, M. (1959) *Morality and the Homosexual.* London, Sands.

47   21   Burton, R. (1885) *Arabian Nights,* Benares (Kamashastra Soc.) Terminal Essay, Vol. x, pp. 205–254.

48   217   Bychowski, G. (1956) 'Homosexuality and psychosis' in Lorand, S. (Ed.) *Perversions.* New York, Random House.

49   122   Calder, W. (1955) 'The sexual offender.' *British Journal of Delinquency, 6,* 26–40.

50 116, 118   California, State of (1954) 'Department of Mental Hygiene.' *California Sexual Deviation Research.*

51   76   Cantor, D. J. (1964) 'Deviation and the criminal law.' *Journal of Criminal Law, Criminology and Police Science, 55,* 441–453

52 183, 234   Cappon, D. (1965) *Towards an Understanding of Homosexuality.* Englewood Cliffs, N.J., Prentice-Hall.

53 209, 213   Caprio, F. S. (1955) *Female Homosexuality.* London, Peter Owen.

54   75   Caprio, F. S. and Brenner, D. R. (1961) *Sexual Behaviour: Psycho-Legal Aspects.* New York, Citadel Press.

55   50   Cattell, R. B. and Morony, J. H. (1962) 'The use of the 16 PF in distinguishing homosexuals, normals, and general criminals.' *Journal of Consulting Psychology, 26,* 531–540.

56   223   Chapman, A. H. and Reese, D. G. (1953) 'Homosexual signs in Rorschachs of early schizophrenics.' *Journal of Clinical Psychology, 9,* 30–32.

References

57   69   Chapman, Diana (1965) 'What is a lesbian?'
            Family Doctor. August 1965, 474–475.
58   202   Chodoff, P. (1966) 'A critique of Freud's theory
            of infantile sexuality.' *American Journal of
            Psychiatry, 123*, 507–518.
59   50   Clarke, R. V. G. (1965) 'The Slater Selective
            Vocabulary Scale and male homosexuality.'
            British Journal of Medical Psychology, 38,
            339–340.
60   126   Clemmer, D. E. (1958) *The Prison Community.*
            New York, Rinehart.
61   123   Clifford, W. (1965) 'Homosexuality by consent.'
            *Justice of the Peace and local Government
            Review, 129*, 597–598.
62   66   Colette, Sidonie Gabrielle (1932) *Ces Plaisirs.*
            Paris, Ferenczi.
63   47   Coppen, A. J. (1959) 'Body-build of male homo-
            sexuals.' *British Medical Journal, 3*, 1443–1445.
64   79   Cornelius, A. R. (1966) 'Crime and the punish-
            ment of crime.' *Excerpta Criminologica, 6*, 1–12.
65   131   Cory, D. W. (1955) 'Homosexuality in prison.
            Journal of Social Therapy, 1, 137–140.
66   93, 103   Cory, D. W. (1960) *The Homosexual in America.*
            2nd ed. New York, Castle.
67   262   Cory, D. W. and LeRoy, J. P. (1963) *The Homo-
            sexual and his Society: A View from Within.*
            New York, Citadel Press, p. 82.
68   226   Craft, M. [Ed.] (1966) *Psychopathic Disorders.*
            London, Pergamon Press.
69   135, 138   Craft, M. (1966) 'Boy prostitutes and their fate.'
            British Journal of Psychiatry, 112, 1111–1114.
70   231   Curran, D. (1943) *Psychological Medicine*, Edin-
            burgh, Livingstone.
71   231   Curran, D. (1947) 'Sexual perversions and their
            treatment.' *The Practitioner, 158*, 343–348.
72   184, 233, 234   Curran, D. and Parr, D. (1957) 'Homosexuality:
            An analysis of 100 male cases.' *British Medical
            Journal, 1*, 797–801.
73   163   Darke, R. (1948) 'Heredity as an etiological factor
            in homosexuality.' *Journal of Nervous and
            Mental Disease, 107*, 251–268

References

74 18, 115   Davenport, W. (1965) 'Sexual patterns in a Southwest Pacific Society.' In Beach, F. A., *Sexual Behaviour*. New York, Wiley.

75   40, 66   Davis, Katharine B. (1929) *Factors in the Sex Life of 2,200 Women*. New York, Harper.

76   50   Dean, R. B. and Richardson, H. (1964) 'Analysis of M.M.P.I. profiles of forty college-educated overt male homosexuals.' *Journal of Consulting Psychology*, *28*, 483–486.

77   29   Denniston, R. H. (1965) 'Ambisexuality in animals.' In Marmor J. [Ed.] *Sexual Inversion*. New York, Basic Books.

78   211   Deutsch, Helena (1944) *The Psychology of Women*. New York, Grune and Stratton.

79   19   Devereux, G. (1937) 'Institutionalised homosexuality of the Mohave Indians.' *Human Biology*, *9*, 498–527.

80   99   Devlin, P. (1965) *The Enforcement of Morals*. London, Oxford University Press.

81   165   Dewhurst, C. J., and Gordon, R. R. (1963) 'Change of sex.' *Lancet*, *2*, 1213–1216.

82   24   Dickinson, G. Lowes (1896) *The Greek View of Life*. London, 23rd edn., Methuen, 1957.

83 123, 138   Doshay, L. J. (1943) *The Boy Sex Offender and his Later Career*. New York, Grune and Stratton.

84   248   Duffy, C. T. and Hirschberg, A. (1965) *Sex and Crime*. New York, Doubleday, Chapter 17.

85   158   Dunn, C. W. (1940) 'Stilboestrol-induced gynecomastia in the male.' *Journal of American Medical Association*, *115*, 2263–2264.

86   100   Dworkin, R. (1966) 'Lord Devlin and the enforcement of morals.' *Yale Law Journal*, *75*, 986–1005.

87 44, 188   East, W. Norwood, *et al.* (1947) 'The sociological aspects of homosexuality.' *Medico Legal Journal*, *15*, 11–23.

88   22   Eglinton, J. Z. (1964) *Greek Love*. New York, Layton Press.

89   164   Ellis, A. (1945) 'The sexual psychology of human hermaphrodites.' *Psychosomatic Medicine*. *7*, 108–125.

References

90   234   Ellis, A. (1956). 'The effectiveness of psychotherapy with individuals who have severe
homosexual problems.' *Journal of Consulting
Psychology*, *20*, 191–195.

91   241   Ellis, A. (1965) *Homosexuality: Its Causes and
Cure*. New York, Lyle Stuart.

92   35   Ellis, H. (1915) *Studies in the Psychology of Sex*.
3rd edn. Vol. II, *Sexual Inversion*. Phila-
delphia, F. A. Davis.

93   131   Epps, Phyllis (1951) '300 female delinquents in
Borstal.' *British Journal of Delinquency*, *1*,
187–197.

94   53   Evans, Jean (1954) *Three Men*. London, Gollancz.

95   268   Eysenck, H. J. (1954) *The Psychology of Politics*.
London, Routledge & Kegan Paul.

96   259   Feldman, M. P. and MacCulloch, M. J. (1964)
'A systematic approach to the treatment of
homosexuality by conditioned aversion.'
American Journal of Psychiatry, *121*, 167–
171.

97 180, 189 Fenichel, O. (1945) *The Psychoanalytic Theory of
Neurosis*. London, Kegan Paul.

98   35, 41   Finger, F. W. (1947) 'Sex beliefs and practices
among male college students.' *Journal of Abnormal and Social Psychology*, *42*, 57–67.

99   125   Fishman, J. F. (1934) *Sex in Prison: revealing sex
conditions in American prisons*. New York,
Padell.

100   267   Flugel, J. C. (1945) *Man, Morals and Society*.
London, Duckworth.

101   158   Foote, R. M. (1944) 'Diethylstilboestrol in the
management of psychopathological states.'
Journal of Nervous and Mental Disease, *99*,
928–935.

102   30   Ford, C. S. and Beach, F. A. (1951) *Patterns of
Sexual Behaviour*. New York, Harper.

103   17   Ford, C. S. and Beach, F. A. (1952) *Patterns of
Sexual Behaviour*. London, Eyre & Spottis-
woode.

104   158   Foss, G. L. (1951) 'The influence of androgens on
sexuality in women.' *Lancet*, *1*, 667–669.

References

105 22, 65 Foster, Jeannette H. (1958) *Sex Variant Women in Literature*. London, Muller.

106 124 Fox, L. W. (1952) *The English Prison and Borstal Systems*. London, Routledge & Kegan Paul.

107 31 Freedman, D. G., *et al.* (1961) 'Critical period in the social development of dogs.' *Science*, *133*, 1016.

108 189 Freeman, T. (1955) 'Clinical and theoretical observations on male homosexuality.' *International Journal of Psycho-analysis*, *36*, 335–347.

109 202 Freud, S. (1905) *Three Essays on the Theory of Sexuality* (Trans. and ed. J. Strachey). London, International Psycho-analytic Library, 1962.

110 205 Freud, S. (1908) 'Character and anal erotism.' *Collected Papers* (trans. Joan Riviere), vol. 2, 45–50. London, Hogarth Press, 1924.

111 219 Freud, S. (1911) 'Psycho-analytic notes upon an autobiographical account of a case of paranoia.' *Collected Papers* (trans. Joan Riviere), vol. 3, 387–416. London, Hogarth Press, 1925.

112 203 Freud, S. (1914) 'On narcissism; An introduction.' *Collected Papers* (trans. Joan Riviere), vol. 4, 30–50. London, Hogarth Press, 1925.

113 204 Freud, S. (1916) 'On the transformation of instincts with special reference to anal erotism. *Collected Papers* (trans. Joan Riviere), vol. 2, 164–171. London, Hogarth Press, 1924.

114 232 Freud, S. (1920) 'The psychogenesis of a case of homosexuality in a woman.' *Collected Papers* (trans. Joan Riviere), vol. 2, 202–231. London, Hogarth Press, 1924.

115 231 Freud, S. (1951) 'Letter to an American mother.' *American Journal of Psychiatry*, *108*, 252.

116 237, 259 Freund, K. (1960) 'Some problems in the treatment of homosexuality.' In Eysenck, H. J. [Ed.] *Behaviour Therapy and the Neuroses*. Oxford, Pergamon Press.

117 117 Freund, K. (1963) *Die Homosexualität beim Mann*. Leipzig, Hirzel.

118 117 Freund, K. (1963) 'A laboratory method for

diagnosing predominance of homo- or hetero-erotic interest in the male.' *Behaviour Research and Therapy, 1*, 85–93.

119   239   Freund, K. (1965) 'On the problem of male homosexuality. *Review of Czechoslovak Medicine, 11*, 11–17.

120   117   Freund, K., *et al.* (1965) 'A simple traducer for mechanical plethysmography of the male genital.' *Journal of the Experimental Analysis of Behaviour, 8*, 169–170.

121   152   Gaaremstroom, J. H. (1940) 'Sexual development of fowls derived from eggs treated with oestradiol benzoate.' *Journal of Endocrinology, 2*, 47–54.

122   88   Gallo, J. J., *et al.* (1966) 'The consenting adult homosexual and the law.' *U.C.L.A. Law Review* (Los Angeles), *13*, 643–832.

123   76   Gallo, J. J., *et al.* (1966) 'Statutory sex provisions.' *U.C.L.A Law Review* (Los Angeles), *13*, 657–685.

124   118,126, 223   Gebhard, P. H., *et al.* (1965) *Sex Offenders.* New York, Harper.

125   121, 256   Gebhard, P. H. (1965) 'Situational factors affecting human sexual behaviour.' In Beach, F. A. (Ed.) *Sexual Behaviour.* New York, Wiley.

126   39   Geddes, D. P. (Ed.) (1954) *An Analysis of the Kinsey Reports on Sexual Behaviour in the Human Male and Female.* London, F. Muller esp. 'The scientific method' by H. H. Hyam and P. B. Sheatsley, pp. 95–120.

127   242   Gershman, H. (1964) 'Homosexuality and some aspects of creativity.' *American Journal of Psycho-analysis, 24*, 29–38.

128   122   Gibbens, T. C. N. (1957) 'The sexual behaviour of young criminals.' *Journal of Mental Science, 103*, 527–540.

129   116   Gibbens, T. C. N. and Prince, Joyce (1963) *Child Victims of Sex Offences.* London, (I.S.T.D.).

130   228   Gibson, Evelyn and Klein, S. (1961) *Murder: A*

References

Home Office Research Unit Report. London, H.M.S.O. Table 36, p. 33.

131 124, 128 Gibson, G. (1966) 'The social worker and the homosexual.' *Consultation on the Church, Society and the Homosexual.* London, 9–11 August (unpublished).

132 28 Gide, André (1939) *Journal 1889–1939.* Paris.

133 41 Giese, H. (1959) *L'Homosexualité de l'homme.* Paris, (Payot).

134 201 Gillespie, W. H., *et al.* (1964) 'Symposium on homosexuality.' *International Journal of Psycho-Analysis, 45,* 366–371.

135 223 Gittleson, N. L. and Levine, S. (1966) 'Subjective ideas of sexual change in male schizophrenics.' *British Journal of Psychiatry, 112,* 779–782.

136 158 Glass, S. J. and Johnson, R. H. (1940) 'Limitations and complications of organotherapy in male homosexuality. *Journal of Clinical Endocrinology, 4,* 540–544.

137 159 Glass, S. J., *et al.* (1940) 'Sex hormone studies in male homosexuality.' *Journal of Clinical Endocrinology, 26,* 590–594.

138 273 Glover, E. (1949) 'Victorian ideas of sex. In B.B.C. Talks.' *Ideas and Beliefs of the Victorians.* London, Sylvan Press.

139 53 Goldberg, P. A. and Milstein, Judith T. (1965) 'Perceptual investigation of psycho-analytic theory concerning latent homosexuality in women.' *Perceptual and Motor Skills, 21,* 645–646.

140 19 Goldman, I. (1963) *The Cubeo, Indians of the Northwest Amazon.* Illinois University Press.

141 158 Golla, F. L. and Hodge, R. S. (1949) 'Hormone treatment of the sexual offender.' *Lancet, i,* p. 1006.

142 98 Gottschalk, J. (1965) 'Counselling the homosexual.' *One Confidential* (Los Angeles), *10,* (No. 4), 3–5.

143 128 Greco, M. C. and Wright, J. C. (1944) 'The correctional institution in the etiology of

References

chronic homosexuality.' *American Journal of Orthopsychiatry*, *14*, 295–307.

144   158   Greenblatt, R. B. (1943) 'Hormonal factors in libido.' *Journal of Clinical Endocrinology*, *3*, 305–306.

145   60   Greenspan, H., and Campbell, J. D. (1945) 'The homosexual as a personality type.' *American Journal of Psychiatry*, *101*, 682–689.

146   130   Greenwald, H. (1958) *The Call Girl*. New York, Ballantine Books.

147   98   Grey, A. (1966) 'Christian society and the homosexual.' *Faith and Freedom*, *19*, No. 56. (Manchester College, Oxford.)

148   92   Group for the Advancement of Psychiatry (1955) *Report on Homosexuality, with particular emphasis on this problem in Governmental Agencies*. Report No. 30, Topeka, Kansas.

149   48   Grygier, T. G. (1957) 'Psychometric aspects of homosexuality.' *Journal of Mental Science*, *103*, 514–526.

150   48   Grygier, T. G. (1958) 'Homosexuality, neurosis and "normality".' *British Journal of Delinquency*, *9*, 59–61.

151   158, 255   Hackfield, A. W. (1933) 'Über die Kastration bei vierzig sexuell Abnormen. *Monatschrift für Psychiatrie und Neurologie*, *87*, p. 1.

152   232, 255   Hadfield, J. A. (1958) 'The cure of homosexuality.' *British Medical Journal*, *1*, 1323–1326.

153   232   Hadfield, J. A. (1966) 'Origins of homosexuality.' *British Medical Journal*, *1*, 678.

154   120   Halleck, S. L. (1965) 'Emotional effects of victimisation.' In Slovenko, R. (Ed.) *Sexual Behaviour and the Law*. Springfield, Ill., Thomas.

155   65   Hamburger, C. (1953) 'The desire for change of sex.' *Acta Endocrinologica*, *14*, 361–375.

156   189   Hamilton, D. M. (1939) 'Some aspects of homosexuality in relation to total personality development.' *Psychiatric Quarterly*, *13*, 229–244.

157   35   Hamilton, G. V. (1929) *A Research in Marriage*. New York, A. and C. Boni.

References

158   32   Harlow, H. F., and Harlow, M. K. (1962) 'Social deprivation in monkeys.' *Scientific American, 207*, 136–146.

159   32   Harlow, H. F. (1965) 'Sexual behaviour in the rhesus monkey.' In Beach, F. A. (Ed.) *Sex and Behaviour.* New York, Wiley.

160   20   Harrison, T. (1937) *Savage Civilisation.* London, Gollancz.

161   99   Hart, H. L. A. (1963) *Liberty, Law and Morals.* London, Oxford University Press.

162   221   Hastings, D. W. (1941) 'A paranoid reaction with manifest homosexuality.' *Archives of Neurology and Psychiatry, 45*, 379–381.

163   89   Haward, L. R. C. (1963) 'The reliability of corroborated police evidence.' *Journal of the Forensic Science Society, 3*, 71–78.

164   134   Hegeler, I. and Hegeler S. (1963) *An ABZ of Love* (transl. E. Krag). London, Spearman.

165   108   Helmer, W. J. (1963) 'New York's "middle-class" homosexuals.' *Harper's Magazine,* March, 85–92.

166   122   Hemphill, R. E., *et al.* (1958) 'A factual study of male homosexuality.' *British Medical Journal, 1*, 1317–1323.

167   46, 86, 191   Henry, G. W. (1941) *Sex Variants.* New York, Harper.

168   129   Henry, Joan (1952) *Who Lie in Gaol.* London, Gollancz.

169   97   Heron, A. (Ed.) (1964) *Towards a Quaker View of Sex* (Revised edn.). London, Friends House.

170   51   Hess, E. H., Seltzer, A. L. and Shlien, J. M. (1965) 'Pupil response of hetero- and homosexual males to pictures of men and women.' *Journal of Abnormal and Social Psychology, 70*, 165–168.

171   197   Hewitt, C. C. (1961) 'On the meaning of effeminacy in homosexual men.' *American Journal of Psychotherapy, 15*, 592–602.

172   35   Hirschfeld, M. (1920) *Die Homosexualität des Mannes und des Weibes.* Berlin, Marcus.

References

173   26, 35   Hirschfeld, M. (1944) *Sexual Anomalies and Perversions.* London, Francis Aldor.

174   171   Holden, H. M. (1965) 'Psychotherapy of a shared syndrome in identical twins.' *British Journal of Psychiatry, 111*, 859–864.

175   206   Holeman, R. E. and Winokur, G. (1965) 'Effeminate homosexuality: A disease of childhood.' *American Journal of Orthopsychiatry, 35*, 48–56.

176   26   Holloway, R. (1813) *The Phoenix of Sodom.* London, J. Cook.

177   42, 232   Home Office (1957) *Report of the Committee on Homosexual Offence and Prostitution* (Wolfenden Report), (Command 247). London, H.M.S.O.

178   96   Home Office (1963) *Report of the Tribunal appointed to Inquire into the Vassall Case and Related Matters* (Command 2009). London, H.M.S.O.

179   33   Home Office (1966) *Criminal Statistics, England and Wales 1965* (Command 3037). London, H.M.S.O. Table A.

180   55   Hooker, Evelyn (1956) 'Preliminary analysis of group behaviour of homosexuals.' *Journal of Psychology, 42*, 217–225.

181   51   Hooker, Evelyn (1957) 'The adjustment of the male overt homosexual.' *Journal of Projective Techniques, 21*, 18–31.

182   52   Hooker, Evelyn (1958) 'Male homosexuality in the Rorschach.' *Journal of Projective Techniques, 22*, 33–53.

183   51   Hooker, Evelyn (1959) 'What is a criterion?' *Journal of Projective Techniques, 23*, 278–218.

184   67, 71   Hopkins, June (1966) Personal Communication. 'Research in Progress.' Cambridge.

185   206   Horney, Karen (1945) *Our Inner Conflicts.* New York, Norton.

186   57   Horowitz, M. J. (1964) 'The homosexual's image of himself.' *Mental Hygiene, 48*, 197–201.

187   63   Housden, J. (1965) 'An examination of the biological etiology of transvestitism.' *International Journal of Social Psychiatry, 11*, 301–305.

References

188   126   Huffman, A. V. (1960) 'Sex deviation in a prison community.' *Journal of Social Therapy* (Medical Correctional Assn., New York), *6*, 170–181.

189   27   Hyde, H. M. (1948) *The Trials of Oscar Wilde.* London, William Hodge.

190   258   James, B. (1962) 'Case of homosexuality treated by aversion therapy.' *British Medical Journal,* *1*, 768–770.

191   258   James, B. and Early, D. F. (1963) 'Aversion therapy for homosexuality.' *British Medical Journal, 1*, 538.

192   216   James, R. E. (1947) 'Precipitating factors in acute homosexual panic (Kempf's Disease) with a case presentation.' *Quarterly Review of Psychiatry and Neurology, 2*, 530–533.

193   80   James, T. E. (1964) 'Law and the sexual offender.' In Rosen, I. (Ed.) *The Pathology and Treatment of Sexual Deviation.* London, Oxford University Press.

194   138   Jefferiss, F. J. G. (1956) 'Venereal disease and the homosexual.' *British Journal of Venereal Diseases, 32*, 17–20.

195   31   Jenkins, M. (1928) 'The effect of segregation on the sex behaviour of the white rat.' *Genetic Psychology Monographs, 3*, 461–471.

196   163   Jensch, K. (1941) 'Weiterer Beitrag zur Genealogie der Homosexualität.' *Archiv für Psychiatrie und Nervenkrankheiten, 112*, 679–696.

197   133   Jersild, J. (1956) *Boy Prostitution.* Copenhagen, G. E. C. Gad.

198   192   Jonas, C. H. (1944) 'An objective approach to the personality and environment in homosexuality.' *Psychiatric Quarterly, 18*, 626–641.

199   103   Jowitt, F. W. (1954) 'Medicine and the law.' (The twenty-eighth Maudsley lecture.) *Journal of Mental Science, 100*, 351–359.

200   167   Kallmann, F. J. (1952) 'Comparative twin study of the genetic aspects of male homosexuality.' *Journal of Nervous and Mental Disease, 115*, 283–298.

201   167   Kallmann, F. J. (1952) 'Twin sibships and the

References

study of male homosexuality.' *American Journal of Human Genetics, 4,* 136–146.

202   131   Karpman, B. (1948) 'Sex life in prison.' *Journal of Criminal Law, Criminology and Police Science, 38,* 475–486.

203   56   Kendrick, D. C. and Clarke, R. V. G. (1967) 'Attitudinal differences between heterosexually and homosexually oriented males.' *British Journal of Psychiatry, 113,* 95–99.

204   71   Kenyon, F. E. (1967) Personal Communication. 'Research in progress.' Oxford.

205   210   Khan, M. M. R. (1964) 'Infantile sexuality in female homosexuality.' In Rosen, I. [Ed.] *The Pathology and Treatment of Sexual Deviation.* London, Oxford University Press.

206   25   Kiefer, O. (1935) *Sexual Life in Ancient Rome* (translated G. and H. Highet). New York, Dutton.

207   35, 37, 77, 233   Kinsey, A. C., *et al.* (1948) *Sexual Behaviour in the Human Male.* London and Philadelphia, Saunders.

208   40, 66   Kinsey, A. C., *et al.* (1953). *Sexual Behaviour in the Human Female.* London and Philadelphia, Saunders.

209   54   Kitsuse, J. I. (1962) 'Societal reaction to deviant behaviour.' *Social Problems, 9,* 247–256.

210   223   Klaf, F. and Davis, C. (1960) 'Homosexuality and paranoid schizophrenia.' *American Journal of Psychiatry, 116,* 1070–1075.

211   221   Klein, H. R. and Horwitz, W. A. (1949) 'Psychosexual factors in the paranoid phenomena.' *American Journal of Psychiatry, 105,* 697–701.

212   206   Klein, Melanie, *et al.* (1952) *Developments in Psycho-analysis.* London, Hogarth Press.

213   76   Klimmer, R. (1965) *Die Homosexualität.* Hamburg, Kriminalistik, pp. 283–285.

214   170   Klintworth, G. K. (1962) 'A pair of male monozygotic twins discordant for homosexuality.' *Journal of Nervous and Mental Disease, 135,* 113–125.

215   52, 221   Koegler, R. R. and Kline, L. Y. (1965) 'Psycho-

therapy research: an approach utilizing auto-
nomic response measurements. *American
Journal of Psychotherapy, 19,* 268–279.

216   206 Kolb, L. C. and Johnson, A. M. (1955) 'Etiology
and therapy of overt homosexuality.' *Psycho-
analytic Quarterly, 24,* 506–515.

217   50   Krippner, S. (1964) 'The identification of male
homosexuality with the M.M.P.I.' *Journal of
Clinical Psychology, 20,* 159–161.

218   39   Kubie, L. S. (1948) 'Psychiatric implications of
the Kinsey Report.' *Psychosomatic Medicine,
10,* 95–106.

219   52   Kuethe, J. L., *et al.*(1964) 'Male-female schemata
of homosexual and non-homosexual peni-
tentiary inmates.' *Journal of Personality, 32,*
23–31.

220   89   Kyler, C. W. (1963) 'Camera surveillance of sex
deviates.' *Law and Order, 11,* 16–20.

221   202 Lagache, D. (1950) 'Homosexuality and jealousy.'
International Journal of Psycho-analysis, 31,
24–31.

222   54   Lambert, K. (1954) 'Homosexuals.' *Medical
Press, 232,* 523–526.

223   14, 40 Landis, C., *et al.* (1940) *Sex in Development.* New
York and London, P. B. Hoeber.

224   118 Landis, J. T. (1956) 'Experiences of 500 children
with adult sexual deviation.' *Psychiatric Quarterly Supplement, 30,* 91–109.

225   17   Landtman, G. (1927) *The Kiwai Papuans of
British New Guinea.* London, Macmillan.

226   162 Lang, T. (1940) 'Studies in the genetic determination of homosexuality.' *Journal of Nervous
and Mental Disease, 92,* 55–64.

227   170 Lange, J. (1930) *Crime as Destiny: A Study of
Criminal Twins* (translated). London, Allen
and Unwin.

228   95   Lawrence, G. H. (1966) 'The psychiatrist, the
polygraph, and police selection.' *Security
World Magazine, 3,* 23.

229   107 Lenzoff, M. and Westley, W. A. (1956) 'The

homosexual community.' *Social Problems*, *4*, 257–263.

230   202   Lewinsky, H. (1952) 'Features from a case of homosexuality.' *Psycho-analytic Quarterly*, *21*, 344–354.

231   22   Licht, H. (1926) 'Das Liebesleben der Griechen.' Dresden, P. Aretz. (Trans.) *Sexual Life in Ancient Greece*. New York, Barnes and Noble, 1952.

232   184   Liddicoat, R. (1956) 'Homosexuality: Results of a survey.' Thesis, University of Witwatersrand. (See *British Medical Journal*, *9*, Nov. 1957.)

233   79   Lindman, F. T. and McIntyre, D. M. (1961) 'The sexual psychopath and the law.' *The Mentally Disabled and the Law*, Ch. x. Chicago, University Press.

234   184   Loeser, L. H. (1945) 'The sexual psychopath in military service.' *American Journal of Psychiatry*, *102*, 92–101.

235   187   London, L. S. and Caprio, F. S. (1950) *Sexual Deviations*. Washington, Linacre Press.

236   189   Lorand, S. (1951) *Clinical Studies in Psychoanalysis*. New York, International Universities Press.

237   31   Lorenz, K. Z. (1958) 'The evolution of behaviour.' *Scientific American*, *199*, 67.

238   30   McBride, A. F., and Hebb, D. O. (1948) 'Behaviour of the captive bottle-nose dolphin.' *Journal of comparative and physiological Psychology*, *41*, 111–123.

239   226   McCord, W. and McCord, Joan (1956) *Psychopathy and Delinquency*. New York, Grune and Stratton.

240   195   McCord, W., McCord, Joan and Verden, P. (1962) 'Family relationship and sexual deviance in lower-class adolescents.' *International Journal of Social Psychiatry*, *8*, 165–179.

241   211   McDougall, Joyce (1965) 'Introduction à un colloque sur l'homosexualité féminine.' *Revue Française de Psychanalyse* *29*, 357–376.

References

242 109, 111 McGee, B. (1966) *One in Twenty*. London, Secker and Warburg, Chapter 11.

243   118 McGeorge, J. (1964) 'Sexual assaults on the children.' *Medicine, Science and Law, 4,* 245–253.

244   99 McIlvenna, Rev. T., *et al.* (1965) *A Brief of Injustices*. Council on Religion and the Homosexual, 330 Ellis Street, San Francisco.

245   54 McKinnon, Jane (1947) 'The homosexual woman.' *American Journal of Psychiatry, 103,* 661–664.

246   251 Mackwood, J. C. (1947) 'A note on the psychotherapeutic treatment of homosexuality in prison.' *Medical Practitioner, 217,* 217–219.

247   252 Mackwood, J. C. (1954) Remedial and educational psychotherapy during penal detention in *The Roots of Crime*, Ed. Norwood East. London, Butterworth, pp. 90–119.

248   21 Malinowski, B. (1929) *The Sexual Life of Savages in Northwestern Melanesia*. London, Routledge.

249   76 Mannheim, H. (1946) *Criminal Justice and Social Reconstruction*. London, Kegan Paul.

250   113 Masters, R. E. L. (1962) *The Homosexual Revolution*. New York, Julian Press.

251   212 Masters, W. H. and Johnson, Virginia E. (1966) *Human Sexual Response*. Boston, Little, Brown.

252   158 Masters, W. H. and Magallon, D. T. (1950) 'Androgen administration in the post-menopausal woman.' *Journal of Clinical Endocrinology, 10,* p. 348.

253 118, 259 Mather, N. J. de V. (1966) 'The treatment of homosexuality by aversion therapy.' *Medicine, Science and the Law, 6,* 200–205.

254   28 Maurois, André (1950) *The Quest for Proust*. London, Jonathan Cape.

255   234 Mayerson, P. and Lief, H. I. (1965) 'Psychotherapy of homosexuals' in Marmor, J. [Ed.] *Sexual Inversion*. New York, Basic Books.

256   270 Mead, M. (1929) *Coming of Age in Samoa*. London, Jonathan Cape.

257   19 Mead, M. (1931) *Growing up in New Guinea*. London, Routledge.

References

258   60   Mead, M. (1935) *Sex and Temperament*. London, Gollancz.

259   61   Mead, M. (1949) *Male and Female*. New York, Wm. Morrow.

260   260   Meyer, A. E. (1966) 'Psycho-analytic versus behaviour therapy of male homosexuals: A statistical evaluation of clinical outcome.' *Comprehensive Psychiatry*, 7, 110–117.

261   193   Miller, P. R. (1958) 'The effeminate passive obligatory homosexual.' A.M.A. *Archives of Neurology and Psychiatry*, 80, 612–618.

262   71   Miller, W. G. and Hannum, T. E. (1963) 'Characteristics of homosexually involved incarcerated females.' *Journal of Consulting Psychology*, 27, 277.

263   235   Mintz, Elizabeth E. (1966) 'Overt male homosexuals in combined group and individual treatment.' *Journal of Consulting Psychology*, 30, 193–198.

264   118   Mohr, J. W., Turner, R. E. and Jerry, M. B. (1964) *Pedophilia and Exhibitionism*. Toronto University Press.

265   165   Money, J., *et al.* (1955) 'Hermaphroditism: recommendations concerning assignment of sex, change of sex, and psychological management.' *Bulletin of John Hopkins Hospital*, 97, 284–300.

266   165   Money, J., *et al.* (1957) 'Imprinting and the establishment of gender role.' *Archives of Neurology and Psychiatry*, 77, 333–336.

267   232   Monroe, R. R. and Enelow, M. L. (1960) 'The therapeutic motivation in male homosexuals.' *American Journal of Psycho-therapy*, 14, 474–490.

268   160   Moore, T. V. (1945) 'The pathogenesis and treatment of homosexual disorders.' *Journal of Personality*, 14, 47–83.

269   163   Morrow, J. E., *et al.* (1965) 'A possible explanation of the excessive brother-to-sister ratios reported in siblings of male homosexuals.' *The*

References

Journal of Nervous and Mental Disease, 140, 305–306.

270   138   Morton, R. S. (1966) *Venereal Diseases.* Penguin Books, p. 128.

271   228   Mowat, R. R. (1966) *Morbid Jealousy and Murder.* London, Tavistock Publications.

272   159   Myerson, A. and Neustadt, R. (1940) 'Androgen excretion in urine in various neuro-psychiatric conditions. *Archives of Neurology and Psychiatry, 44,* 689.

273   189   Nash, J. and Hayes, F. (1965) 'The parental relationships of male homosexuals.' *Australian Journal of Psychology, 17,* 35–43.

274   26   Nathan, P. (1943) *The Psychology of Fascism.* London, Faber.

275   125   Nelson, V. F. (1933) *Prison Days and Nights.* Boston, Little Brown.

276   189, 232   Neodoma, K. (1951) 'Homosexuality in Sexological practice.' *International Journal of Sexology, 4,* 219–224.

277   62   New York Academy of Medicine Report (1966) 'Change of sex on birth certificates for transsexuals.' *Bulletin of the New York Academy of Medicine, 42,* 721–724.

278   132   Nice, R. W. (1966) 'The problem of homosexuality in corrections.' *American Journal of Corrections, 28,* 30–32.

279   223   Norman, J. P. (1948) 'Evidence and clinical significance of homosexuality in 100 un-analysed cases of dementia praecox.' *Journal of Nervous and Mental Disease, 107,* 484–489.

280   191   O'Connor, P. J. (1964) 'Aetiological factors in homosexuality as seen in R.A.F. psychiatric practice.' *British Journal of Psychiatry, 110,* 381–391.

281   54   O'Connor, W. A. (1948) 'Some notes on suicide.' *British Journal of Medical Psychology, 21,* 222–228.

282   121   Ollendorff, R. (1966) *Juvenile Homosexual Experience and its Effect on Adult Sexuality.* New York, Julian Press.

References

283   18, 20   Opler, M. K. (1965) 'Anthropological and cross-cultural aspects of homosexuality.' In Marmor, J. (Ed.) *Sexual Inversion.* New York, Basic Books.

284   97   Oraison, M. (1952) *Vie chrétienne et problèmes de la sexualité.* Paris, Conferences Laenec (withdrawn).

285   206   Ovesey, L., *et al.* (1963) 'Psychotherapy of male homosexuality: Psycho-dynamic formulation.' *Archives of General Psychiatry, 9,* 19–31.

286   249   Owensby, N. M. (1940) 'Homosexuality and lesbianism treated with metrazol.' *Journal of Nervous and Mental Disease, 92,* 65–66.

287   95   Packard, V. (1964) *The Naked City.* London, Longmans (Penguin Books Edition 1966), Ch. III. 'How to strip a job-seeker naked.'

288   163   Pare, C. M. B. (1956) 'Homosexuality and chromosomal sex.' *Journal of Psychosomatic Research, 1,* 247–251.

289   163   Pare, C. M. B. (1965) 'Etiology of homosexuality.' In Marmor, J. (Ed.) *Sexual Inversion.* New York, Basic Books.

290   170   Parker, N. (1964) 'Homosexuality in twins; A report on three discordant pairs.' *British Journal of Psychiatry, 40,* 489–495.

291   169   Pastore, N. (1949) 'The genetics of schizophrenia.' *Psychological Bulletin, 46,* 285–302.

292   104   Paul, R. (1965) 'Problems of psychosexual orientation.' *Guy's Hospital Reports, 114,* 333–336.

293   154,159, 160   Perloff, W. H. (1965) 'Hormones and homosexuality.' In Marmor, J. (Ed.) *Sexual Inversion.* New York, Basic Books.

294   231   Planansky, K. and Johnston, R. (1962) 'The incidence and relationship of homosexual and paranoid features in schizophrenia.' *Journal of Mental Science, 108,* 604–615.

295   76   Ploscowe, M. (1951) *Sex and the Law.* New York, Prentice Hall.

296   109   Plummer, D. (1963) *Queer People.* London, W. H. Allen.

297   232   Poe, J. S. (1952) 'The successful treatment of a

References

40-year-old passive homosexual.' *Psychoanalytic Review*, *29*, 23–33.

298 75 Poupart, J. M. (1965) 'Les problèmes de la delinquance sexuelle.' *Reveue de Droi Pénal et de Criminologie*, Bruxelles, *8*, 807–836.

299 163 Pritchard, M. (1962) 'Homosexuality and genetic sex. *Journal of Mental Science*, *108*, 616–623.

300 19 Querlin, Marise (1965) *Women Without Men*. London, Mayflower Books, p. 113.

301 96 Radcliffe Report (1962) *Security Procedures in the Public Service* (Command 1681). London, H.M.S.O., pp. 18–19.

302 11, 160 Rado, S. (1940) 'A critical examination of the concept of bisexuality.' *Psychosomatic Medicine*, *2*, 459–467.

303 80, 118, 227 Radzinowicz, L. (1957) 'The state of the Law.' *Sexual Offences. Ch. xvi* London, Macmillan.

304 170 Rainer, J. D., *et al.* (1960) 'Homosexuality and heterosexuality in identical twins.' *Psychosomatic Medicine*, *21*, 251–258.

305 245 Ramsey, G. V. (1943) 'The sexual development of boys.' *American Journal of Psychology*, *56*, 217–233.

306 63 Randell, J. B. (1959) 'Transvestitism and transsexualism: A study of 50 cases.' *British Medical Journal*, *2*, 1448–1452.

307 120 Rasmussen, A. (1934) 'Die Bedeutung sexueller Attentate auf Kinder unter 14 Jahren für die Entwicklung von Geisteskrankheiten und Characteranomalien.' *Acta Psychiatrica et Neurologica*, *9*, 351–433.

308 31 Rasmussen, E. W. (1955) 'Experimental homosexual behaviour in male albino rats.' *Acta Psychologica*, *11*, 303–334.

309 135, 138 Raven, S. (1960) 'Boys will be boys.' *Encounter*, *86*, (November), 19–24.

310 202 Regardie, F. I. (1949) 'Analysis of a homosexual. *Psychiatric Quarterly*, *23*, 548–566.

311 116 Reifen, D. (1966) 'Sex offenders and the protection of children.' *Canadian Journal of Corrections*, *8*, 120–132.

References

312   225   Reinhardt, J. M. (1957) *Sex Perversions and Sex Crimes.* Springfield, Ill., C. Thomas, 209–215.

313 135, 138   Reiss, A. J. (1961) 'The social integration of queers and peers.' *Social Problems, 9,* 102–120. Reproduced in Ruitenbeek, H. M. (1963) *The Problems of Homosexuality in Modern Society.* New York, Dutton.

314 225, 227, 248   River, J. P. de (1958) *Crime and the Sexual Psychopath.* Springfield, Illinois, C. Thomas.

315   80   Robinson, K. (1965) 'Parliamentary and public attitudes.' In Rosen, I. (Ed.) *The Pathology and Treatment of Sexual Deviation.* London, Oxford University Press.

316 62, 109   Roditi, E. (1962) *De L'homosexualité.* Paris, Sedino, p. 29.

317 217, 223   Rosanoff, A. J. (1938) *Manual of Psychiatry and Mental Hygiene.* (7th edn.) New York, John Wiley.

318   221   Rosenfeld, H. (1949) 'Remarks on the relationship of male homosexuality to paranoia.' *International Journal of Psycho-analysis, 30,* 36–47.

319   41   Ross, R. T. (1950) 'Measures of the sex behaviour of college males compared with Kinsey's results.' *Journal of Abnormal and Social Psychology, 45,* 753–755.

320   242   Rubinstein, L. H. (1958) 'Psychotherapeutic aspects of male homosexuality.' *British Journal of Medical Psychology, 31,* 14–18.

321   223   Ruskin, S. H. (1941) 'Analysis of sex offenders among male psychiatric patients.' *American Journal of Psychiatry, 97,* 955–968

322   218   Saltzman, L. (1965) ' "Latent" homosexuality.' In Marmor, J. [Ed.] *Sexual Inversion.* New York, Basic Books.

323   64   Savitsch, E. de (1958) *Homosexuality, Transvestism and Change of Sex.* London, Heinemann Medical Books.

324   250   Schneck, J. M. (1950) 'Some aspects of homosexuality in relation to hypnosis.' *Psychoanalytic Review, 37,* 351–357.

325   138   Schofield, M. (1964) 'Social aspect of homo-

References

sexuality.' *British Journal of Venereal Diseases*, *40*, 129–134.

326   83, 118   Schofield, M. (1965) *Sociological Aspects of Homosexuality: A comparative study of three types of homosexuals.* London, Longmans.

327   219   Schreber, D. P. (1903) *Memoirs of my Nervous Illness* (translated and edited by Ida Macalpine and R. A. Hunter). London, Wm. Dawson, 1955.

328   249   Schrenck-Notzing, A. von (1892) *Die Suggestions-Therapie bei Krankhaften Erscheinungen des Geschlechtsinnes mit besonderer Berücksichtigung der conträren Sexualempfindung.* Stuttgart, von Ferdinandenke.

329   267   Schur, E. M. (1965) *Crimes without Victims: Deviant Behaviour and Public Policy.* Englewood Cliffs, N.J., Prentice-Hall.

330   202   Schwarz, H. (1952) 'A case of character disorder.' *Bulletin of the Menninger Clinic*, *16*, 20–30.

331   230, 238, 260   Scott, P. D. (1964) 'Definition, classification, prognosis and treatment.' In Rosen, I. [Ed.] *The Pathology and Treatment of Sexual Deviation.* London, Oxford University Press.

332   197   Sears, R. R. (1965) 'Development of gender role.' In Beach, F. A. [Ed.] *Sex and Behaviour.* New York and London, Wiley.

333   250   Selling, L. S. (1947) 'Extra-institutional treatment for sex offenders.' In Lindner, R. M. and Seliger, R. V. [Ed.] *Handbook of Correctional Psychology.* New York, Philosophical Library, p. 228.

334   159   Sevringhaus, E. L. and Chornyak, J. (1945) 'A study of homosexual adult males (17-ketosteroid assays).' *Psychosomatic Medicine*, *7*, 302–305.

335   47   Sheldon, W. H. (1949) *Varieties of Delinquent Youth.* New York, Harper.

336   78   Sherwin, R. V. (1965) 'Sodomy.' In Slovenko, R. *Sexual Behaviour and the Law.* Springfield, Ill., Thomas.

References

337   166   Slater, E. (1962) 'Birth order and maternal age of homosexuals.' *Lancet, 1.* 69–71.

338   49   Slater, E. and Slater, P. (1947) 'A study in the assessment of homosexual traits.' *British Journal of Medical Psychology, 21,* 61–74.

339   247   Slovenko, R. (1965) *Sexual Behaviour and the Law.* Springfield, Ill., C. Thomas.

340   217   Smalldon, J. L. (1933) 'The etiology of chronic alcoholism.' *Psychiatric Quarterly, 4,* 640–641.

341   124   Smith, A. Heckstall (1954) *Eighteen Months.* London, Allan Wingate.

342   69   Socarides, C. W. (1965) 'Female homosexuality.' In Slovenko, R. [Ed.] *Sexual Behaviour and the Law.* Springfield, Ill. C. Thomas.

343   184   Soddy, K. (1954) 'Homosexuality.' *Lancet, 267,* 541–546.

344   259   Solyom, L. and Miller, S. (1965) 'A differential conditioning procedure as the initial phase of the behaviour therapy of homosexuality.' *Behaviour Research and Therapy, 3,* 147–160.

345   42   Spencer, S. J. G. (1959) 'Homosexuality among Oxford Undergraduates. *Journal of Mental Science, 105,* 393–405.

346   231   Stanley-Jones, D. (1947) 'Royal Society of Medicine symposium on homosexuality.' *Medical Press.* September, p. 213.

347   252   Stanley-Jones, D. (1947) 'Sexual inversion; an ethical study.' *Lancet, i,* 366–369.

348   257   Stevenson, I. and Wolpe, J. (1960) 'Recovery from sexual deviations through overcoming non-sexual neurotic responses.' *American Journal of Psychiatry, 116,* 737–742.

349   249   Stone, M. B. (1964) 'Homosexuality in a borderline mental defective; Rehabilitation through hypnosis and re-education.' *Pennsylvania Psychiatric Quarterly, 4,* 42–53.

350   211   Storr, A. (1964) *Sexual Deviation.* Harmondsworth, Penguin Books.

351   248   Sturup, G. K. (1960) 'Sex offenses: the Scandinavian experience.' *Law and Contemporary Problems* (Duke University), *25,* 361–375.

References

352   126   Sykes, G. (1958) *The Society of Captives*. Princeton, University Press.

353   23   Symonds, J. A. (undated *c.* 1891) *A Problem in Modern Ethics, being an Enquiry into the Phenomenon of Sexual Inversion.* London (cited in P. L. Babington bibliography of Symonds, London, Castle, 1925, p. 75).

354   94   Szasz, T. S. (1965) 'Legal and moral aspects of homosexuality.' In Marmor, J. (Ed.) *Sexual Inversion*. New York, Basic Books.

355   138   Tarr, J. D. F. (1962) 'The male homosexual and venereal disease.' *G. P. (Kansas)* 25, 91–97.

356   252   Taylor, F. J. (1947) 'Homosexual offences and their relation to psychotherapy.' *British Medical Journal*, 2, 525–529.

357   236   Taylor, F. Kräupl (1965) 'Homosexuality' (Correspondence). *British Journal of Psychiatry*, *III*, 196–197, 548–549

358   195   Taylor, F. Kräupl (1966) *Psychopathy, its Causes and Symptoms*. London, Butterworths.

359   26, 74   Taylor, G. R. (1953) *Sex in History*. London, Thames & Hudson.

360   49   Terman, L. M. and Miles, Catherine C. (1936) *Sex and Personality*. New York, McGraw Hill.

361   53, 206   Thompson, Clara (1947) 'Changing concepts of homosexuality in psycho-analysis.' *Psychiatry*, *10*, 183–189.

362   248   Thompson, G. N. (1949) 'Electro-shock and other therapeutic considerations in sexual psychopathy.' *Journal of Nervous and Mental Diseases*, *109*, 531–539.

363   221   Thornton, N. (1948) 'Some mechanisms of paranoia.' *Psycho-analytic Review*, *35*, 290–294.

364   199   Tiller, P. O. (1967) 'Parental role division and the child's personality development.' In Dahlstrom, E. *The Changing Roles of Men and Women*. London, Duckworth.

365   30   Tinbergen, N. (1964) 'Aggression and fears in the normal sexual behaviour of some animals.' In Rosen, I. [Ed.] *The Pathology and Treatment*

of Sexual Deviation. London, Oxford University Press.

366   123   Tolsma, F. J. (1957) *De betekenis van de verleiding in homefiele ontwikkelingen*. Psychiatrijuridical Society, Amsterdam.

367   118   Toobert, S., *et al.* (1959) 'Some factors related to pedophilia'. *International Journal of Social Psychiatry, 4,* 272–279.

368   92   United States Senate Committee (1950) *Employment of Homosexuals and Other Sex Perverts in Government*. Senate Document 241, 81st Congress, 2nd Session, Dec. 1950.

369   272   Unwin, J. D. (1934) *Sex and Culture*. Oxford.

370   227   Walker, N. (1965) *Crime and Punishment in Britain*. Edinburgh, University Press.

371   129   Ward, D. A. and Kassebaum, G. G. (1965) *Women's Prison: Sex and Social Structure*. Chicago, Aldine.

372   192   West, D. J. (1959) 'Parental relationships in male homosexuality.' *International Journal of Social Psychiatry, 5,* 85–97.

373   127   West, D. J. (1963) *The Habitual Prisoner*. London, Macmillan.

374   118   West, D. J. (1965) *Murder followed by Suicide*. London, Heinemann.

375   134   West, D. J. (1967) *The Young Offender*. Duckworth & Penguin Books.

376   94   West, L. J. and Glass, A. J. (1965) 'Sexual behaviour and the military law.' In Slovenko, R. (Ed.) *Sexual Behaviour and the Law*. Springfield, Ill., Thomas (Cites Fry and Rostow).

377   128   Westwood, G. (1952) *Society and the Homosexual*. London, Gollancz.

378   10, 107, 123, 194   Westwood, G. (1960) *A Minority*. London, Longmans.

379   117   Westwood, G. (1960) *A Minority, op. cit.,* p. 159.

380   52   Wheeler, W. M. (1949) 'An analysis of Rorschach indices of male homosexuality.' *Journal of Projective Techniques, 13,* 97–126.

381   90   Whitaker, B. (1964) *The Police*. Penguin Books.

382   189   Whitener, R. W. and Nikelly, A. G. (1964).

References

'Sexual deviation in college students.' *American Journal of Orthopsychiatry*, *34*, 486–492.

383   103   Wildeblood, P. (1955) *Against the Law*. London, Weidenfeld & Nicolson.

384   103   Wildeblood, P. (1956) *A Way of Life*. London, Weidenfeld & Nicolson.

385   106   Wilkins, L. T. (1964) *Social Deviance*. London, Tavistock.

386   67   Winner, Albertine L. (1947) 'Homosexuality in women.' *The Medical Press*, *218*, 219–220.

387   64   Wolf, C. (1958) 'Operations for change of sex.' In Savitsch, E. de., *Homosexuality, Transvestitism and Change of Sex*. London, Heinemann Medical Books.

388   256   Wolpe, J. (1958) *Psychotherapy by Reciprocal Inhibition*. Stanford, Stanford University Press.

389   235   Woodward, Mary (1958) 'The diagnosis and treatment of homosexual offenders.' *British Journal of Delinquency*, *9*, 44–59.

390   46   Wortis, J. (1937) 'A note on the body-build of the male homosexual.' *American Journal of Psychiatry*, *93*, 1121–1125.

391   46, 61   Wortis, J. (1940) 'Intersexuality and effeminacy in a male homosexual.' *American Journal of Orthopsychiatry*, *10*, 567–569.

392   159   Wright, C. A. (1935) 'Endocrine aspects of homosexuality. *The Medical Records*, (New York), *142*, 407.

393   155   Young, W. C. (Ed.) (1961) *Sex and Internal Secretions*. Baltimore, Williams and Wilkins.

394   223   Zamansky, H. S. (1958) 'An investigation of the psycho-analytic theory of delusions.' *Journal of Personality*, *26*, 410–425.

395   30   Zuckerman, S. (1932) *The Social Life of Monkeys and Apes*. London, Kegan Paul.

INDEX

Abreaction, 255
Abstinence, 97, 246, 251
'Active' role, 13, 49, 61, 126, 130
Adolescent conduct, 42, 104, 116, 121–123, 200, 206, 244–245, 266, 270
Age of consent, 75, 80, 83
  origin, 69, 122, 143, 181, 206, 236, 255, 263, 266
  peak attraction, 114, 116–118, 203
Ageing homosexuals, 58
Aggression-submission, 30, 60, 156, 199, 206, 218, 264
Albany Trust, 112
Alcoholism, 217
Alienation, 55–57, 106–108, 243–244, 267
Anal fixation, 204–206
Animal sex, 29–32, 155–156
Anthropological data, 17–21, 60–61, 115, 199, 270, 272
Arabian Nights, 21–22
Aversion treatment, 257–260

Behaviour therapy, 256–260
Berdache, 19, 199
Bible, The, 22, 73, 97
Bisexuality, 11, 40, 183, 214–215, 234–236, 265
Blackmail, 86, 90, 103, 247
Broken homes, 194
Brothers, excess of, 162–164
Buggery, 13, 61, 77–78, 82–83, 140
'Butch' lesbians, 104, 130

California, 52, 112, 117, 131, 248
Camera surveillance, 89
Case histories, 141–150, 179, 219–220, 225, 256
Castration, 153, 247–248
  complex, 176, 179, 181
Causes, multiplicity of, 45, 188, 202, 212, 261–2 66
Child molesting. See Paedophilia
  rearing, 187, 189, 194–197, 202, 207, 226, 264, 269–271
  seducers, 116
  victims, 120

Children, sex stimulation of, 115
Christian attitudes, 73–74, 96–99
Chromosome abnormalities, 151–152, 161–163, 226
Civil disabilities, 91–96, 267
Clubs for homosexuals, 110–112
Conversion prospects. See Cure
Covert homosexuals, 15, 208, 216, 234
Crime and homosexuality, 59, 71, 86, 90, 103–104, 134, 213, 214, 216–217, 223–229, 247, 252
Criminal statistics, 33–34, 82, 118
Cultural causes, 199–120, 263, 269–271
Cure, prospects of, 230–237, 259–260
  spontaneous, 233, 256–257, 266

Death penalty, 21, 24, 26, 73, 250
Decadent societies, 234, 272
Definitions, 10–13
Denmark, 248
Deportation, 93
Depressive reactions, 54, 87, 213, 238, 242
Detection by tests, 49–53, 94–95
'Dildol', 14
'Directories' for homosexuals, 108, 109
Divorce, 78
Drug addiction, 71

Electro-convulsant treatment, 248
Entrapment, 88–90
Exclusive homosexuality. See Obligatory homosexuality
Exhibitionism, 182, 265
Extortion racket. See Blackmail

Facultative homosexuals, 11, 125–128, 135–136, 182–183, 261
Fellatio, 13, 62
Feminine identification, 45, 59, 62–64, 127, 197–199, 236
Fetishism, 121, 182, 208, 265
Forces, homosexuals in the, 24, 83–84, 93–94, 191–192

Index

Freudian theory, 15–16, 176–180, 183, 185, 189, 201, 202–206, 210, 218, 219–222, 263
Frigidity, 178, 181

'Gay' society, 107–113
Greek homosexuality, 22–24, 201
Guilt feelings, 53–54, 102, 179, 181, 214, 242–243, 254

Heredity, 167–171, 207, 262
Hermaphroditism, 65, 161–166
Heterosexual feelings forgotten, 181
Historical personages, 26–28, 44
Holland, 104, 111, 267
Homophile organizations, 110–113
Homosexual panic, 216–217, 229, 230, 242
    partnerships, 57–58, 211
    society, 106–113
Hormones, 153, 155–160, 247
Hypnotic treatment, 249

Identification with parent, 179, 198
Importuning, 75, 83, 131, 253
Impotence, 68, 154, 176, 181, 234
Imprinting, 31, 121
Incest. See Oedipus
Indecency, 77–78, 81, 82
Incidence, male, 33–39, 41–42
    female, 40–41
Institute of Sex Research, Indiana, 65, 118, 223
Inter-sexuals, sex preferences of, 164–165
Institutionalized homosexuality, 18–20, 119
Intolerance, 102–106, 267–268

Jealousy, 202, 213, 217–218, 228–229

Kempf's disease, 216–217
Kings of England, 27–28
Kinsey rating scale, 36, 68, 233, 234
Koran, The, 79

Latent homosexuality, 218, 242
Law:
    American, 72, 76–79, 93–94
    English, 79–84
    European, 74–76
    Religious, 73–74, 79
Law enforcement, 84–90
    reform, 79, 82–83, 99–101, 267

Law Reform Society, 88
Law and morals, 99–101, 123, 267
Lesbianism, 12–13, 40–41, 54, 65–71, 77, 112, 207–214, 239, 241
Literature, lesbian, 65–66, 69
Love-making methods, 13–14, 67

Magazines for homosexuals, 112–113
Mannerisms, 45, 59
Marriage, 67, 68–69, 119, 137, 239–241, 270
Masculine protest, 70, 262
    temperament, 60–61
Masculinity, excessive, 49, 126, 201, 217, 262
    tests, 49–50
Maternal age, 166
    influence, 142, 145, 148, 171, 180, 188–196, 199, 208–211, 236
Mental hygiene, 271, 273
    illness. See Paranoid schizophrenia
    subnormality, 227
Metrazol treatment, 249
Minorities Research Group, 67, 112
Minority attitudes, 106–107, 108, 113–114, 243, 262
Model Penal Code, 79
Moslem codes, 62, 72–73, 79
Mother-bound men, 142, 145, 148, 171, 180, 188–196, 199, 236

Narcissism, 59, 203
Neurotic personality traits, 71, 183–185, 213–214, 237, 242
Novels and plays, 69, 105–106, 136, 217, 241

Obligatory homosexuality, 10–11, 36, 42, 145, 183, 206, 234, 262–263, 266
Occupational choice, 44, 57, 93, 95
Oedipus Theory, 176–180, 183, 185, 189, 210, 264
Oestrogen Therapy, 247
Orgasm, female, 212
Orgies, 111–112

Paedophilia, 114–120, 131, 224, 247, 265
Paranoid attitudes, 243–244
    schizophrenia, 219–223

Index

Parents. *See* Maternal/Paternal influenc

Parents' gender preference, 164–165, 171, 209–210

'Passive' role, 13, 49, 61, 68, 126, 130

Paternal influence, 171, 189–196, 211, 236

Personality of homosexuals 45, 48–53, 70–71, 183–186

Perversions, variety of, 11–12

Physique of homosexuals 44–47, 61, 213

Police methods, 85–90, 133

Polygraph detector, 95

Pornography, 113

Prevention, 266–273

Primitive cultures, 17–21, 60–61, 115, 199, 270, 272

Prison, behaviour in, 70–71, 124–131

effects of, 129, 251

Promiscuity, 41, 71, 107, 112, 138–140, 146, 262

Prosecution, immunity from, 85

policy, 77–78, 83, 90

Prostitution, female, 68, 71, 104

male, 49, 75, 76, 132–138

Psychiatric opinions, 188

Psycho-analytic theory, 15–16, 172–186, 189, 201–212, 218, 219–222, 263

treatment, 231–236, 253–254

Psychopathic offenders, 78–79, 93, 94, 225–226, 248

Psychotherapy, short term, 254–255

Public attitudes, 9–10, 37, 39, 102, 269

Regression, 200, 207, 214, 266

Religious teachings, 22, 62, 72–74, 79, 96–99, 251

Repression, Freudian, 173, 185, 216–218, 242

Research, difficulties of, 10, 167

Resistance to cure, 232, 237, 253–254

Roman Catholic views, 97, 98

Romans, 25

Rorschach projection test, 51, 52, 71

Sadism, 224–225, 227

Samoan culture, 269–270

Security risks, 92, 95–96

Seduction, effects of, 121–123, 129, 131, 138, 250, 256–257

Segregation of sexes, 30–31, 127–129, 252

Sex arousal, 14, 41, 212

Sex, change of, 62–65, 152, 162–163, 219

education, 271

learning, 31–32, 154–155

object choice, 15–16, 154, 160, 187

role attitudes 50, 62–64, 70, 71, 156, 164–166, 176, 196–201, 262

reversal. *See* Hermaphrodites, Trans-sexualism

Sexual Offences Act, (1956) 80–81 (1967) 82–84

Sexual psychopath law, 78–79, 93–94

Socio-sexual role. *See* Sex role

Shamans, 20

Sodomy. *See* Buggery

Sodomitical sin, 97

Solon's laws, 24

Spontaneous cure, 233, 266

Students, incidence among, 42

Suicide, 54–55, 87, 99, 238

Surgery, 64, 247

Temperament of homosexuals, 48–53, 70–71, 183–185

Templars, 26

Trans-sexualism, 62–65

Transvestitism, 63, 70

Traumatic experiences, 212, 255

Treatment aims, 237–246

behaviouristic, 256–260

methods, 247–260

prison, 251–252

success rates, 230–237, 259–260

Tribadism, 14

Twins, 167–171, 262

'Unconscious' homosexuality, 216–218, 242

Vassall case, 96

Venereal disease, 138–140

Vice squads, 90

Violence, 118–119, 126, 211, 216–217, 223–229

Whistling ability, 46

Wolfenden Report, 9, 42, 86, 103, 232

Printed in the United States
130262LV00006B/56/P